# CHILDREN AND OUR GLOBAL FUTURE

# CHILDREN AND OUR GLOBAL FUTURE

*theological and social challenges*

## KRISTIN HERZOG

The Pilgrim Press
Cleveland

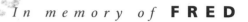

*In memory of* **FRED**

a n d

*in hope for* **LUCY**

The Pilgrim Press, 700 Prospect Avenue, Cleveland, Ohio 44115-1100
thepilgrimpress.com

© 2005 Kristin Herzog

Chapter 3 appeared in a slightly different form in *A.R.T.S.: The Arts in Religious and Theological Studies*, 14, 2 (2002): 36–42, and is reprinted with permission.

10   09   08   07   06   05         5   4   3   2   1

Library of Congress Cataloging-in-Publication Data

Herzog, Kristin, 1929–
    Children and our global future : theological and social challenges / Kristin Herzog
      p.  cm.
    Includes bibliographical references and index.
    ISBN 0-8298-1678-X (pbk. : alk. paper)
    1. Children (Christian theology)   I. Title.

BT705.H47   2005
200'.83—dc22

                                      2005053467

# CONTENTS

# ILLUSTRATIONS

*Each of us, whether we
have children or not, gives birth
to the next generation.*

— JOAN CHITTISTER, O.S.B.

# PREFACE

✦

During the five years of research on the topic of this study, countless friends and acquaintances have inspired and supported me. Three New Testament scholars critiqued the biblical chapter and made valuable suggestions: D. Moody Smith, Wolfgang Schrage, and Sharon Ringe. The chapter on the child in world religions was first presented in a session at the American Academy of Religion in 2001, and the responses gave me many new ideas. Leela Prasad provided me with most interesting bibliographic suggestions for this chapter, and Teresa Berger made helpful comments about it. Marcia Bunge read a large part of the first draft of the whole manuscript and caused me to improve the connection between text and topic and the organization between chapters. Elisabeth Moltmann-Wendel kindly commented on this first draft. My Peruvian friends were invariably helpful in giving me information, especially Luis Reinoso, Efraín Llanco, Pedro Uchuya, and—as a Peruvianized North American—Bernard "Pete" Byrne. Emilie Townes efficiently connected me with many womanist scholars concerned with the place of the child in theology.

As an independent scholar I have benefited greatly from conferences of the National Coalition of Independent Scholars and my local Independent Scholars' Association of the North Carolina Triangle.

Since members of these groups come from a wide variety of academic fields and religious or nonreligious backgrounds, their responses to a mainly theological issue were stimulating. I also appreciated the support of Dean L. Gregory Jones of the Duke University Divinity School in enabling me to continue my late husband's exchange program with Latin America by taking small groups of theology students for teaching or cultural immersion to Peru. In addition these projects were made possible through the superb leadership and friendship of the Reverend Dr. Mark Wethington, who for about sixteen years has taken pastors, students, and lay people to Peru and has hosted Peruvians in this country. The Reverend Para Drake also contributed to these exchanges for several years. Gustavo Gutiérrez—when he happened to be in Lima—and the people of the Instituto Bartolomé de las Casas have always graciously shared with our visiting groups their knowledge of the Peruvian situation.

My summers in Germany were continuously enriched by the kind neighborliness and friendship of Wolfgang and Elisabeth Schrage. I made constant use of their great home library. My sister Ruth Karwehl has regularly supplied me with information from German sources, and my brother and sister-in-law, Hans-Martin and Brigitte Karwehl, were especially helpful concerning information on Asian religions and on art resources.

There are many others to whom I am grateful for various kinds of support: Hannah and Edward J. Neugaard, M. Douglas and Blair Meeks, Jörg Rieger, Mary McClintock Fulkerson, Lothar and Lilo Schreiner, Frederick Trost, Waltraud Schmidt-Wegner, Mark and Margot Pickett, Katherine Bartlett, Sally Malek, Tom and Polly Harris, Rosanna Panizo, Kitty Dixon, Esther Hammer, Martin Keiper, Kimberly Vrudny, Brigitte and Hermann Schmidt, and Liselotte Schrader Woyke. I sensed correctly at first sight that Ulrike Guthrie would be an excellent editor to work with, and the whole team at The Pilgrim Press matched her efficiency and kindness.

Then there are those to whom I am most closely tied: my daughter, Dagmar Herzog, and her husband, Michael Staub, keep energizing me by their amazing intellectual pursuits and the unwavering love and support for their daughter Lucy, whose courage, affection, and love of life outweigh her handicaps. Finally, anybody who has known

Frederick Herzog (1925–1995) will sense that his life, love, and work have inspired every line of this book.

Concerning technicalities, I hope that readers will not mind the fact that many of my sources are German and some are Latin American. I live three months of each year in Germany and at least one or two weeks annually in Peru. Since our lives and our scholarship are increasingly determined by global events, I assume that sources from different continents will be helpful in giving a wider view.

When I talk about "children," I often include all young people under the age of eighteen. This is how the International Labor Organization, UNICEF, and other organizations use the term, and it is the only way we can work for the legal protection of young people according to the International Convention on the Rights of the Child. However, when I talk of "the child" in reference to Jesus of Nazareth's use of the word, I have the small child in mind: its playfulness, energy, curiosity, vulnerability, lack of pretension or deception, contentment in being dependent on love and care, and closeness to body and nature. In many cases, the difference between younger and older children will be fluid—as it is in the New Testament, where even grownups are "children of God."

*Durham, North Carolina*

# INTRODUCTION

➤ ✦ ◄

## The Child as Fact and Fiction, Victim and Savior

This study urges theologians and interested lay people in churches, schools, and universities to take children seriously in the construction of theology and in our life as people of faith and conscience. We are increasingly aware that life on this globe is fragile and that children as the most vulnerable human beings need our special care and commitment. At the same time, however, children have proven that they are influential agents and actors locally and globally, for good or for bad. It is therefore surprising that until recently theology has continuously relegated them to fields like Christian education and pastoral theology and has been oblivious to them in systematic theology, church history, and biblical theology. Even liberation theologies or ecumenical studies have largely been centered on adults. While theologians have tried hard to wrest some meaning from the events of September 11, 2001, in which almost three thousand people were killed in a day, few pay any attention to the estimated thirty thousand children under age five who die *every* day around this globe from *preventable* causes, according to UNICEF statistics.[1] Should that not be of concern to theologians?

Traditionally children have not been seen as an important part of our daily lives. In fact, they have been kept out of areas of adult business and decision making, while being courted by advertisers and hugged by political campaigners. There are certain places in the world where most people do not like to take children: prisons, battlefields, houses of prostitution, late-night bars, porno shops, gun shows, shooting galleries, and drug-infested neighborhoods. It is not only fear for their physical or psychological health that keeps grown-ups from introducing them to those places, but children seem to represent the conscience of human beings who keep them at a distance from "adult" and "adulterous" affairs. We know, however, that children are actually present in all these environments. In recent years alone, the Kosovo war, the wars in Afghanistan and Iraq, the crises in Liberia, Sierra Leone, and the Sudan, and countless other conflicts have proven again that children are massively involved in war—both as victims or recruited killers. Child abuse is pervasive in family situations even more than in public places, including churches. Guns and drugs are available to children within their homes and schools. Child prostitution is widespread in all parts of the world, especially where poverty reigns. Many of our consumer goods are produced by child labor. Businesses exploit children as consumers, and beauty pageants train them to act like adults before they are even in school.

We know all of this, but we still prefer to see children as relatively innocent and in need of protection from the worst parts of the adult world. Even when we learn that a child in our neighborhood can kill— as has happened in U.S. and European schools—we consider this a horrible exception within the world of children, and we try to "fix" *their* world instead of our own, which they are merely imitating.

We react to children emotionally on the basis of popular notions of childhood, memories of our own experiences as children, or ideas perceived to be of biblical origin, avoiding thereby the reality of our present predicaments. Children touch us more deeply than most adults. That is why entrepreneurs, politicians, and fund-raisers of nonprofit organizations try to attract our interest, our votes, and our money by presenting sentimental images of children: the sweet, the charming, the needy, those with disabilities. These images move us to help, protect, and enjoy them, or to rediscover in them what we have forgotten or suppressed.

For Christians, there is the additional influence of images from our religious upbringing: pictures of Jesus surrounded by children, often depicting a text that has incorrectly and sentimentally been connected with infant baptism:

> People were bringing little children to him, in order that he might touch them; and the disciples spoke sternly to them. But when Jesus saw this he was indignant and said to them, "Let the little children come to me; do not stop them; for it is to such as these that the kingdom of God belongs." (Mark 10:13–14)

Besides pictures we might remember sermons at Christmas time concerning Isaiah's prophecy that the "peaceable kingdom" will be led by a child. The idea that a child will save the world and bring peace is, however, not only present in the Jewish or Christian Scriptures; it has deep historical roots in many cultures and religions of the world. The legends surrounding the birth of the Buddha contain some images that have a striking resemblance to those in the story of Jesus' birth in the Gospels.[2] The benevolent, elephant-headed Hindu god Ganesa, depicted with vitality and humor in thousands of images, was born in an even more miraculous way than Jesus or Buddha, and his mother Parvati was immediately sure that this child would be venerated above all other gods.[3] The Islamic faith, which clearly distinguishes the divine and the human realms and considers it impossible that God would have a son, nevertheless accepts Jesus' virgin birth and describes miracles that Jesus performed as a child. Even in pagan antiquity we find, for example, in Heraclitus and Virgil, visions of a savior child who will bring peace and happiness to nature and to human beings.[4]

Yet there is a profound clash between images of the child as savior and the overwhelming contemporary and historical evidence of the child as victim. At the beginning of the new millennium, one in six children in the United States lives in poverty.[5] One-and-a-half million U.S. children have a parent in prison.[6] In 1999, six to seven million U.S. children were taking mood-altering drugs like Ritalin,[7] and meanwhile Europe has caught up with this trend. An estimated three hundred thousand child soldiers are being trained to kill in Africa, Asia, and Latin America.[8] About 246 million children between ages five and seventeen years work for starvation wages to enable their families' survival or well-being.[9] An estimated one million children were forced into sexual trafficking during the year 2000.[10] Fifteen million children have been orphaned by AIDS.[11] About 4.5 million children worldwide have died from AIDS during the past twenty-three years.[12] Six hundred thousand children under age five are estimated to have died in Iraq during the time of U.S. sanctions,[13] and nobody has yet counted the dead, crippled, and orphaned children among the many thousands of Iraqis who have become victims of violence in recent times.

I pondered the clash of images between the child as savior and as victim when in November of 1998 I attended the annual conference of the American Academy of Religion in the midst of Florida's Disney World, the "Magic Kingdom" constructed to allow us to become children again.[14] Marian Wright Edelman gave a splendid lecture on theology's need to be concerned about children, and a group of black womanist theologians were the first to take up her challenge in presentations at the same conference. I realized then that theology had been concerned with many people at the underside of history: women, racial and ethnic groups, people of different sexual orientations, the poor, and people with disabilities. Moreover, many theologians had learned to care deeply about animals and the ecosystem. However, theology had never put a child in its center the way Jesus did, according to Mark 9:36:

> Then he took a little child and put it among them; and taking it in his arms, he said to them, "Whoever welcomes one such child in my name welcomes me, and whoever welcomes me welcomes not me but the one who sent me."

While practical theology and Christian education have certainly been concerned with childhood issues, systematic theology has remained concentrated on adult persons. Church history has for centuries dealt with quarrels about the baptism of children and their presumed innocence or inherited sinfulness; exegesis has interpreted Jesus' words about children in standard commentaries on the synoptic Gospels. Until very recently, however, theology in its core has never been serious about centering its message in the realm of God as represented in a child, the way Jesus is reported to have done it: "Truly I tell you, whoever does not receive the kingdom of God as a little child will never enter it" (Mark 10:15).

Before we therefore make up for this deficit and deal seriously with the child in theology, we have to ask what we mean by a "child," statistically as well as theoretically. Since UNICEF and the International Labor Organization (ILO) refer to children as any young person under eighteen years of age, and since the United Nations Convention on the Rights of the Child does the same, I will here also follow this definition. Different societies have various ways of legally defining the age of "children." Since no government wants to be accused of imprisoning or killing children, the age limits often change: in South Africa, childhood ends at ten years of age, and in England today a ten-year-old has criminal responsibility;[15] Israel has lowered the legal criminal age from sixteen in 1987 and fourteen in 1988 to twelve more recently, because of the escalating violence by children in the Intifada.[16] I use the UNICEF limit of eighteen years because it plays an important role in international efforts to curb the devastating effects of exploitative child labor, child prostitution, involvement of children in armed combat, and other abuses. However, when I talk about Jesus' words and actions concerning children, I assume that he had the small child in mind, as I explained in my preface.

More complex is the theoretical definition of childhood. Ever since Philippe Ariès asserted that the Middle Ages had no concept of childhood, portraying children as little adults, and that children simply grew up as companions of adults without being—like modern children—their doting parents' center of attention, scholars have debated his thesis.[17] Lloyd de Mause, for example, saw the history of childhood completely differently. He contended that Ariès painted too positive a picture of medieval parents and children. He emphasized pervasive child abuse in the past and more loving care of children in the present.[18] I cannot do justice here to this very important controversy, but what certainly remains Ariès's greatest contribution is the idea that childhood is differently constructed in every age. There is no essential and no universal childhood. What was considered necessary discipline in one age is considered child abuse in another. What was healthy, frank sexual play between adults and children in Ariès's estimation, is considered unacceptable behavior in De Mause's opinon.[19]

Some of these enormous changes are simply caused by technological advances. What in antiquity used to be a cruel abandonment of sickly or unwanted children can be considered a primitive way of population control that today is achieved by technical means of family planning and abortion. Other differences in popular perception are grounded in social and economic circumstances. For example, Nancy Scheper-Hughes has described how poor women in Brazil who do not know how to feed one more child might still today allow a sickly baby to die, and how this practice then becomes a culturally sanctioned act.[20] Not only does every age define childhood differently, but, as psychologists and sociologists remind us, every culture and every individual constructs different "figurations" of what a child is.

Childhood can be "a highly valued feature of adulthood. For example, the turn back to one's childhood to repair the adult or to reclaim 'the child within' (as in many psychotherapeutic techniques) has become a familiar response to adult problems . . . ."[21] In the nineteenth century theories of infantile development were often linked to theories of race. For Herbert Spencer, a developmental human history is visible in the child. He saw children as little savages, not innocents, and for him "race and sex were explicitly identified as bodily traits that would both indicate and correlate with differences in mental development. . . . Like Darwin's biography, Spencer's observations about the child in the domestic space opened out onto a colonial world of human differences. The 'lower races' had fewer mental powers—like children."[22]

It is clear, then, that "invocations of the child . . . are historically and culturally specific."[23] Childhood reflects the needs, fears, and wishes of adults. "The child has, in a real sense, become a myth, and become mythologized. . . . Myth denies the complexity of history and historical construction; it gives them the simplicity of essences."[24] Advertisements that use the images of pretty children to lure us into another shopping spree or get us to donate to a charity make use of this myth. Even our statistics of child mortality, birthweight, or household size can be just "stories," and our own children may be a tapestry of texts of childhood.[25] However, being aware of the social construction of childhood does not help us to deal with the burning issues of children around the globe unless we also realize that "there are . . . material realities which we ignore at our peril."[26] It is important to get away from biological determinism, but we might also run "the risk of abandoning the embodied material child."[27] Nature and nurture can never be separated. Our figurations and fictions have an effect on the concrete well-being of children, and their "bodily needs are . . . mediated, adapted and controlled by human society."[28]

What remains important is the difference of children in terms of class, gender, ethnicity, region, and religion. However local or global our outlook might be, we have to take these differences into consideration, just as feminism in the seventies had to learn that sisterhood is not global or universal, but decisively varied. With these premises in mind we have to challenge theology to listen to children "for a change." It was a change of heart that Jesus had in mind when he asked grown-up men to "become like children."

**1**

# THEOLOGY'S HISTORIC NEGLECT OF AND RECENT INTEREST IN THE CHILD

→ ✦ ←

For Systematic Theology the child is still neither a factor nor a topic of scholarly reflection; neither did it take up the idea of a theology oriented in the child, nor did it pursue the task of a theological anthropology of the child.[1]

Child rearing, as the responsibility largely of women, has not been regarded as a serious theological topic. Hence, the subject of children as a religious issue was placed under the less prestigious area of Christian education.[2]

Until very recently, the field of systematic theology in the twentieth century has been largely silent on the question of children.[3]

Studies of the child in theology can learn much from the evolution of women's studies in theology. It took many years of intensive research and writing on the hidden or forgotten role of women in history before theologians became widely aware of the issue and sensitive to its implications. Dictionaries of church and theology have learned in recent decades to add entries for "Women," but entries for "Child" or

"Children" are frequently still missing.[4] In the pioneering volume *The Child in Christian Thought,* Marcia Bunge points out that children do not play a role in the way systematic theologians treat central theological themes.[5] In the same book, Bonnie Miller-McLemore declares that children as subjects in their own right have figured very little in theologians' ruminations about human nature and salvation. Even in feminist theology, she states, one has to read "between the lines" in writings on motherhood and the family or discern a "subtext" in order to find out that there is indeed a concern for children, especially "a material appreciation of the labors of love, a psychological grappling with early developmental issues, a spiritual understanding of the gifts of children, and a political declaration of the vulnerabilities and rights of children."[6] Feminist theologians have more directly dealt with childhood when they tried to discover the roots of child abuse.[7]

Childhood has, however, not always been neglected in the history of Christian thought, as Marcia Bunge's collection of articles proves. From Chrysostom, Augustine, and Thomas Aquinas to Luther, Calvin, and John Wesley; from Schleiermacher to Karl Barth, children have appeared in theological works. Hardly anywhere, however, can we discover a stance as radical as that attributed by the Gospels to Jesus of Nazareth: the child as model for our life and faith and as representative of Godself.

Centering theology in children does not mean falling back upon our tendency to put human beings high above—and separate from—everything else in the universe. On the contrary, we can learn from a child to live and think ecologically, because children do not build nuclear reactors or weapons of mass destruction; they are more vulnerable than grownups to air pollution and poisoned food; they are intimately tied to their immediate locality—without dreams of global domination. This has nothing to do with innocence, but with the reality of utter dependence. The small child is so dependent on us that it teases love and care out of us. It elicits a gentleness and concern that we usually do not bestow on our adult friends. Our stewardship of the earth becomes more intense when we know that a child's life hangs in the balance, and our sense of responsibility for a fragile cosmic web becomes stronger in the presence of a child.

This need for responsibility can on the one hand easily lead to a frantic social activism; on the other, our sense of the child's intuitive trust and wholeness might cause us to plead for a childlike spirituality. Both activism and spirituality play an important role, but separated from each other they will lead to moralism or individualistic piety. Putting a child at the center of theology will mean instead acknowledging that our relationship with God finds expression in our relationship with children. Martin Luther has compared the unity of "faith" and "good works" to the inseparability of fire and warmth: the one simply results from the other. Likewise spirituality and praxis, vision and action concerning children cannot be separated. The necessary interweaving of both is a human truth that does not only pertain to the Christian faith.

Many religious traditions, including Christianity, see a divine presence in the child and expect a "redeemer child" to save the world; many also emphasize the concrete responsibility for children. In keeping my heart and mind open to visions of other cultures and religions, past and present, I would like to gain a better understanding of my own Christian tradition: What did Jesus mean by tying divinity to childhood and true life to the "welcoming" of children in God's name? How did his vision relate to the Hebrew prophets' tradition of the redeemer child? Was Jesus' concrete closeness to children unique in the history of religions, as one exegete has claimed?[8] And why would a man like Karl Marx praise Jesus' love of children?[9] What are the political implications of a redeemer child that is expected to bring peace?

We know that Isaiah did not prophesy a "spiritual" messiah child, but a concrete "prince of peace" who on King David's throne would realize God's rule on earth. Jesus also did not talk about some metaphysical realm of God being represented in a child, but in all three synoptic Gospels his words about children appear in the context of the disciples' quarreling about who might be the greatest among them. He puts a "real" child among them and declares that "the least among all of you is the greatest" (Luke 9:48). Related Gospel passages make it clear that Jesus was here not just speaking about spiritual conditions, but that he had concrete political practices in mind. For example, when James and John want to have priority seating in the "kingdom," or realm of God, he declared,

> You know that among the Gentiles those whom they recognize
> as their rulers lord it over them, and their great ones are

tyrants over them. But it is not so among you; but whoever wishes to become great among you must be your servant, and whoever wishes to be first among you must be slave of all (Mark 10:42–44, par. Luke 22:24–26).

In the social order here described, power is grounded in those who lack official authority and who are found in the lowest social rank, like children and servants. In the phrasing of the Beatitudes, it will be the "poor in spirit," the "peacemakers," and the "meek" who will "inherit the earth."

When it comes to the relationship between children—"the meek"—and peacemaking, feminist theology is especially challenged to resist traditional notions of weakness, servanthood, and childlikeness, because women have been "lorded over" in patriarchal systems by being pushed into these categories. Also, the expected redeemer child was always a male, even though the Hebrew Bible portrays many strong women leaders like Deborah or Esther, and even though the prophets already knew that the Spirit will be poured out on "all flesh," and "your sons and your daughters shall prophesy" (Joel 2:28). Our task is, then, to discern how Jesus preached and lived a model of power-sharing in which human beings—without gender distinction—do not expect from others what they don't want to embody themselves. As Judith Gundry-Volf puts it, "The point is not self-negation arising out of powerlessness; rather it is the exercise of power motivated by love, in order to live a truly human life and accomplish social change."[10] By embracing children in a "motherly" way, even if they come to him, so to speak, from the street, Jesus shows his total disregard for the traditional notions of gender and class in his time. There are many other aspects of gender relations to which a theological discussion of childhood must pay attention, especially in view of the remaining immense gender gap in the situation of children around the globe today.[11] Gender issues are only one part of the overwhelming needs of children in our world that push us from reading the Bible to reading the "signs of the times" (Matt. 16:3) in our present situation.

This move from theology to social reality is inevitable if we take biblical words about children seriously. Robert Coles is right in stressing the political importance of children,[12] and we could have known all along from biblical figures like Pharaoh or Herod that children have played a political role to the extent that they were sometimes slaughtered en masse by rulers fearful of losing their power. In the twentieth century Hitler abused children in a different way: "Arian" women were decorated for bearing many children for the "Führer" and his wars, while Jewish and other unwanted children were murdered. Remembering the silence of most Christians during that time, we are reminded that theology has overlooked the intimate relationship between the child as redeemer, social agent, and victim. It has failed to remind dictators that a government that victimizes children or turns them into social agents of an ideology can never bring peace and "redemption" to a society.

In what sense, then, can a child today be a redeemer? At a panel discussion on school issues in my home city of Durham, North Carolina, in 2001, the Jewish director of Durham Congregations in Action, a consortium of about fifty-six congregations, two synagogues, and one mosque, cooperating in the social work for the city, declared that we must take seriously the education and nurture of every single child, because there might be a president or a messiah among them. I would like to rephrase that to say: we have to take seriously every child because each one represents the messiah—God's future. Welcoming a child redeems our obsession with adult notions of greatness and individualism that harm our communal life. The child as redeemer teaches us interdependence and trust in relationships, reminding us of Jesus' vulnerable openness to those around him.

Such reflections about the child's role in theology are not completely new; they simply have multiplied and intensified during the last years. I would like to give credit here to many pioneers in the field who made it possible for "the child" to have slowly entered theological reflection. Among the concerned authors are some early forerunners: in Germany, Gerhard Krause edited a small but important book, *Kinder im Evangelium (Children in the Gospel)* in 1973, and the Swiss theologian Hans-Ruedi Weber published *Jesus and the Children: Biblical Resources for Study and Preaching* in 1979.[13] Diana Wood in 1994 edited a volume that is important for church history, *The Church and Childhood*.[14] *Concilium* brought out a collection of essays on the subject in 1996.[15] Besides the previously mentioned volume edited by Marcia Bunge, *The Child in Christian Thought*, which is mainly historically oriented, the January

2000 issue of *Theology Today* contained a wide variety of articles on childhood issues, as did the *Interpretation* issue of April 2001. *The Sewannee Theological Review* devoted its Christmas 2004 issue to "Children and the Kingdom." Judith Gundry-Volf not only contributed to Marcia Bunge's volume, but also wrote about children in the Gospels in *Theology Today* and *Interpretation.*[16] Bonnie Miller-McLemore has been concerned with children in several works and has called attention to the fact that they "represent one of the least heard of all marginalized groups."[17] Pamela Couture pointed to the often hidden fate of children in poverty and its pastoral and political implications.[18] In Germany, Peter Müller did an extensive exegetical study of children in the New Testament.[19] Two German publications of 2002 have greatly enriched the theological research on children. *Gottes Kinder,* part of the series *Jahrbuch für biblische Theologie,* written by seventeen contributors, covers a wide variety of issues, from legal and sociological considerations to exegesis of Old and New Testament texts.[20] A volume edited by Rüdiger Lux combines biblical interpretations with representations of the child in art, philosophy, pedagogy, and Greek literature.[21] David H. Jensen's *Graced Vulnerability* is a superb theological study of childhood.[22]

While some of these publications are equally important for both sides of the Atlantic, there are also issues specific to a certain geographic context. Jacquelyn Grant realized early on that ministry with African American youth could not simply be based on traditional European American theologies.[23] Joan Martin and Evelyn Parker have worked on issues of public education and work with adolescents from a womanist point of view.[24] The Interdenominational Theological Center in Atlanta brought out an excellent journal issue, "Embracing Children of the World: Persons, Society and Culture—Transitions and Transformation," emphasizing, for example, the special needs of urban minority children and youth and the interaction between young Jews, Muslims, and Christians.[25]

The child thus appears in theology within different contexts. There is also a difference in theoretical presuppositions about children. For example, Danna Nolan Fewell has contributed an impressive postmodern perspective to the interpretation of the Hebrew Bible for children.[26] She freely blends innovative exegesis with poetry, plays, and short sketches of children's observations. Besides such individual works, there is finally also institutional progress. The first two American

Academy of Religion consultations on "Childhood Studies and Religion" that took place at the conferences in Atlanta in November 2003 and in San Antonio in 2004 proved theology's growing awareness of the need for scholarship in this field and are being continued. The Protestant churches of Latin America and the Caribbean have expressed great interest in common research and action concerning the children of their continent where more than 40 percent of the population is under the age of eighteen. In September 2002, fifty-five leaders of these churches gathered in Barba de Heredia, Costa Rica, and a second consultation took place November 13–15, 2003, in Buenos Aires, with the goal of gaining a deeper biblical and pastoral understanding of childhood and children.[27] In Tegucigalpa, Honduras, a consultation took place in February 2004, discussing the urgent problem of new legislation concerning delinquent street children.[28] In Norway the faculty of theology at the University of Oslo and the Norwegian Research Council are involved in a comprehensive research project titled, "'As a Little Child'? An Investigation of Perceptions of Children and Childhood in Early Christianity, Related to the General Culture of Antiquity."[29]

Theologians might take note that scholars of other disciplines have in recent years clearly centered their research on the child. Outstanding among them is the psychologist Robert Coles, with his early series *Children of Crisis* and the later volumes, *The Political Life of Children* (1986) and *The Spiritual Life of Children* (1990). Nancy Scheper-Hughes placed the child in the center of her anthropology. Her *Death without Weeping: The Violence of Everyday Life in Brazil* (1992) is as moving as it is intellectually sharp, and the volume she edited with Carolyn Sargent, *Small Wars: The Cultural Politics of Childhood* (1998), successfully shatters popular images of "family values." Like Coles, Scheper-Hughes knows that childhood issues cannot be separated from politics.

Art historians have found that some of the most famous modern painters, like Pablo Picasso, Paul Klee, Wassily Kandinsky, Gabriele Münter, and Henri Matisse, have derived much of their originality from observing and admiring children's drawings.[30] Museums now feature exhibits on the child in contemporary art. A very large exhibit in Koblenz, Germany, in the summer of 2000 showed paintings, sculpture, and photography concerning "Children of the Twentieth Century."[31] New York's Museum of Modern Art in the fall of 2000 ex-

hibited a collection called "Innocence and Experience," which concentrated on the dark side of childhood, the mysterious, fascinating, or
frightening child on the threshold to adulthood.

Legal scholars, like theologians, still have a long way to go in focus-
ing their attention on children. Elise Boulding wrote in 1979: "I do not
know of any country where there is any body or case of statutory law
setting forth the rights of children. . . . There is no legal agreement on
'who is a child.'"[32] Times have changed. The International Convention
on the Rights of the Child has been ratified by 191 nations (unfortunately not by the United States and Somalia). But "there are surpris-
ingly few legal scholars who focus in some general sense on the rights
of the child," as Katherine Bartlett, dean of the Duke University Law
School, stated in 2000.[33] She also pointed to exceptions: various scholars have written articles in law reviews on legal representation, surro-
gate parenthood, child custody, or objections by parents to medical
treatment of children.[34] In recent times the media have increasingly discussed the legal difficulties of punishing children for serious crimes, especially since the trial of the Washington area sniper Lee Malvo, and
the continuing research of psychologists and lawyers will be needed to
find an ethical solution to this complex problem. Another issue being
researched intensely is immigration law for children.[35] Within the medical community, there has been increasing research on the uncertain effects of "adult" medications for children, the overuse of Ritalin, and the
possibly deadly consequences of antidepressants for young people.

The scholarship on childhood done by historians is of course of
special importance to theologians. I have already mentioned Philippe
Ariès's classic work, *Centuries of Childhood*, which has been variously
criticized during the last decades. Yet it remains a pioneering volume
by reminding us that the concept of childhood is as much a construct
as are concepts of sexuality, child abuse, or adolescence.[36] Barbara
Tuchman echoes some of Ariès's ideas in her book, *A Distant Mirror*.[37]
However, the whole issue of what historically constituted child abuse
or child neglect remains unresolved. A new approach to documenting
history has been presented in the volume *Childhood in America*, edited
by Paula S. Fass and Mary Ann Mason.[38] It is an anthology documenting four hundred years of childhood in the United States. One could
even call it a collage of very different documents such as newspaper

accounts, fiction, memoirs, and academic essays. Gender, race, and class differences are taken into account.

Finally, even philosophy has concerned itself with children, and some scholars have described children as philosophers. Outstanding in the United States is the work of Gareth B. Matthews.[39] I will talk in chapter 6 about Helmut Hanisch's article on children as philosophers and theologians.[40] Both authors emphasize the importance and complexity of children's questions, questions that cannot be answered by a simple "true" or "false," nor indeed by any adequate reply. Their value lies simply in a continuous questioning and searching. Christopher Phillips, the founder of the popular "Socrates Café" movement, likes to philosophize with children. "Philosophy is important for kids of all ages," he says; "it gives them this great chance to sculpt their moral code, to figure out clearly who they are and who they want to be."[41]

All these examples could inspire theologians to focus their scholarship on children. In fact, the excellent recent volume *Rethinking Childhood* that draws on a variety of academic fields contains an article by Eileen W. Lindner, "Children as Theologians."[42] The most compelling reason, however, for theologians to be attentive to children is not their increasing importance in scholarly inquiries and public discussion, but the fact that they are at the heart of the biblical message. The Hebrew people knew that their future always depended on passing on their story and their faith to the next generation, and they expected a child to bring the final peace. Jesus' life is an expression of what it means to be a "child of God" and to discover God's presence in every child. "The gospels inform us that, far from signifying a condition to be overcome or transcended in order to obtain fulfillment, childhood . . . is the goal of Christian striving."[43] Our close reading of biblical texts regarding children has to be combined with historical, systematic, and practical reflections, because the topic invites a merging of the traditional theological disciplines.[44] What all the fields have in common is the basic representation of the child as our future.

Dietrich Bonhoeffer ended his theological study of "Act and Being" with some thoughts on this aspect of childhood.

> Willingness to be determined by the future is the eschatological possibility of the child. The child sees itself, in all fear and wonderment, gripped by the onrush of things to come, there-

fore it can live only for the present, but the grown man, willing to be determined by the present, lapses into the past, into himself, into death and guilt. It is only out of the future that the present can be lived. [45]

"With every child, a new life begins, original, unique, incomparable," says Jürgen Moltmann. "With every beginning of a new life, the hope for the reign of peace and justice is given a new chance."[46] We can add: with every adult who in the midst of our technologically and scientifically managed world "becomes like a child," eternal life breaks into the universe. Becoming like a child and thereby being close to God is also a basic conviction in Elisabeth Moltmann-Wendel's theology. It is not death that is the final goal of our life, she says with Hannah Arendt, but being born.[47] In her autobiography she speaks of her childhood as a time of feeling safe in the shadow of Jesus.[48] Grace Jantzen, also inspired by Hannah Arendt, suggests, "Taking birth as the centre of our imaginary will direct our attention to *this* world, to our connection, through the maternal continuum, with all others who have been born."[49] "With every new human being—provocatively stated—a piece of liberty comes into the world," states Karin Ulrich-Eschemann in reference to Hannah Arendt.[50]

In view of all these voices and especially in light of the biblical witness, we might ask with Robin Maas,

> How is it, then, that such a fundamental aspect of revelation should continue so consistently ignored, sentimentalized, suppressed? Why do we steadfastly resist the obvious implications of Jesus' teachings on childhood and even more, *his own childhood,* as a sign not of the beginning of our spiritual quest but, in a very real sense, as its *consummation?*[51]

Seeing childhood as fulfilled life, as goal and gift of life, not a stage to be overcome, is not just a Christian idea. There is a Hasidic saying: "When a child walks down the road, a company of angels goes before him proclaiming, 'Make way for the image of the Holy One.'"[52] And the Babylonian Talmud says, "Take care of the children of the poor, for from them will the Torah arise."[53] For the Jewish pediatrician Janusz Korczak, who refused to leave the children entrusted to him and who died with them in the concentration camp Treblinka in 1942, a child was "a sacred being to receive the mysterious God who thus offers future."[54] Korzcak also saw that it is the child in us that is nurtured when we care for children and that we can seek in the child the undiscovered part of ourselves.[55] This idea is not far from what the Buddhist Thich Nhat Hanh said in a Christmas meditation in 1996. He suggested that the child in us is the Holy Spirit, the Spirit of the Buddha, that has to be reborn again and again, helping us to live in the present moment, without worries or fears about the future.[56] To state it in the words of Bruno Schulz, we have to "mature into childhood." Schulz, a Polish Jew, was a writer and visual artist who became a victim of a Nazi massacre. In a letter to Andrzej Plesniewicz he wrote,

> If it were possible to reverse development, to attain the state of childhood again, to have its abundance and limitlessness once more, that "age of genius," those "messianic times" promised and sworn to us by all mythologies would come to pass. My ideal goal is to "mature into childhood."[57]

The child is the embodiment of divine spirit in different religious traditions. "Becoming like a child" is, for example, the goal of Taoists. Muslims, according to Muhammad, come back from a pilgrimage to Mecca like a newborn child. Tamil Hindus sing praises to their greatest gods by imagining them as babies or toddlers. We can learn from all these traditions without creating a religious melting pot. By revitalizing our own Christian tradition by its "childhood roots," we can have helpful dialogues with other faith traditions.

Was Jesus' attitude toward children unique? Yes and no. "Who is not unique?" asks the Buddhist Thich Nhat Hanh. Jesus is unique and yet present in every child on this earth. He is unique in having pronounced more forcefully and radically what other religions have also said about childhood. Moreover, he lived what he preached, showing what it means to live like a child of God, living a vulnerable life, beautiful like the lilies of the field and yet so risky that it could lead him to cry like a child to his Abba: "My God, my God, why have you forsaken me?"

Keeping our eyes focused on this "child of God" can propel us into action, working towards a world where thirty thousand children do not have to die tomorrow.

# 2

# THE CHALLENGE
# OF OUR TRADITION

## *Biblical Resources*

And a little child shall lead them. (Isa. 11:6)

Truly I tell you, unless you change and become like children,
you will never enter the kingdom of heaven. (Matt. 18:3)

Almost eleven million children worldwide die annually before
their fifth birthday from mostly preventable and treatable diseases.
Four million die in their first month of life.[1]

## THE CHILD IN THE HEBREW BIBLE

Theological concern for children is today inspired by two sources: the
challenge of biblical texts at the center of our tradition, and the present
situation of children around the world that indicates a global crisis.
Both the Jewish and the Christian traditions envision a child as God's
future for this world, whether as expected Messiah-King or as the Christ

child who will bring peace, and both plead for taking care of children. In view of these visions, the UNICEF statistics and other indicators pointing to a children's world of violence and war, hunger and homelessness, appear overwhelming. How can we profess our faith and yet remain idle in the face of so much suffering and injustice? Knowing that any kind of Christian activism will remain shallow if it is not rooted in the biblical witness and empowered by its spiritual energy, we will first turn to the ancient texts that so many generations have considered sacred guides.

There are images of children in the Hebrew Bible that indicate how Israel cherished children as YHWH's blessing: the baby Moses in a reed basket who will liberate the oppressed Israelites (Exod. 2); the boy Samuel who listens to God's voice and becomes a "trustworthy prophet" (1 Sam. 3:20); the young shepherd David who can kill a giant and play the lyre to banish King Saul's "evil spirit" (1 Sam. 16–17). While sons were valued much more than daughters because they would guarantee continuation of the family line and financial as well as cultic status, children in general were God's promise that the covenant would last for generations to come.

> *Sons are indeed a heritage from the LORD,*
> *the fruit of the womb a reward.*
> *Like arrows in the hand of a warrior*
> *are the sons of one's youth.*
> *Happy is the man who has his quiver full of them.*
> *He shall not be put to shame*
> *When he speaks with his enemies in the gate.* (Ps. 127:3–5)

The first lines of this text can easily be put into inclusive language, but the following warlike imagery indicates that sons were especially valued as defenders in a precarious nomadic or "pioneer" existence. In contrast to our society that shows increasing "fatherlessness" and singleness, life in Israel was determined by the family and its male head. Children were often considered ignorant, mischievous, and in need of discipline (2 Kings 2:23–24; Prov. 22:15; Wisdom 12:24–25), but they could also be seen as proclaiming God's glory in their very being and thereby representing a divine protection:

> *You have set your glory above the heavens.*
> *Out of the mouths of babes and infants*

*you have founded a bulwark because of your foes,*
*to silence the enemy and the avenger* (Ps. 8:1b–2)

Infertility was considered a terrible burden or even a curse and a large number of children the greatest blessing. Hannah, the mother of Samuel, suffered greatly because "the LORD had closed her womb" (1 Sam. 1:5ff.), and only when she conceived we are told that "the LORD remembered her" (1 Sam. 1:19). But there is no single pattern of family life in the Hebrew Bible and, in spite of the challenge of Genesis 1:28 to "Be fruitful and multiply," no *absolute* command for fertility. Isaiah 56:3b–5 clearly states:

*Do not let the eunuch say,*
*"I am just a dry tree."*
*For thus says the LORD:*
*To the eunuchs who keep my sabbaths,*
*who choose the things that please me*
*and hold fast my covenant,*
*I will give, in my house and within my walls,*
*a monument and a name*
*better than sons and daughters.*

Similarly Isaiah 54:1 proclaims:

*Sing, O barren one who did not bear;*
*burst into song and shout,*
*you who have not been in labor!*
*For the children of the desolate woman will be more*
*than the children of her that is married, says the LORD.*[2]

God's love for Israel is portrayed as a parent's love for a child:

*When Israel was a child, I loved him,*
*and out of Egypt I called my son.*

· · · · · · · ·

*. . . it was I who taught Ephraim to walk,*
*I took them up in my arms;*
*but they did not know that I healed them.*
*I led them with cords of human kindness,*
*with bands of love.*

*I was to them like those*
*who lift infants to their cheeks.*

*I bent down to them and fed them.* (Hos. 11:1, 3–4)

Infants in ancient Israel were first tended by their mother, but after two or three years the father took over the most important part of the education of a son, namely the teaching of the Torah. Though boys became part of the Covenant on their eighth day by circumcision, they were "unfinished" members of the community until they had studied and practiced the Torah. At the annual Passover ritual the youngest son would ask for the meaning of the celebration, and the father would answer the way Scripture commanded: "When your children ask you in time to come, 'What is the meaning of the decrees and the statues and the ordinances that the LORD our God has commanded you?' then you shall say to your children, 'We were Pharaoh's slaves in Egypt, but the LORD brought us out of Egypt with a mighty hand'" (Deut. 6:20–21; cf. Exod. 13:14; Josh. 4:6, 21). Passing on the Torah to the next generation was at the heart of Israelite faith:

> *Tell your children of it*
> *and let your children tell their children,*
> *and their children another generation.* (Joel 1:3; cf. Ps. 78:3–4)

Girls on the other hand learned household and agricultural skills or business deals concerning the land from their mother. At the age of ten to fifteen years they were given in marriage.[3] Child labor was important in Israel's early time for the household's economic survival.

> As early as age five or six, both boys and girls might be assigned tasks of fuel gathering, caring for younger children, picking and watering garden vegetables, and assisting in food preparation. . . . By the age of thirteen, children typically reached nearly full adult labor input in farm households.[4]

In Israel's later history there was also an appreciation of children's play (Zech. 8:5), but discipline, especially for sons, was always valued so highly that from today's point of view it appears cruel:

> *Do not withhold discipline from your children;*
> *if you beat them with a rod, they will not die.*

*If you beat them with the rod,*
*you will save their lives from Sheol.* (Prov. 23:13–14)

A harsh agricultural and pioneer situation in early Israel made strict authority within the kinship group necessary for survival, and we find similar views throughout antiquity in various cultures.[5]

The common ancient practice of abandoning newborn children, especially girls, who were sickly, handicapped, considered superfluous, or too great a burden, was not practiced in Israel. A famous papyrus of the year 1 B.C.E. shows a letter written by an Egyptian migrant laborer who tells his pregnant wife to cast out the newborn if it is a girl. In Rome, the newborn child was placed before the father's feet. Unless he lifted it up and acknowledged it, it was exposed, which meant that it died or was picked up by strangers to be trained as a slave or prostitute.[6] No such child exposure is known to have happened in Israel. While children were cherished, they were not idealized. In Psalm 51 David is said to have confessed that he was "born guilty, a sinner when my mother conceived me." It was only through instruction and strict guidance that the child would become a responsible adult, because "the inclination of the human heart is evil from youth" (Gen. 8:21; cf. 6:5).

## THE EXPECTED MESSIAH CHILD

The appreciation of children in Israel has to be seen against the background of the one child who—as a future ruler—was expected to bring peace and final deliverance. This is the vision proclaimed in the book of Isaiah:

*For a child has been born for us,*
*a son given to us;*
*authority rests upon his shoulders;*
*and he is named*
*Wonderful Counselor, Mighty God,*
*Everlasting Father, Prince of Peace.*
*His authority shall grow continually,*
*and there shall be endless peace*
*for the throne of David and his kingdom.* (Isa. 9:6–7)

*A shoot shall come out from the stump of Jesse,*
*and a branch shall grow out of his roots.*

*the spirit of the LORD shall rest on him,*
*the spirit of wisdom and understanding,*
*the spirit of counsel and might,*
*the spirit of knowledge and the fear of the LORD.*

. . . . . . . . . . .

*He shall not judge by what his eyes see,*
*or decide by what his ears hear;*
*but with righteousness he shall judge the poor,*
*and decide with equity for the meek of the earth.*

. . . . . . . . . .

*The wolf shall live with the lamb,*
*the leopard shall lie down with the kid,*
*the calf and the lion and the fatling together,*
*and a little child shall lead them.*
*The cow and the bear shall graze,*
*their young shall lie down together;*
*and the lion shall eat straw like the ox.*
*The nursing child shall play over the hole of the asp,*
*and the weaned child shall put its hand on the adder's den.* (Isa.11:1–8)

Christians have traditionally turned these lines into Christmas texts and interpreted them as announcing the coming of Christ. The prophecies from the eighth century B.C.E. were, however, either announcing the birth of a child and future king at the Davidian royal court or celebrating the ascent of a prince to the throne of David.[7] In any case, the future king "is not merely an ordinary person elevated to regal status through covenant with YHWH. He is, rather, a miraculous figure, and his accession is an event that transforms ordinary reality and ushers in the reign of justice traditionally associated with YHWH's own lordship." The prince assumes the status of God's son, "exchanging, as it were, human for divine paternity."[8] Perhaps the prophetic announcement of the royal child's birth was later used as an enthronement hymn. The point is that Israel did not separate spiritual and political peace and well-being. It inherited ideas of divine kingship from Egyptian traditions in which a transcendent deity acts in human history. But whereas in Egypt the prince was considered the physical son of a god, in Israel he was seen as adopted by YHWH as the legitimate representative on earth who ruled not by his own, but by YHWH's power (Ps. 2:7; 89:27f.; 2 Sam. 7:14). Probably Isaiah was speaking to a political crisis: parts of the northern kingdom had just been lost to Assyrians, and the people feared that YHWH had finally abandoned them to their enemies. Into this situation Isaiah proclaims the faithfulness of YHWH evident in the birth of a child who will be a just and wise ruler. So this is not the prophecy of a transcendent event, relating to "eternal salvation," but of a fulfilled history. Terms like "everlasting father," "endless peace," and "forevermore" (see Psalm 45) relate in the ancient oriental tradition to the quality and continuity of kingship, not to an endless chronology. Kings always were considered to have "eternal life."[9]

The prophecy's unity of politics and salvation is beautifully captured in the famous painting by the Quaker Edward Hicks, "The Peaceable Kingdom." Hicks inserts into the picture of peacefully playing animals and children a scene of William Penn making a treaty with Native Americans.[10] Human beings are here intricately interwoven with nature, and adult "business" is inseparable from the well-being of children, other creatures, and the land they live on. Whether we relate the Isaiah prophecies to Jesus or not, we should not ignore their concrete historical and ecological implications. When a ruler is concerned about the "poor" and the "meek of the earth" (Isa. 11:4); when there is no corruption or favoritism (11:3–5), not only people will benefit, but so will all of creation. Even a little child will be able to lead wild animals, and infants will be able to play around poisonous snakes (11:6–8).

We may consider this a utopian vision, but Israel was not alone in its expectation of a Golden Age in which a child would become a savior king whose reign would bring peace to all creation. We can find that image throughout antiquity, for example, in a fragment of Heraclitus and in the fourth Eclogue of Virgil.[11] I will later refer to similar images in the religious traditions of Asia. In the course of Israel's history the images of the child as savior and the child as victim were merged in a rabbinic story. Rabbi Juda said, "See how God loves the little children. When the Sanhedrin moved into captivity, the Shekinah did not follow, and she also did not follow the guards of the priests. But when the little children were forced into captivity, the Shekinah went along with them."[12] The closeness of children and divinity turns into an eschatological vision of childhood in the *Book of Jubilee:* "Then there will be no old people and persons tired of life, because they will all be children and young people."[13]

## THE MYSTERY OF THE ABRAHAM-ISAAC STORY

In view of all these savior-like images of children we might well ask how the ancient Israelites could have even remotely considered child sacrifice. While there was no abandonment of sickly or superfluous children as in other societies, there is some indication that Israel struggled with the issue of child sacrifice. The best-known example is Abraham's call to sacrifice his son (Gen. 22:1–19). In the Jewish tradition it is called "The Binding of Isaac." The story has been interpreted by some theologians as providing a pattern for blind obedience and child abuse, foreshadowing Christianity's controversial dogma of God sacrificing his son to atone for the world's sins.[14] The issue has to be seen in a larger context. It is well known that child sacrifice appears to have occurred in all cultures of antiquity. In the pre-Inca Andean cultures, the most beautiful and flawless children were sacrificed on sacred mountains to the sun god, as it is depicted, for example, on a pottery vessel from the Mochica culture of the northern coast of Peru.[15] Jon D. Levenson has traced the history of child sacrifice in Judaism and Christianity. He thinks that only at a relatively late stage of Israel's history child sacrifice was branded as counter to the will of YHWH and thus idolatrous. Jeremiah 19:5–6 clearly sees the practice as pagan slaughter, to be totally rejected by faithful Israelites. Ezekiel 20:25–31, like the book of Jeremiah written around the turn of the sixth century B.C.E., similarly condemns it, letting YHWH declare, "I gave them statutes that were not good . . . in order that I might horrify them, so that they might know that I am the LORD." That child sacrifice was known and often acceptable at a certain stage in Israel's history is obvious from the story of Jephtha's daughter (Judg. 11:29–40), but in contrast to the Abraham story, Jephthah was never *commanded* to sacrifice his daughter; he just made a foolish vow. Levenson suggests that the substitution of an animal was not a later stage of sacrifice, but had in fact always been an option. Abraham is not commanded to sacrifice a ram, but is allowed to.

What the later stage of sacrifice entailed was a sublimation or transformation: in Numbers 8:16–19 the Levites are taking the place of the firstborn sons. They are dedicated to the Lord, not killed. Gradually even a monetary contribution for the firstborn could take the place of killing him or making him a Levite (Num. 3:46–48; 18:15–18). Levenson concludes that the binding of Isaac does not only express the aversion to child sacrifice, but also continues the cultic tradition that the firstborn belongs to God. In addition, it was interpreted as an initiation story: Isaac willingly accepts his own imminent death; he is thereby passing into adulthood and becoming the next patriarch. Rabbinic literature continues the idea of Isaac's complete readiness for the sacrifice, and this tradition became important for martyrs.[16] Abraham's readiness to sacrifice his son becomes connected with the Passover sacrifice, just as in Christianity the eucharist is a reenactment of Jesus' final meal before his sacrificial death. "Both the Jewish and Christian systems of sacrifice come to be seen as founded upon a father's willingness to surrender his beloved son and the son's unstinting acceptance of the sacrificial role he has been assigned in the great drama of redemption."[17]

It is not surprising, then, that these foundational stories have been interpreted and misinterpreted in multiple ways throughout history. Conscientious or overly ambitious rulers and other patriarchs have sent their sons into war or other dangers, and the sons uncomplainingly risked their lives because the father's command seemed to imply a divine command and a proof of courageous, virtuous manhood. Unfortunately, in many such cases no angel prevented the son's death, and the victim did not become a savior as in the Isaac story, where the almost sacrificed child becomes the ancestor of the child savior: Matthew 1:2 traces Jesus' ancestry to Abraham and Isaac. There is no reason, however, to blame the story for the way it has been interpreted and to see in the binding of Isaac the pattern of a tyrannical father or an abused child. What we see is a dilemma that even a conscientious parent today could get into. When under a tyrannical or misguided regime a father has to send a son to war and likely to death in battle, he might be persuaded to consider this a divine command for a sacrifice by violence.[18] As in the rabbinic tradition, the victim then becomes a celebrated martyr. We have many contemporary examples in fathers of military men (and women) of various nations or in suicide bombers. While a case can be made for emergency situations where violence and sacrifice are needed to prevent greater violence, the death of many eighteen-year-old soldiers and countless Iraqi children in the war in Iraq is another reminder that people of faith are still confused about what sacrifice God might demand of them and their children. The God of Israel and of Jesus of Nazareth is a God of life who struggles for the *life* of children, not their sacrifice.[19]

Not everybody of course will draw this conclusion from "the binding of Isaac," and the story will always remain an ancient tale wrapped in mystery. But, as Phyllis Trible has pointed out, there are innumerable varieties of child sacrifice in cultures not informed by the Abraham story, and therefore we cannot make the story responsible for various horrors of our history and society.[20] Just recently a deeply religious mother in Texas killed two of her children and wounded the third because she had psychotic delusions, believing she was divinely chosen by God to kill her children as a test of faith and then serve as a witness when the world ended.[21] In case she had Abraham and Isaac in the back of her mind, some church must have failed to teach her that Abraham's vision and understanding of God were limited by his time and his culture, that they are not to be imitated, but to be seen as a stage in the spiritual and ethical grappling of humankind or even, as Frank Crüsemann puts it, as "a process between God and God."[22] There are other stories that indicate that the mind of YHWH is not immutable, but responds to human thought and action, as when Noah's faithfulness is followed by the divine decision that the flood will never be repeated (Gen. 8:21), or when Abraham's stubborn pleading for Sodom and Gomorrah elicits the promise that even ten people of integrity can save the cities from destruction. In trying to discern God's will, we have to see biblical characters as our challenging dialogue partners, not templates or models of action.[23]

The story of Abraham and Isaac has, however, become paradigmatic in the later Hebrew as well as the Christian tradition. Isaac, the "beloved son" of Abraham, is the ancestor of God's beloved child Israel (Hos. 11:1–4). For Christians, Isaac as the son risking to be sacrificed can point to the life of Jesus who in the Gospel of Matthew is called "servant" of God with direct reference to the Suffering Servant of Isaiah 42 (Matt. 12:17–20).[24] In this metaphoric network childhood is merged with servanthood and victimization with salvation. The

Suffering Servant is, however, not a passive or weak human being who acts like a docile child. "He will bring forth justice to the nations" (Isa. 42:1); "he will not grow faint or be crushed" (42:4).

> *The LORD GOD helps me;*
> *therefore I have not been disgraced;*
> *therefore I have set my face like flint.* (Isa. 50:7)

Such integrity and strength will later characterize those who, according to the apostle Paul, "are children of promise, like Isaac" (Gal. 4:28). This is a metaphoric line that leads us from consideration of the child in the Hebrew Bible to the child in the New Testament. There are, however, other connecting links to be considered, and they touch on the gender issue.

## PLAYFUL SOPHIA

In view of the dominance of male images of the child in the Hebrew Bible, we might consider the female "underground" that can also be discovered and that affects our understanding of savior figures in ancient Israel. While the expected Messiah was male, the prophet Joel proclaimed that God will pour out the divine spirit on "all flesh":

> *Your sons and your daughters shall prophesy,*
> *your old men shall dream dreams,*
> *and your young men shall see visions.*
> *Even on the male and female slaves,*
> *in those days, I will pour out my spirit.* (Joel 2:28–29)

More important, the female *sophia*, the personified wisdom figure of Proverbs and other Wisdom literature, shows some childlike features and teaches human beings to be true children of God. *Sophia* probably influenced Jesus' teaching and certainly shaped the way the Gospels and especially the Johannine writings understood the Christ.

> *The Lord created me at the beginning of his work,*
> *the first of his acts of long ago.*
> *Ages ago I was set up,*
> *At the first, before the beginning of the earth.*
>
> .   .   .   .   .   .   .   .   .   .   .   .   .   .

*Before the mountains had been shaped,*
*before the hills, I was brought forth—*
*When he established the heavens, I was there,*

.   .   .   .   .   .   .   .   .   .   .   .

*when he marked out the foundations of the earth,*
*then I was beside him, like a master worker;*
*and I was daily his delight,*
*rejoicing before him always,*
*rejoicing in his inhabited world*
*and delighting in the human race.* (Prov. 8:22–31)

The birth imagery in these lines: "created" (or "conceived") in 8:22 and "brought forth" in 8:24 tells us that God brings forth a child, so to speak, as the first step in creating the world and then has this child participate in the ordering of the universe, working, as it were, in interdependent partnership.[25] Traditionally the "master worker" image in 8:30 has been translated as "little child," but there is much uncertainty connected with the Hebrew word *'amôn*. The translation "little child" relates the word to Egyptian parallels where the goddess Maat, ruler of cosmic and social order, plays before her father, the creator god.[26] Other translators see the word as meaning "architect's plan," a blueprint for the cosmos, or they think the grammar may be read differently, meaning "Then I was with [God], the master worker."[27] However, the preferred reading today is "master worker" in terms of a female force codesigning the creation; a female underside, so to speak, of the (grammatically male) Logos at the beginning of John's gospel. Otto Plöger translates the "master worker" as "foster child" (*"Pflegling"*), a ward or minor, in whose playful attentiveness YHWH delights.[28] Even if the term "master worker" were to refer to an *adult* female cocreator, the description of the way this power is brought forth and codesigns creation elicits the aura of a child's playful imagination and children's sheer delight in life itself, "a spotless mirror of divine power and an image of God's goodness" (Wisdom 7:26). In Philo, Sophia is the "daughter of God," and Philo is the link to the Gospel of John that begins in 1:1–18 with a wisdom hymn to the Logos.[29] Sophia and Logos are parallel in Wisdom 9:1–2, and both are all-powerful, without thereby diminishing God's power, which they express in different ways.[30] John

1:12 declares that those who "receive" the Logos will also receive the power to become "children of God." We will later see in the New Testament that "receiving" or "welcoming" a child means receiving Jesus and thereby receiving God (Mark 9:37; Luke 9:46).

Jesus is the child and envoy of Sophia and ultimately Sophia herself, especially in the Gospel of Matthew.[31] The Gospel of John substitutes the stories of Jesus' birth and infancy with the description of the Logos who was rejected by the world. An apocalyptic text describes Sophia as looking for a home among human beings—like the Logos of John 1:11 or like the infant Jesus in Luke 2:7—but not finding it returning to her heavenly home and taking her place among angels.[32] In the book of Wisdom, Sophia is seen, like the Logos, as all-powerful, all-seeing, all-knowing (Wisdom 7:17–24). However, in contrast to the very male, warrior-like, sword-wielding Logos (Wisdom 18:15–16; 22), Sophia is felt like the breath of life itself, knowing the ways of wind, plants, and animals, energizing and illuminating the whole creation with her eternal splendor, and causing people to become "friends of God and prophets" (Wisdom 7:17–30).[33] Sophia's spirit converts human beings into true children and is understood by children. A Qumran psalm praises Wisdom for proclaiming God's power to "those lacking judgment"—and these certainly include children:

> For, wisdom has been granted
> So that YHWH's glory can be proclaimed
> And so that his many deeds can be recounted
> Has she been taught to man:
> So that his power can be proclaimed to ordinary people
> So that his might can be explained to those lacking judgment:
> Those found to be far from his gates.[34]

Such Wisdom texts prove that Israel's visions of its past and future reached beyond the expectations of a male redeemer child on the throne of David. We can also assume that the daily life of children in ancient Israel was much more visible, colorful, and influential than what we can read in the available texts written by educated males.[35] It is certain, however, that children were seen throughout antiquity and also in the Hebrew Bible as unfinished creatures who could become full human beings only by having adults train and discipline them.

While in all societies they were certainly cherished on the personal level, in legal and cultic matters they did not count.[36] In Israel children were not permitted to enter the temple, and only at age twenty could young men enter the outer court of the temple.[37] Girls were generally not taught the Torah and therefore had even less cultic importance. In comparison with Roman customs, however, where children were often not even given names, but only numbers, and where child abandonment was frequent, children in Israel were considered a special blessing. From Exodus through the Psalms and the prophets, the mandate to care for orphans—as for widows—is often emphasized.[38] More radically, Psalm 8:1b–2 proclaims the power of crying infants as a protection against enemies.

> *You have set your glory above the heavens.*
> *Out of the mouths of babes and infants*
> *you have founded a bulwark because of your foes,*
> *to silence the enemy and the avenger.*

The cry of a newborn child is the first intensely awaited sign of its life and vitality. The crying of infants is an insuppressible challenge, and yet it does not force a decision, but leaves adults the freedom to respond. Anthropologists have observed children as peacemakers in social conflicts, because their mere appearance often slows down aggression while not *forcing* the enemies to reconcile.[39] The existence of Israel's children represented a guarantee of Israel's future and therefore a protection.

In this environment of children as protectors and saviors of a suffering, chosen people and at the same time as victims of legal and cultic neglect, Jesus grew up in a traditional Jewish setting, in an ambiguous family situation and in an occupied country constantly threatened by political crisis. There is at least the possibility that his own childhood may have influenced his later view of children.

## THE CHILD IN THE NEW TESTAMENT

Before dealing with Jesus' startling words about children, we might consider what we can discern or assume about his own childhood. Since, for example, on any given Sunday in countless Christian worship services worldwide the virgin birth is professed, we have to inquire into its origin and meaning. If Jesus Christ was as truly human as he was truly God, his birth and childhood must have affected his life and teaching. However, our inquiry is a difficult one: not only do we know very little about Jesus' birth and childhood, but the few orientation points that the New Testament provides are considered myths or legends by many contemporary scholars.

Nevertheless, some tentative conclusions can be drawn from a variety of sources. Andries van Aarde, for example, has scrutinized the available canonical and noncanonical texts, the Egyptian, Roman, and Hellenistic literature and practices surrounding and permeating Israel in Jesus' time, and the work of the theological critics evaluating all of this today. He comes to the conclusion that Jesus grew up as a fatherless child in Galilee, as such was socially and ritually discriminated against as a "bastard" child, underwent John the Baptist's baptism in order to rid himself of the "systemic" sin of which he was accused, thereby becoming suddenly certain that God was his father, and from then on preached the good news of God's fatherhood to all the downtrodden people he gathered around him, for example, street children who were nobodies in his society and often fatherless, and women who were without patriarchal protection.

Van Aarde further argues that "neither Paul nor Mark seem to know anything about either Joseph or Mary's virginity," even though they are the earliest canonical sources, and "no known father played a role in the life of the historical Jesus."[40] He traces the figure of Joseph, whom he considers legendary, to the Joseph of the Hebrew Bible and the tradition praising him as the model of a kind and forgiving man. The idea that Joseph adopted the boy Jesus and stayed with Mary in order to save her from "public disgrace," but without having sexual relations with her before Jesus' birth (Matt. 1:19, 25), may have grown out of the widely known assumption that divine beings were born from virgins, and it also related to the prophecy of Isaiah 7:14 that a "virgin" (a term used in the Septuagint translation, but in the original Hebrew simply indicating a young woman of marriageable age)[41] shall bear a son. Such considerations, according to Van Aarde, do not imply that Mary was a woman of questionable morals. The child Jesus may have been conceived by rape or seduction or by liaison with a "foreigner" from the multicultural borderland around Nazareth who was not considered a true Israelite and therefore caused the child to be treated as a nobody in terms of the strict purity laws of the Jerusalem priesthood. In fact, the Joseph tradition of the northern tribes stood in tension with the Judaic southern priestly power structure, since the northerners had mixed with Samaritans and pagans. "Since the post-exilic marriage reform measures (see Neh. 9–10; Ezra 9–10) and certainly also during the first century, there was an insistence on the basis of priestly purity codes that male Israelites divorce 'foreign' women. The result was 'fatherlessness,' or in other words, 'illegitimacy.'"[42] A pregnant woman who was abandoned by her husband was often given the label "whore." The genealogy of Matthew 1 gives the fatherless child Jesus the legitimation of descent from Abraham and David to Joseph who adopted the child. The location of Jesus' birth in Bethlehem and the flight to Egypt are, according to Van Aarde, legends that connect the child to David's city and, through the story of Herod's infanticide, emphasize the opposition between the Jerusalem royalty and the descendants of Joseph in the northern kingdom.

I cannot do justice here to Van Aarde's detailed arguments, but I appreciate his attempt to go beyond the usual assumption that we simply do not know anything about Jesus' birth and childhood that is historically verifiable. While I regard many of his conclusions as mere speculations, he may have contributed an interesting perspective to an understanding of Jesus' view of childhood and fatherhood. Jane Schaberg had much earlier (1987) pointed out that the creative act of God described as "virginal conception" does not necessarily replace human paternity.[43] She suggested that Joseph, whom she does not consider as legendary as does van Aarde, had two alternatives to explain the pregnancy of Mary: rape or seduction. A raped woman could be divorced or the marriage could be completed. A seduced woman was to be stoned together with her partner. Joseph first chooses divorce as the best legal option, but then he follows the angel's advice to take Mary as his wife—which removed the suspicion of seduction or adultery, but not of rape.[44] Both Schaberg and Van Aarde emphasize that children born of unlawful unions would be lifelong misfits who would suffer serious discrimination. They were forbidden marriage with priestly families, Levites, legitimate Israelites, and even with illegitimate descendants of priests. They could not hold public office nor participate in court decisions. "Their families' share in Israel's final redemption was vigorously argued."[45]

Van Aarde goes beyond interpreting the meaning of "virginal conception" to emphasize what he considers the merely shadowy or legendary existence of Joseph. John P. Meier, writing about a decade before Van Aarde, strongly disagrees with Schaberg and points out that the precise origins of the idea of virginal conception remain obscure and that any claim of Jesus' illegitimacy must remain speculative, going back to polemics of the first centuries after Christ.[46] However, he acknowledges the paradox of Jesus being virginally conceived and yet being the Son of David through Joseph, his legal father, according to Matthew 1:1–18, since lineage was traced through the father, whether biological or adoptive. He considers the Infancy Narratives unreliable for historical information about Jesus and thinks it likely that the brothers and sisters of Jesus were true siblings.[47]

What this controversy amounts to in terms of Jesus' relationship with children is simply the *possibility* that he faced discrimination because his birth may have appeared to be dubious. If fatherless children were at the bottom of the lower classes—even as grownups they could not enter the temple and were not allowed to marry a pure Israelite woman—children with uncertain paternity may also have faced prejudice. Since Jesus mostly gathered around him the downtrodden, the poor, and the disabled, it is not unreasonable to suppose that he himself may have experienced a marginalization that made him sensitive to others being discriminated against, for example, children without legitimate fathers, who were probably numerous in the multicultural Galilean community where impoverished peasants were hardly able to pay their taxes.

> Jesus had been conceived in Galilee, a land of many Roman soldiers. They easily took the native women to bed; some went freely and others were forced. Is this not the way of all . . . conquering soldiers?
>
> Jesus was a *mestizo*. . . . He appeared to be a half-breed. A scandal to all the pious and the pure of society.[48]

Most scholars agree that Jesus did have Joseph as foster father, but he disappears from the synoptic stories after the boy Jesus was found by his "parents" in the temple at age twelve (Luke 2:41–45). Even there only his mother is reported as speaking to him and is said to have afterwards "treasured" the experience. Joseph may have died early, but the silence about him in the earliest sources is remarkable in view of the importance of fathers in first-century Mediterranean culture. Mark 3:32 mentions only his mother and brothers; some versions of Mark 6:3—not chosen in the New Revised Standard Version—mention "the carpenter." Later on, Jesus is known as Mary's son, although the late-written Gospel of John describes him as "son of Joseph whose father and mother we know" (John 6:42). It is clear that he must have had a tense relationship with his family, since he acts rather strange toward his mother, and the family considers him crazy (John 2:4; Matt. 12:48–50; Mark 3:33f.; John 7:5; Mark 3:21). "[He] may have counted on considerable resistance within families against following him or professing loyalty to him," as suggested by the dire predictions of family conflicts in Mark 13:9–13 and Luke 12:51–53.[49]

Such texts indicate that Jesus was no advocate of "family values" in terms of the biological family, although we do not know whether, for example, the harsh sayings of Luke 14:26 or Matthew 10:21, 37 are truly Jesus' words: "Whoever comes to me and does not hate father and mother, wife and children, brothers and sisters, yes, and even life itself, cannot be my disciple," and the apocalyptic warning, "Brother will betray brother to death, and a father his child, and children will rise against parents." These statements have to be compared with the various New Testament stories in which Jesus heals or raises from death the child of a loving parent, or with the scene at his crucifixion where he compassionately tells his mother that his beloved disciple will now be her son (John 19:26f.). Also, Jesus did affirm the Decalogue's mandate to honor one's parents (Mark 10:19). However, many of his sayings indicate a total reversal of values. What he called the kingdom of God or the rule of God— and what a secular person might call justice and integrity—should never be disregarded because of blood relationships, he insists. What the faithful disciples receive in the end "a hundredfold" will be new and different relationships (Mark 10:29f.), because Jesus' "family" consists of those who do God's will (Mark 3:35; Matt. 25:40).

Jesus' assessment of family relationships was, then, devoid of any idealism. Likewise he appears to have seen children in a very realistic way. When he observed them playing in the market place, he realized that they were as hard to satisfy and as difficult to coax into cooperation as grownups:

> But to what will I compare this generation? It is like children sitting in the marketplaces and calling to one another, "We played the flute for you, and you did not dance; we wailed, and you did not mourn." For John came neither eating nor drinking, and they say, "He has a demon"; the Son of Man came eating and drinking, and they say, "Look, a glutton and a drunkard, a friend of tax collectors and sinners!" Yet wisdom is vindicated by her deeds. (Matt. 11:16–19)

Considering the import of this passage that stubbornness and narrow-mindedness are to be found in persons of all ages, along with the fact that Jesus is nowhere said to have talked about an innocence peculiar to children,[50] it is all the more astonishing that he apparently saw children as worthy of special blessing and caressing, as models for our relationship with God, and as representatives of Godself.

### Children as Worthy of Special Blessing and Caressing

The most popular and easy to understand text concerning Jesus and children describes his insistence on being close to them. However, even this simple assertion is immediately complicated by the connection of these nobodies with the realm of God and with our adult relationship to God, not just to children. So if we consider three different aspects of Jesus' words about children, we have to keep in mind that they are intricately related. Most people like to bless and caress children, but few—even among believers—see them as models of our being in the world or as representing Godself. We can rationally dissect the reported words of Jesus, but, more important, we can let them interrogate and challenge us, sensing their ancient mystery while considering their interpretation and use throughout history.

The basic text of describing the scene of children to be brought to Jesus is, in its earliest form, Mark 10:13–15.

> People were bringing little children to him in order that he might touch them; and the disciples spoke sternly to them.

> But when Jesus saw this, he was indignant and said to them, "Let the little children come to me; do not stop them; for it is to such as these that the kingdom of God belongs. Truly I tell you, whoever does not receive the kingdom of God as a little child will never enter it." And he took them up in his arms, laid his hands on them, and blessed them.

For many centuries this has been a popular baptismal text, and it has inspired artistic renderings from Lucas Cranach's *Christ Blessing the Children* to sentimental Sunday school posters. Cranach the Elder, a friend of Martin Luther, portrayed only mothers bringing the children, thereby echoing Luther's new emphasis on ordinary women's daily lives.[51] But the text, also in its parallels of Matthew and Luke, says nothing of mothers or parents. The children may have been brought in, so to speak, from the street, as Van Aarde assumes, or may have come with any member of the typical extended family. The disciples could have reacted against the children's possible lack of ritual cleanliness or may have considered them too insignificant to disturb the master. Jesus' anger is mentioned only one other time in the Gospels (Mark 3:5), and his command, "Do not stop them" or "Let be!" occurs also in the story of the woman pouring a precious ointment on his head (Mark 14:6): "Let her alone."[52] Jesus refuses any rules concerning the way people approach him.

As a biblical basis for baptizing children, this text became famous in Reformation times and was used against the Anabaptists. Today, however, most exegetes are convinced that it had nothing to do with baptism and should at best be used only for a blessing ritual.[53] Jesus' blessing of the children may go back to a custom of children being brought to famous rabbis to be blessed, but Jesus *touched* them, "took them up in his arms, laid his hand on them." The term used in verse 13 for "touching" occurs more than thirty times in the four Gospels and almost always in healing stories.[54] Jesus sees body and soul as a whole; his blessing is never just a spiritual ritual, but an affirmation of the whole person's needs. Embracing children who seem to come to him from nowhere, he acts in a feminine, motherly way. The kingdom—or domain, realm, or rule—of God belongs to children, he is said to have stated. We would at most have expected it the other way around: they belong to God's realm. No, we have to learn: God's world is their world.

The following sentence (v. 15) is thought by scholars to have been inserted later: "whoever does not receive the kingdom of God as a little child will never enter it." Translators are still divided on how to read the phrase grammatically: receiving the realm of God the way a child would receive the realm, or, receiving the realm the way we would receive a child. The first reading is usually preferred. Luke 18:17 repeats the same sentence, but Matthew (18:3–5) adds, "unless you change," and he relates Jesus' statement directly to a discussion about greatness, concretely illustrated by Jesus' pointing to a real child.

## Children as Models for Our Relationship with God

In the Gospel of Mark we find this controversy in a *wider* context of the story about Jesus blessing children. Mark 9:33 tells us that the disciples "argued" about "who was the greatest" among them, and also Luke (9:46) refers to this discussion. Mark 10:37 even states that James and John frankly asked for the best places in heaven, and Matthew adds that their mother (piously, ambitiously, or foolishly?) pleaded for them to be able to sit at Jesus' right and left side in his "kingdom" (Matt. 20:20f.). In correcting the disciples' notions, Jesus does not merely talk about a child as a metaphor for a spiritual condition. He becomes concrete by putting a child "among them" (Matt. 18:2) or "by his side" (Luke 9:47), with Mark adding that he took it "in his arms" (9:36). He reverses traditional educational ideas: this is not a child to be instructed, but "the child becomes the lesson."[55] The disciples are the ones who need instruction:

> Truly I tell you, unless you change and become like children, you will never enter the kingdom of heaven. Whoever becomes humble like this child is the greatest in the kingdom of heaven. Whoever welcomes one such child in my name welcomes me. (Matt. 18:3–5)

Becoming like a child here has nothing to do with innocence, naiveté, or anti-intellectualism. After all, Jesus wanted his followers to be "wise as serpents" (Matt. 10:16). We are not supposed to acquire a certain attitude, but to envision with astonishment *God's* attitude of caring for "the least," for those who without merit or pretension simply take for granted, and enjoy, being loved and cared for. Children are not in control of anything, and we can "change" (Matt. 18:2) our addiction to achievement, property, power over others, and calculation of merits by "letting go and letting God," realizing that actually we live like a child, dependent on grace.

This realization will be called by the Gospel of John "being born from above" (John 3:3). There it does not refer to children, but to human rebirth, and this is of course also the point of the texts on "becoming like children" in the other Gospels. Nicodemus wonders how anybody can "be born after having grown old." "Can one enter a second time into the mother's womb and be born?" (v. 4). Jesus tells him that "no one can enter the kingdom of God without being born of water and Spirit" (v. 5). The water here is certainly a reference to baptism, but it is also an indication that rebirth is not just a spiritual event; like water it is the essence of life itself, of the natural world and bodily existence. Entering God's realm means constantly growing and changing like a child, not struggling for independence, success, and heaven's reward for virtue, but realizing absolute interdependence and vulnerability. Merit is irrelevant in the life of an infant. No child can survive without being cared for and living in community. Our self before God is a corporate self, not an individualistic one.

While, then, the idea of rebirth, radical change, and becoming like a child is present in all four Gospels, it occurs in different contexts. In Mark 10 the passage about Jesus blessing children and seeing in them the realm of God follows the discussion with the Pharisees about marriage and divorce, and afterwards the story of the rich young ruler is added. The emphasis is on a kind of catechetical instruction on how, within the realm of God, we have to regard marriage, property, and children. Luke lets the stories about the pleading widow and the Pharisee and publican precede the word about Jesus and the children, and also here the story of the rich young ruler is added with the ending, "How hard it is for those who have wealth to enter the kingdom of God" (18:24). Luke seems to focus on humility, justice, and empty hands before God. This context makes it especially important to reflect on the meaning of a childlike "humility" today.

Becoming like a child does not mean self-abasement. It is especially hard for women to be "humble" or "childlike," since for ages they have been told that they are helpless and in need of guidance like children, and that they should show humility. But the pleading widow of Luke 18:1–8 is a strong, unbending character struggling for justice, and the tax collector forcefully acknowledges the truth about himself. Receiving the realm of God like a child receives it has nothing to do with weakness. We know that even infants have a strong will to assert their needs. Their love of life, their constant urge to discover something new, their eagerness to return the love they receive never show signs of weakness. Being like a child means thriving on community, receiving and giving the sheer love of life, celebrating a continuing birth. "When a woman is in labor, she has pain. . . . But when her child is born, she no longer remembers the anguish because of the joy of having brought a human being into the world" (John 16:21).

Elisabeth Moltmann-Wendel has repeatedly emphasized Hannah Arendt's idea that "natality" ("Natalität") should be the goal and end of our life, and not death.[56] The fragile infant is powerful in its oneness with nature; it does not overwork, overeat, or oversleep, but follows instinctively the rhythm of its needs for growth. If as grownups we were to follow this rhythm instead of competing for domination of others, we would be sharing power and enabling others, not from a sense of false humility, but of a justice inherent in the communal life of all creation.

Jesus lived this life and expected it to be lived by ordinary human beings, even politicians:

> You know that among the Gentiles those whom they recognize as their rulers lord it over them, and their great ones are tyrants over them. But it is not so among you; but whoever wishes to become great among you must be your servant, and whoever wishes to be first among you must be slave of all. For the Son of Man came not to be served but to serve, and to give his life a ransom for many. (Mark 10:42–45)

Just as with the term "humility," we may have a problem with the ancient concepts of a "slave" and of a "ransom for many." The Greek word for "child" (*pais*), which originally meant a small or little child, an "unimportant" creature,[57] was also used for "servant" or "slave." Slaves in ancient Israel had certain rights, and even in a secular context "slave" could be a humble self-description. Moses, David, and the prophets are called servants or slaves of God.[58] When in Mark "the Son of Man," sometimes interpreted as "the true human child" is called a servant, it means that Jesus was understood as representing the true human condition before God, a condition of receptivity and interdependence, the condition of a child who is vulnerable to the point of being made a victim and yet a "ransom for many." That does not mean a return to a scholastic atonement theory—God needing some "satisfaction" in view of our sins—but the realization that Jesus embodied for us what it means to live like a child of God. That kind of life is risky business, a matter of life and death "for many," because human beings want to be grownups and would like to be "almighty," like those Romans who put Jesus to death when he refused to be a slave of any earthly power structure. Welcoming Jesus in a child and like a child means welcoming a life of tough choices, faithful resistance, and endless hope, thereby becoming a beacon of life "for many." Even more, it means inviting Godself into our life.

### Children as Representatives of Godself

To Matthew's sentence, "Whoever welcomes one such child in my name welcomes me," Mark adds, "and whoever welcomes me welcomes not me but the one who sent me" (Mark 9:37; cf. Luke 9:48). So it becomes unmistakably clear that we are not just receiving or welcoming a child because Jesus told us to take care of the needy. It is Godself we are meeting in a child, the vulnerable God who is present in every fragile creature. "Truly I tell you, just as you did it to one of the least of these who are members of my family, you did it to me" (Matt. 25:40). The New Testament stories describing Jesus' birth—whether legendary or not—give us the same message: incarnation happens where we least expect and detect it, in a poor refugee child, under terrifying political circumstances, in a little-known corner of the world. But Jesus carries the matter one step further: *every* child is God's representative and God's "good news" to us. How does that relate to Jesus' life?

Judith Gundry-Volf has related Jesus' words about children to the Passion narrative that follows them in Mark 10. She suggests that

> the immediate context for Jesus' identification with the little child is the passion prediction that Mark records in 9:31: 'the Son of Man is to be betrayed into human hands, and they will

kill him, and three days after being killed, he will rise again.'
Here Jesus identifies himself as a suffering and rejected figure.
. . . He is given over to death. This description likens him to
the little child, for the deprecation of children in the ancient
world was expressed not only by social rejection but even
more drastically by exposure or infanticide at the hands of
one's own family. . . . Jesus' teaching that whoever receives a
little child in his name receives Jesus, thus reverberates with
the ominous tones of the passion prediction.[59]

By lovingly cradling a child in his arms, Jesus points his disciples
to a "'feminine' model of community," Gundry-Volf asserts, because
women were the primary caretakers of children in Jesus' time—as they
are today. Women would also be the ones who stayed with Jesus when
he was rejected and killed like an abandoned child. Even if we cannot
be certain about the relationship between Jesus' view of children and
his own passion experience, it is clear that he challenges the preoccu-
pation with honor in the first-century Mediterranean world where
children had no status or honor, no economic or social worth, regardless of the private love of their families. "Ascribed worth is stood on its
head," and Jesus' followers are asked "to . . . stand in solidarity with
these 'nobodies.'"[60] This reversal of values is bound to reverberate at
the very core of theology.

In recent years, theology has tried to get away from a triumphalist
stance that in the past has fostered imperialism. The emphasis has
been instead on a kenotic theology, on the self-emptying of Christ described in Philippians 2:6–8:

> who, though he was in the form of God,
> did not regard equality with God
> as something to be exploited,
> but emptied himself,
> taking the form of a slave,
> being born in human likeness.
> And being found in human form,
> he humbled himself
> and became obedient to the point of death—
> even death on a cross.

As Origen phrased it, "God's Wisdom entered a woman's womb, was born an infant, and wailed like crying children."[61] Similarly Augustine would state that pagans could not accept that in the infant Jesus "God lay hidden within the body of a wailing child."[62] In Russian Orthodox theology "not only Jesus *leaves his glory behind*, but the entire Godhead is caught up in the self-emptying process."[63] Annie Dillard has expressed this thought in terms of contemporary spirituality:

> Faith would be that God is self-limited utterly by his cre-ation—a contraction of the scope of his will; that he bound himself to time and its hazards and haps as a man would lash himself to a tree for love. . . . That God is helpless, our baby to bear, self-abandoned on the doorstep of time, wondered at by cattle and oxen. Faith would be that God moved and moves once and for all and 'down,' so to speak, like a diver, like a man who eternally gathers himself for a dive and eternally is diving, and eternally splitting the spread of the water, and eternally drowned.[64]

We are allergic these days to the thought that obedience, suffering, and humility bring redemption, and especially to the idea that Jesus did all that "for us." But "emptying" oneself can be understood in very different ways. Gershom Sholem has explained the idea of *tzimtzum* (contraction) in the mystical tradition of the Kabbalah: in the begin-ning there was only Infinite Light. This divine light veiled or con-tracted itself in order to create a space for creation.[65] The self-emptying God withdraws the divine glory in order to create an "other" to be in relation with. God draws into Godself, so to speak, making room for the world like a pregnant mother for her child and continuing to do so. God's first act was not one of revelation or expansion, but of a veiling, a concentration, or a retreat. In Christian terms God withdraws into a fragile human baby that cannot live without being in relation, being nurtured and loved and returning love.

Jesus' life mirrors God's self-emptying, keeping within the bound-aries of what is truly human. The purpose of such a life is not a glori-fication of suffering—Jesus asked that he would be spared the cup of suffering (Mark 14:36)—but limiting oneself to love and justice as "the heartbeat of God" brings about suffering through those who want only to expand, be in charge, or be autonomous, instead of emptying themselves. This type of humility is not weakness or lacking self-esteem; it indicates instead—according to the root of the word—being as close to the *humus* (earth) as a child; it means "staying with the physical, embodied, rhythmic growth processes of the natural world,"[66] something that Buddhists have always seen as liberating. It means restraining or limiting oneself not as self-punishment or obedient sacrifice, but—like the *tzimtzum*-God—breathing in to make room for the other and breathing out to join the other in blessing life-in-relation. "Just to be is a blessing, just to live is holy," said Abraham Joshua Heschel.[67] Children are experiencing early on that birth itself and life's limitations are painful, but after blurting out their pain, they are eagerly continuing their lust for life, not being concerned with their utter dependence. They lack pretension, and they delight in giving and receiving love.

In welcoming a child, Jesus says, we face the being of Godself: inconspicuous, vulnerable, and powerful in eliciting our compassion and cooperation. The child thereby also becomes the representative of other "little ones" in whom we meet God: the poor, disabled, or oppressed who trust the God Jesus proclaimed. Hurting one of these means denying life itself: that person might better be drowned with a millstone around his or her neck! (Matt. 18:6; Luke 17:2). We may be shocked at these drastic words reportedly spoken by Jesus concerning someone guilty of hurting a "little one." However, biblical words and stories are bound to "disrupt" our logical thinking.[68] We should be just as shocked that Plato considered children—together with women, slaves, and animals—to be creatures without reason, and that Aristotle saw the child on the same level as (psychologically) sick, bad, violent, intoxicated, or lower-class human beings, incapable of true feelings.[69] In view of such philosophical opinions at the root of Western culture, we can stand in awe of the radical reversal of values that Jesus of Nazareth introduced into this world when he pointed to God's presence in the child. Those who harm the "little ones," he seems to say in the millstone passage, place themselves outside the true human community. Becoming like children and welcoming all "little ones" means being in communion with God and all creation.

## THE DOUBLE CORE OF THE BIBLICAL CHALLENGE

The two aspects of the New Testament message concerning children, that is, becoming like them and caring for them, have their roots in Israel's faith. Becoming a true child of God was Israel's communal destination, and welcoming children was part of this realization.

> *Can a woman forget her nursing child,*
> *Or show no compassion for the child of her womb?*
> *Even these may forget,*
> *Yet I will not forget you.* (Isa. 49:15)

Israel is God's beloved child (Hos. 11:1), and those Israelites who love YHWH know that they are known, loved, and blessed from the womb on:

> *You knit me together in my mother's womb.*
> *I praise you for I am fearfully and wonderfully made.* (Ps. 139:13b–14a)

> *Before I formed you in the womb I knew you,*
> *and before you were born I consecrated you.* (Jer. 1:5)

Any concrete nurture and care for children in Israel grew out of this conviction. Likewise in the New Testament the realization that we are in a true relationship with God only when we are as trusting, open, receptive, and loving as children, "naturally" implies care for real children. What we are will be mirrored in what we do and vice versa. We are, so to speak, on the same level with children, learning from them while guiding and nurturing them.

That was not always the way the early church understood Jesus' words. In the apostolic letters of the New Testament children are still seen to be on the lower ranks of a patriarchal household, required foremost to be obedient (Eph. 6:1, citing the Decalogue). The apostle Paul refers to children as examples of immaturity and childish ways (1 Cor. 13:11; 14:20), but he also admonishes his readers that "children ought not to lay up for their parents, but parents for their children" (2 Cor. 12:14). "There is some tension between this ideal [of showing Christian love within the structures of family and society] and the occasional uncritical acceptance of the patriarchal and authoritarian structure of the ancient extended family in which, for example, the father is responsible for the education of the children."[70] The admonition to children to obey their parents "in the Lord" is balanced by the admonition to fathers not to provoke their children to anger (Eph. 6:4; cf. Col. 3:21). The apostle Paul mentions that "we were gentle among you, like a nurse tenderly caring for her own children" (1 Thess. 2:7), and the Johannine letters emphasize that God is love, and if we love God, we will love all of God's children (1 John 5:2). While these words refer to adults, they certainly influenced the way real children were viewed. The unity of adult self-understanding and concern for children is also apparent in the apocryphal Gospel of Thomas, which sees adults as "children of light" and at the same time regards real children as representing divine knowledge:

> Jesus saw some babies nursing. He said to his disciples, "These nursing babies are like those who enter the Kingdom." (Gospel of Thomas, 22)

> Jesus said, "The man old in days will not hesitate to ask a little child seven days old about the place in life, and that person will live." (Gospel of Thomas, 4)[71]

God's people, then, have come a long way from the time they thought that the rod of discipline was the best means by which to bring up a child (Prov. 22:15) and from the notion that children do not count until they are grown and taught. Yet even in Israel's earliest times and in the early church's most precarious diaspora situations, there was the sense that being close to God meant being a child—as a people or as an individual—and caring for children.

Jesus' two-sided message about "becoming like children" and "welcoming children" can never be separated. He radicalized this double core of the biblical witness by emphasizing that we welcome Godself in welcoming a child and by expecting from men the same commitment as from women: to lack pretension and the desire to dominate others, to embrace infants, to wash feet, to heal the sick, to gather loved ones like a mother hen (Matt. 23:37), or to appreciate the blunt truth blurted out by children (Matt. 21:14–16). As a true child of God he could appear insensitive toward his own family when they did not understand him, but he honored many loving parents whose sons and daughters were sick or had died and gave their children new life: the daughter of Jairus, the young man of Nain, the daughter of the Syrophoenician woman, the son of the official of Capernaum.[72] He did not regard equality with God as something to be exploited (Phil. 2:6), but lived a life as risky as that of the lilies of the field or of an abandoned child. Like a desperate child he would call to his *abba*: "My God, my God, why have you forsaken me" (Mark 15:34), and yet end with: "into thy hands I commend my spirit" (Luke 23:46).

In living and dying like a true child of God and seeing God's presence in children, Jesus has been considered by some scholars as unique in the history of religions in this regard. I have referred in chapter 1 to such comments by Ulrich Luz and Milan Machoveč. We have to probe these statements and look at other religious traditions to draw at least some tentative conclusions. In the shrinking global village, where seemingly small ethnic and religious conflicts can quickly set a whole continent on fire, we cannot afford to close our eyes to the faith and culture of other nations. In fact, the biblical witness challenges us to discover the presence of God's reign in every child on earth, not just in the children within our synagogues, mosques, churches, and countries.

# 3

# OPENING OURSELVES
# TO OTHER TRADITIONS

➤➤ ✳ ◄◄

## *The Child in Words and Images of World Religions*

Hold the young in awe.[1]

What piqued my interest in exploring how a variety of religious traditions value children was Ulrich Luz's observation in his commentary on the Gospel of Matthew (1997) that Jesus' attitude toward children is unique in the history of religions.[2] When I realized that the Czech philosopher Milan Machoveč in *A Marxist Looks at Jesus* had earlier expressed this view and had also commented that Karl Marx had a special appreciation for Jesus' attitude toward children, I was hooked on the issue.[3] Having learned from early feminist theologians that Christians too easily see Jesus as absolutely unique in his time in "liberating women," I wanted to probe this matter: what did other so-called world religions or their founders teach about children, and what images expressed their understanding of childhood?

First, however, I would like to define what I mean by "world religions." I realize that the use of the term "religion" for anything from

Judaism and Christianity to Buddhism and Native American rituals is ambigous and controversial. Having grown up with a strong dose of Karl Barth's theology, I do not share the liberal notion that one religion is as good as another or that we can pick and choose aspects of many of them in order to mix our individual concoction. Our search for truth should be anchored in a strong communal tradition that is nevertheless open to constant communication with people of other faiths and cultures to whom we give and from whom we receive.[4] I grew up as a Lutheran, have been a member of the United Church of Christ for over four decades, and have always believed in the Methodist principle of the "quadrilateral" in drawing theological conclusions: combining Scripture, tradition, experience, and reason.[5] In the age of globalization, our experience is being challenged to grow, partly because our neighborhoods are changing. For example, there are now more than nine hundred thousand Hindus living in the United States.[6] In European cities, Muslim minarets are increasingly visible between the steeples of Christian churches. "Religion" is always an ambiguous term. Native American languages do not have a word that would represent this Western concept.[7] For Hindus, the word *dharma* can express righteousness, justice, faith, duty, and a religious or social obligation, but it does not cover all that is sacred for Hindus. There are sacred times, places, omens, architecture, music, trees, and plants in the Hindu tradition, and much of this is not covered by the Western notion of "religion."[8] Richard Horsley has convincingly shown how religion is related to empire.[9]

With all this ambiguity, "there is a need to find a new common ground between religions based on the sense of the sacred that links us all together and which can inspire commitment to the common good of the earth."[10] In this sense I will talk about "religious traditions" or "world religions." I would like to indicate here only in a sketch, as it were, where theology might go if it were to explore the relationship of spirituality and childhood in very different social and spiritual locations around the globe.

In this research I found it especially helpful to work with images, because not all spiritual traditions are "religions of the book." Also, "by decolonizing methodologies, by dismantling the authority paradigms based on texts alone, and by understanding indigenous knowledge systems . . . we begin to explore the intersection of 'globalization past' with 'globalization present.'"[11] So I begin with images and texts derived from the Christian and Hebrew Scriptures and then consider other religions.[12]

The German painter Emil Nolde in his picture *Jesus and the Children* got it right: according to the gospel writers Jesus did not just piously bless an audience of children; he became one of them. He called for them (Luke 18:16), "he took them up in his arms, laid his hands on them, and blessed them" (Mark 10:16).[13] They were expressly brought to him "that he might touch them" (Mark 10:13; Luke 18:15). Jesus is "indignant" when the disciples want to keep the children away. Did they consider them to be ritually unclean street children? Too insignificant to take the master's time? We are not told.[14] All three synoptic gospels agree that the child in Jesus' terms is not, as it was assumed in antiquity and is often considered today, an unfinished being that has to be shaped and taught lessons to become an adult. On the contrary, the child is the lesson, and the disciples are the ones who need instruction.[15] "And calling to him a child, he put him in the midst of them, and said, 'Truly I tell you, unless you change and become like children, you will never enter the kingdom of heaven" (Matt. 18:2–3; cf. Mark 10:15; Luke 18:17). Even more radical is Jesus' notion that in receiving or "welcoming" a child, we receive or welcome God: "Whoever welcomes one such child in my name welcomes me, and whoever welcomes me welcomes not me but the one who sent me" (Mark 9:37; cf. Luke 9:48, Matt. 18:5). Emil Nolde beautifully captures in this picture the essence of the gospel. We only see Jesus' back because the point of the story is the reflection of divine love in the faces and movements of the children. He lovingly bends toward them, not only "welcoming" them, but letting himself be received enthusiastically, thus showing what it means to be a child of God.

As we might guess from the way Nolde depicts the faces of the disciples, Jesus' attitude is social and political dynamite. According to Mark 9:33–37, his words about children are a reaction against the disciples' quarrel as to who might be the greatest among them, and in the following chapter the political implications become clear: "You know that among the Gentiles those whom they recognize as their rulers lord it over them, and their great ones are tyrants over them. But it is not so among you; . . . whoever wishes to be great among you must be your servant" (Mark 10:42f.; cf. Luke 22:25f.). That children have political relevance is clear from the stories about Pharaoh and King Herod: massive killing of babies can be a political tool of dictators. Jesus' disciples certainly were no evil politicians, but Nolde shows how disgruntled they are when not they themselves but children are declared to be the representatives of God's reign. There is no gesture of bending down, no look into the children's faces. They stand judgmentally upright, their dark bodies contrasting with the vibrant colors indicating love and life issuing from Jesus and the children, who appear in close communion with him.

Lukas Cranach, a friend of Martin Luther, in the early sixteenth century shows in his painting *Christ Blessing the Children* that there is a gender aspect to the disciples' anger: where there are children, there are women who get in the way![16] The lively contact Jesus has in this picture with two naked babies and a throng of women and children stands in stark contrast to the separate male talk behind his back. The bodiliness of Jesus' message and the realistic spontaneity with which he is received by women and children leaves the disgruntled disciples without control. The very nakedness of the little intruders and the uninhibited gestures of so many women must be an affront to their imagined authority.

There is no indication that Jesus saw children as being innocent, but in seeing a relationship between childlikeness and God, he tapped the roots of an ancient wisdom. We have seen in the previous chapter that since antiquity, the divine was often envisioned in the form of a child who would become a ruler and bring peace to the world. We find that idea in Heraclitus and Virgil[17] and also in modern-day Tibet. In 2000, the media reported that the fourteen-year-old Ugyen Trinley Dorje, recognized as the reincarnation of the sixteenth Karmapa, the spiritual ruler of the Karama Kagyu religious order, had fled from his monastery to exile in India, because Chinese authorities had prevented him from getting an appropriate Buddhist training in Tibet, even though the Dalai Lama and the Chinese government had agreed in 1992 to recognize him as the chosen lama. He had been selected as a seven-year-old child by ancient rituals. "Until then I was a perfectly normal child," he stated in a 2001 interview. The Dalai Lama was enthroned at the age of four. While Karmapas are traditionally expected to bring spiritual as well as political peace, Ugyen Trinley Dorje has expressed his desire to concentrate on contributing to world peace through Buddhist teachings and cultural traditions and leave concrete politics to more experienced monks.[18]

Thus contemporary realities are not so distant from ancient prophecies like the familiar one in Isaiah 9:6 and 11:6:

> *For a child has been born for us, a son given to us;*
> *authority rests upon his shoulders,*
>
> .   .   .   .   .   .   .   .   .
>
> *The wolf shall live with the lamb,*
> *the leopard shall lie down with the kid,*
> *the calf and the lion and the fatling together,*
> *and a little child shall lead them.*

I mentioned in chapter 2 that these verses actually celebrate the ascent of a prince to the throne of David, although Christians have seen them as prophesying Christ's coming. The famous American painting by the Quaker preacher Edward Hicks, *The Peaceable Kingdom*, from around 1840–45, captures the political implications of Isaiah's prophecy by inserting into the picture William Penn making a treaty with the Indians.[19] At the same time it indicates an ecological vision of peace. The animals stand out as majestic beings; the promised child who shall "lead" is not the only child enjoying the blessings of the scene, and the all-encompassing landscape constitutes a necessary part of the harmony. The child who leads is a child who unites creation.

The image of the child as savior and peacemaker is also visible in the earliest pictures of Christ as a young shepherd boy. A statue from the first half of the fourth century, from the Vatican Museum in Rome, shows similarities to representations of Apollo and Dionysos. These early Jesus pictures show no imperial dress or gestures. Only the long hair indicates —according to the conventions of the time—that this is a divine youth. There is no triumphalism, but childlike simplicity and humility.[20]

Later pictures of Jesus' birth, youth, and preaching have much in common with the legends surrounding Gautama Buddha at his birth, variously dated around 500 or 400 B.C.E. Both are said to have been born "outside" and in a nonsexual way: Gautama in a grove, emerging from his mother's side, Jesus in a stable. Queen Maya was not a virgin, but as a married woman she was under a vow of celibacy because of an approaching festival when she carried the child. She was on her way to her parents when unexpectedly she went into labor. Without any pain to Maya, the child emerged from her hip while she was holding on to the branch of a tree. In one of the woodcuts describing the event, the hand gesture of the newborn indicates his intention to become a teacher for the world. Four gods, among them the four-faced Brahman, receive and adore the child.[21] Some legends indicate that during her pregnancy Maya had a dream about her child being a future ruler, and, before her overjoyed husband, sang a song that reminds us of Jesus' mother Mary's song (Luke 1:46–55). The world was flooded with light at the Buddha's miraculous birth; celestials played music and threw flowers. Sages prophesied the destiny of this special child. Nobles and princes came to pay their respects. The future Buddha had already watched these foreign people honoring him while he was in the womb, seeing them as if he were looking through silk. The hour that he was born, the blind received their sight; the deaf and mute conversed in ecstasy of the things that were to come; the lame walked; prisoners were freed, and even the cries of the beasts were hushed as peace encircled the earth. The newborn Gautama immediately took seven steps and uttered the words, "This is my last birth."[22] Queen Maya died seven days after giving birth and was "taken to heaven." Her sister became the second wife of the king and brought up Gautama. She became as influential as Mary in the story of Jesus. The twelve-year-old Buddha got lost when he felt compassion for a wounded bird; likewise the twelve-year-old Jesus could not be found when he felt the need to be in his "father's house." Some scholars have suggested that the infancy narratives of Matthew and Luke and of some apocryphal gospels contain Buddhist and Hindu subtexts, deriving either from direct influence, from Gnostic connections, or from commonalities in the human psyche.[23]

There are even similarities in the birth of the Jesus child and the birth of the Hindu god Ganesa, the elephant-headed divinity often shown as a child or youth. Ganesa is a powerful symbol of vitality, humor, and benevolence, represented in thousands of pictures and statues, and prayed to by millions as the remover of obstacles. His kindness is boundless, and his knowledge is inexhaustible. What connects him with Jesus and the Buddha is his very miraculous birth and its universal consequences. There are many versions of the story of his birth in the Puranas.[24] One of them records that the goddess Parvati, who ardently wanted a son, repeatedly asked her husband Siva to fulfill her wish.

> One day when she insisted more than usual, Siva, exasperated, grabbed a piece of Parvati's sari and knotted it so as to give it the shape of a child. The piece of cloth which was on Parvati's knees suddenly stirred by itself; and when she untied the knot, she found a child hidden there.[25]

But suddenly the head of the boy fell to the ground, and a heavenly voice declared," You must choose a new head belonging to a being of superior quality." Siva was then able to obtain the head of the white elephant from the paradise of Indra, the god of gods. To Parvati's joy he put it on his son to bring him to life again. Meanwhile the hordes of gods came to greet Ganesa.[26] In most versions of the story the goddess Parvati gives birth without the intervention of her husband, god Siva. She is the one "whose breasts have never been suckled." A Bengalian miniature of the nineteenth century shows him as a royal child in the lap of his goddess mother.[27] He carries a crown and a scepter and has four arms indicating his manifold powers. (Other representations of Ganesa show him with up to twenty arms.) His mother is seated on a sacred lotus flower and also rests her foot on lotus; it is the pink lotus that blooms during the day. Pink, red, yellow, and golden are traditionally Ganesa's colors. He is patting a little mouse, which is not just one of his attributes, but—in other representations—one of his "vehicles." He is sometimes represented as riding on a giant rat ("a symbol of coiled-up energy," as Martin-Dubost remarks), and sometimes on a mouse, a lion, a serpent, or a peacock. "The mouse is . . . comparable to the intellect. It is able to slip unobserved . . . into rice and sugarcane fields, rich granaries, stealing the most precious treasures from humans."[28] My illustration 6 shows an apparently tiny elephant-headed baby whose power derives from the eight-armed Parvati.

Once again we see here the divine, royal child, being born in a supernatural way and bringing peace and happiness to millions of devotees who believe in the eternal power and kindness of this baby that will also be a demon-slaying savior. Westerners have a hard time understanding the way Hindu art and rituals combine deities, humans,

animals, and objects in one intimate universe. We easily sentimental-
ize ox and ass at the stable or the humble donkey on which Jesus rode
into Jerusalem, but we cannot picture Jesus riding on a mouse or having the head of an animal. Obviously these images derive from a pre-
Christian era, but they also indicate the continuing difference between
Eastern and Western sensibilities. Highly technologized societies have
lost some of the sense of mystery and ambiguity, because they have favored rationality and control, thereby losing ties to the world of fero-
cious or kind animals and forgetting extraordinary dreams or visions.
It takes the art of a Marc Chagall to immerse us again in such an archaic world where we merge with angels and animals.[29]

The enduring intuition of a special child as savior and peacemaker
was in Jesus' proclamation turned into a vision of the child as model
for every person's relationship to God. There is not only one child to
be adored or expected, but ordinary, individual lives are to be transformed by contemplating the life of this child and all children.
Childhood is now not something to grow out of, but a state to aspire
to. While founders and members of other religions may not have
spelled this out as precisely as Jesus, many of them have a vision of
"becoming like a child" to be "saved."

We can see glimpses of such a vision when we look back thirty-five
hundred years to Egypt's Pharaoh Akhenaten and his wife Nefertiti.
The sculpted limestone representation depicting them as playing with
three of their daughters is an amazing statement of royal family life.[30]
Akhenaten was the first emperor to introduce monotheism into our
world. He ruled for seventeen years, and probably Nefertiti ruled with
him. I think this scene shows not only the royal couple as stately incarnation of the sun god Aten, but it expresses their childlike playfulness and their joyful devotion to the three daughters who seem to be
energized as much as their parents by the divine rays of grace. The
sun's rays end in human hands touching the holy family. Such pictures
were displayed on home altars in private chapels. Here, 1,350 years before Christ, a couple appears to "welcome" children—to use Jesus'
term. As ruling adults they play with them and show affection while
trusting that together with their children they are divinely blessed.
Another sculpture of this time that remained unfinished even shows
Akhenaten kissing one of his daughters sitting on his lap.[31]

An even more amazing connection between common childhood and divinity can be found in Hinduism. Krishna is an eternally youthful child. John Stratton Hawley in his book *Krishna the Butter Thief* explains the Hindu fascination with the child Krishna, a breaker of boundaries, an irresistible charmer, an incarnation of endless energy, clowning cleverness, and deep compassion.[32] He elicits love as well as fear, fascination as well as horror, because he is uncontrollable. He churns the cosmic milk ocean, and with his constant activity he hinders the work of his mother Yasoda, a poor cowherd woman, who ties him down to a mortar stone. That causes the boy to tremble like a lotus, and the gopis—young women who show a partly amorous, partly parental love for him—protest that the punishment is too harsh. Hawley comments that present-day Indians are very reluctant to punish their children corporally. They generally believe that children up to the age of five cannot really sin. "Krishna, the archetypal child, invades our ordered world because we invite him." Since he is a child, he cannot be expected to act in a civilized way. He simply has to be loved. His thievery actually has salvific power: it erases the sin of thievery in others. How can anybody restrict him when he already restricted himself to enter this world! He is actually an ocean of purity, auspiciousness, goodness, and compassion.[33] His incarnation is a playful process. "Hindus have long affirmed that the gods created the world in an act of play and that they continue to play through it."[34] This idea is not completely alien to the Christian world. Jürgen Moltmann has described "Play as Symbol of the World":

> The genesis of the world and the order of everything in that world have the character of play. In play, gods and human beings give themselves up to the world in its wholeness. In play, the world displays its beauty. As play, the world hovers over the abyss.[35]

In a similar way Huston Smith sees the Hindu worldview:

> The world is *lila*, God's play. Children playing hide and seek assume various roles that have no validity outside the game. They place themselves in jeopardy and in conditions from which they must escape. Why do they do so when in a twin-

kling they could free themselves by simply stepping out of the game? The only answer is that the game is its own point and reward. It is fun in itself, a spontaneous overflow of creative, imaginative energy. So too in some mysterious way must it be with the world. Like a child playing alone, God is the Cosmic Dancer, whose routine is all creatures and all worlds. From the tireless stream of God's energy the cosmos flows in endless, graceful reenactment.[36]

Whether Krishna as a little boy steals butter or Krishna as teenager steals the hearts—and clothes!—of milkmaids, he lives out the human protest against the finality of the cosmic ordering process and the erection of boundaries. If Krishna steals, he does so for love, and the whole cosmos belongs to him anyway.

A different way of connecting common childhood and divinity is found in the devotional poetry of South India, where the Tamil language is spoken. Tamil literature contains a special genre, the *pillaittamil*. As Paula Richman has shown, in these poems an extraordinary being, a deity, prophet, saint, or hero, envisioned in the form of a baby, is praised. Venerating a deity in the form of a child is an ancient Hindu tradition which emphasizes *bhakti*, intimate devotion. An interesting parallel can be found in the legendary tradition of the Virgin of Guadalupe. Juan Diego, who had the vision of the divine Virgin, calls her "my little girl." Mexican-Americans frequently make diminutive any person for whom they feel special affection.[37] In the stylized and yet often humorous *pillaittamil* poems, the baby god and the powerful adult god that this child became are praised at the same time.[38] Again it is a childlike spirit of devotion to a deity that reminds us of Jesus' words about "becoming like children" to enter God's realm. There are *pillaittamils* from the twelfth century on until today, and their subjects range from the Hindu god Murukan, the warrior son of Siva, to the prophet Muhammad, the baby Jesus, and contemporary political figures and movie stars. These poems can have around one hundred verses. The structure is highly conventionalized. One standard component is the moon verse in which the moon is invited or even urged to play with the child. *Pillai* means child or baby. The writers of these poems are males who take the voice of a woman and describe domestic scenes. Addressing a god and ruler of the universe as a child indicates nearness, intimacy, and accessibility, and this genre has a long history in Hindu literature. Unlike Sanskrit, Tamil is a "mother tongue," tapping powerful emotions and the roots of childhood and adolescence. One poem portrays the god Murukan as a helpless baby tenderly cared for by his mother, but in the end Murukan's powerful demon-killing is described. There is even a reflection on Murukan's young wife. Present and future are conflated. In 1985, Arul Cellatturai, an engineer, wrote a *pillaittamil* to baby Jesus. "Adult Jesus is always kept in a high elevated position," he stated, "[but] there is no fear to approach child Jesus."[39] Taking the voice of a mother and writing for Christians and non-Christians alike, he portrayed Jesus as a Tamil child, observing his own long-awaited son. The poem expresses wonder at the miracles of modern science. Its message is that Jesus continues to be born every moment in the minds of his devotees.[40]

Such literature has its roots in a culture that cherishes and enjoys children in a special way. Margaret Travick, who described life and love in a Tamil family, observed:

> Childhood is made much of in Tamil Nadu. People love to decorate their walls with pictures of little babies, to worship child gods, to create literary images of children in many different genres, and to play with children—not, as with some of us, because they believe that the child requires this kind of attention, but rather, it would seem, because the adults themselves enjoy it.[41]

Reality, according to Hindu belief, can be known only through archaic, unconscious, preverbal processes of sensing and feeling, an intuition of the fundamental rhythms of the universe.[42] That might partly explain the importance of children within the Hindu world, because they live within these "fundamental rhythms." It also explains the desire to merge the psyche of the adult and the child and the need to preserve or rediscover the child in the mature person. In Buddhism this desire is turned into spiritual practice.

The Buddhist Thich Nhat Hanh talked about the "child in us" as he celebrated Christmas with Christians. "We celebrate the birth of a child," he said. "But we have to look into ourselves. There is a child in us to be born. Our practice is to allow the child to be born every moment of our daily life."[43] "Redemption" and "resurrection" are daily practices.

> And we practice in such a way that Buddha is born every moment of our daily life, that Jesus Christ is born every moment of our daily life—not only on Christmas day, because every day is Christmas day, every minute is a Christmas minute. The child within us is waiting each minute for us to be born again and again.[44]

How do these thoughts connect with the historical Buddha? At first sight he does not appear very child-friendly according to the traditional stories describing his life. When his son was born, he considered him "another bond to tie me," and neither wife nor child could keep him from becoming a wandering ascetic to seek deliverance from suffering. But when later he had worked out the Noble Eightfold Path, it included "Right Effort," meaning charity and kindness toward all living things; and when his son was seven years old, the Buddha began to become a kindly father, teaching the son through simple examples from everyday life.[45] That kind of teaching has continued throughout the centuries in Buddhist countries. At four years of age boys usually undergo a ceremony to introduce them to the ideals of humility and simplicity. Young men spend part of their life in a monastery even if they later take on secular professions.

The Buddha's teaching focused above all on forgetting the illusions of the ego. In contrast to Hindu belief in an enduring self that continues to go through cycles of rebirth, the Buddha suggested that the self is nothing but a bundle of ephemeral conceptions that do not survive death. Continuing rebirth only happens as long as we cling to the ego's illusions and desires. Human beings, he taught, consider the self as something solid that prevails, but all ideas of "this is me," "this is mine," or "this is what I want to achieve" are illusory and lead to suffering. If we lose the thirst of the ego with its obsessions and possessions, we can overcome suffering. In contrast to the early Hinayana teachings, in Mahayana Buddhism not only some select persons can achieve this salvation, but all are saved, even those who are not aware of it. They only have to awaken to the fact that greed, pride, hate, and suffering do not touch their true being and can be overcome by awareness and right practice.

The process of emptying oneself of all wrong desires is here certainly not the same emptying that the apostle Paul talks of in describing Jesus' humbling himself in Philippians 2, but there are some points of contact: an earthbound humility, a lack of pretension, a life of trust and integrity. Emptiness for the Buddha describes that which is imperishable, eternal, and indescribable. The goal of the Buddha to give up the illusions of the ego can remind us of Jesus' admonition to "become like children," because the small child is content and happy in being dependent and cared for; it lives in the moment and does not yet yearn for greatness and domination.

The Buddha's goal of nirvana, a "nothing" of indescribable delight, is, then, a longing for "rebirth." It is not the rebirth of a wandering soul suffering through one incarnation after another, but a spiritual rebirth within this life, a last birth ending all suffering. Explaining his enlightenment, the Buddha described it as an awakening to the true knowledge of life: when he suddenly saw the light, it was like a chicken emerging from the breaking egg shell.[46] Such new birth is not something to cling to for a purely personal salvation. Especially in the Mahayana tradition, which has fewer ties to the historical Gautama Buddha, a Buddha is one of many all-gracious beings who in their childlike happiness help others to attain nirvana. Among the ethical principles of such saints is the loving care of children.

This aspect of Buddhist faith is represented, for example, in pictures of a Tibetan Buddhist *arhat*. *Arhats* are saints who have achieved nirvana. One of them, Hvasang, is often depicted with children around him whom he protects from thieves and thugs. The humor of such a potbellied, Santa-Claus-like figure indicates the childlike joy of the *arhat* in being surrounded by children.[47] Hvasang is always shown as laughing, and some of his attributes are a rosary or fruits, and a sack of provisions. He is considered a generous spender of alms, his roundness indicating that he has lots to give away. Children trustingly climb around him.

When we move from such colorful, sensual portrayals of divine beings to the Islamic world, we are first of all chastened to get away from images. The Islamic tradition discourages any depiction of the divine, whether as a child or as an adult. It is even more than Judaism and Christianity a religion of the Book and the Word. The words of the Koran are recited in a child's ear at birth for a blessing.[48] The

Koran denies a divine sonship of Jesus—Allah is beyond all "begetting"[49]— but accepts Jesus' virgin birth and records the miracles performed by the child Jesus who could already speak while still an infant in a cradle and who could fashion birds out of clay.[50] Muhammad's own birth—570 C.E.—is described in legends like those that surrounded Jesus, the Buddha, and Hindu gods: the night of his birth animals began to talk, thrones of kings were turned over, wild animals brought the news from east to west, and the air was filled with angels, bright light, and sweet fragrances.[51] However, Muhammad did not see himself as a savior or messiah, but simply as a prophet proclaiming a new faith. The center of his message is contained in the word "Islam": "submission" to Allah. Islam is the youngest of all great world religions and is more closely involved in history and in everyday social and political life than those religions that originated in prehistoric, vaguely known times. The revelations of the Hebrew Bible and the Christian New Testament are seen as being partly confirmed and partly surpassed by the final and absolute truth of the Koran. Muhammad is the latest and greatest prophet.

Growing up in Mecca, a city of many religions and a lively caravan trade, the young man became acquainted with pagan Arabic pilgrims to the holy Kaaba as well as Jews and Christians. So it is not surprising that we find these very different elements in the Koran. Whether the whole sacred book was written down during his lifetime is uncertain, but according to tradition the archangel Gabriel dictated the words during Muhammad's visions. What is of interest concerning children in the Koran is the fact that there are rules that can be considered progressive for Muhammad's time. There is at least a beginning of equality for boys and girls: abandoning female babies—a common practice for population control in Muhammad's time—is strictly forbidden.[52] Girls can be educated, because men and women are equal before Allah.[53] The prostitution of slave girls is abolished.[54] Wives, daughters, and sisters receive the right to some inheritance.[55] Above all, the care for orphans is commanded repeatedly,[56] made urgent by the fact that Muhammad himself grew up as an orphan. As a father he is said to have been so sensitive toward children that one time he did not get up from prayer after a child had climbed on his back lest he hurt the little one.[57] Important in our context is the fact that "the *hajj* [pilgrimage to

Mecca] is regarded by Muslims as a form of resurrection or rebirth. Tradition asserts that a person returns from a sincerely performed *hajj* free from all sins, as on the day when he or she was born."[58] So here we find a different form of the idea of having to become like a child,

The *hajj* also has another aspect that relates to the Muslim understanding of childhood: the concluding rite of the pilgrimage is the Feast of Sacrifice that commemorates Abraham's sacrifice of a ram instead of his son. I have indicated in chapter 2 that "The Binding of Isaac" is a foundational story for three faiths: Judaism, Christianity, and Islam. Bruce Feiler has beautifully described how Abraham could be at the center of an interreligious dialogue contributing to a better understanding of all three traditions. Each one of them interprets the story of the almost-sacrifice of Abraham's son in a different way. Each one has taken the text and—in Feiler's opinion—used it as a pretext in order to prove some superiority or justify some practice. It is "the most debated, the most misunderstood, and the most combustible event in the entire Abraham story."[59] In the Koran (sura 37) Abraham tells his son that he had a dream of sacrificing him, and he asks the son's advice concerning what to do about it. The son replies that he should do whatever God orders. So the father does prepare the boy for the sacrifice, but God calls out and saves him from carrying out the deed. The point is that both father and son are submitting themselves to God's will. Interestingly, the unnamed "son" is considered by later Islamic interpreters to be Ishmael, not Isaac. Early biographers of Muhammad have traced the lineage of the prophet's tribe to Ishmael, who was said to have grown up in Mecca.

This "Islamization" of the story highlights another point: the Koran is interested in the childhood of Abraham. Already as a boy "Ibrahim," as he is called here, recognizes that there is only one God and refuses to serve idols. Feiler calls him the first monotheist.[60] Thus the Koran praises the faith of the child Abraham as well as the child Isaac (or Ishmael). However, in regard to the older Abraham, some readers might join Feiler in asking, "Is that the model of holiness, the legacy of Abraham: to be prepared to kill for God?" "Abraham, I was discovering, is not just a gentle man of peace. He's as much a model of fanaticism as he is for moderation."[61] Did he blur the line between faith and violence and cause people to elevate violence to the standard of piety? We can admire his faith and courage, but the relationship to his son remains ambiguous.

It is exactly this relationship between the generations and the avoidance of conflict in society that concerned the founder of another world religion: Confucius. While many of the stories of Muhammad's life are shrouded in legend and mystery, it is even more difficult to unearth details of Confucius' life in order to discern how he regarded children. He lived around 500 B.C.E., probably a little earlier than the Buddha. The typical legends surrounding a divine birth have also been told in his case: angels hovered over the house when he was born, and heavenly music sounded in the air.[62] He grew up to become an administrator and later a wise teacher, trying to show rulers and average people how human relationships could be deepened and strengthened. Recent research has shown that Confucius was not the dry bureaucrat that he seemed to be, for example, in the estimate of imperial China's rulers or their more recent Communist heirs. The rituals that he valued so highly were originally tied to cosmic processes. Hierarchies of families and states were, like wind and stars, determined by natural rhythms to which human beings could adapt. The submission of the child to parents and forebears was not the obedience of a slave, but another kind of humility toward "heaven," which did indeed play a role in Confucius' worldview.[63] The honoring of the ancestors had been the center of religious life in China for many centuries before Confucius. The binding force of the Chinese family was the conviction that every person is an important link in an endless chain from past to future. "Being filial," that is, to find one's place like a child in the family and the line of ancestors, is, according to the Confucian *Analects*, a political activity, because it affects society at large.[64] Filial piety is, however, not just filial conduct. It can be expressed in any number of ways, whether prescribed by *li*, the Confucian concept of ritual, or not. The important point of all Confucian ethics is that the self is essentially interpersonal, and self-realization is fundamentally social and interactive.[65] Also, *li* is not to be understood as consisting of strict, formal rules.

> *Li* are those meaning-invested roles, relationships, and institutions which facilitate communication, and which foster a sense of community . . . . They are a social grammar that pro-

vides each member with a defined place and status within the family, community, and polity. *Li* are life forms transmitted from generation to generation as repositories of meaning, enabling the youth to appropriate persisting values and to make them appropriate to their own situations.[66]

As we have seen earlier in the reflection on Jesus' understanding of the child as model for adults, childhood is characterized by a total interdependence, which stands in contrast to our Western notion of individualism. Confucius too sees the child as a link in a chain or tapestry of relationships, and "ritual" is the happy practice of interaction. As the picture "Confucius Playing at Presenting a Sacrificial Vessel" shows, ritual appears like a playful activity founded on childlike awe and love.[67]

In case we still find Confucius too much focused on hierarchies and proper social conduct, we can learn that another wise founder of a religious tradition presented the same criticism within Confucius' time and culture. Lao-tsu also lived around 500 B.C.E. According to legend, he wrote the famous Tao Te Ching, an ancient Chinese text that has its roots in a shamanistic heritage and combines mysticism, folk wisdom, political instruction, and cosmology. It is likely that many sages contributed to it between the seventh and the second centuries B.C.E.[68] If Confucius focused on societal order, political engagement, and the rituals that would keep human beings in harmony with their destiny, Lao-tsu distrusted all hierarchies in family and society and was concerned with the whole human being as part of the cosmic order, the Tao, meaning the Supreme Reality or the all-pervasive substratum of life.[69] It can be compared to the Logos of St. John's gospel. It is nameless, eternal, and indescribable. Life is meaningful if a human being focuses on this life-force, carefully observes nature and the body, and becomes like a child, "supple as a newborn" (verse 10).

*One who embraces Tao*
*Becomes pure and innocent*
*Like a newborn babe*
*Deadly insects will not sting him*
*Wild beasts will not attack him*
*Birds of prey will not strike him*

.   .   .   .   .   .   .   .   .

> *Yet his vitality is full*
> *His inner spirit is complete.* (Verse 55)

As in Jesus' message, things are turned upside down in the Tao te Ching: the gentle overcomes the hard; the small and weak is in fact the strong. The soft water can erode the hard rock (verse 78). "In Taoism . . . ultimate reality is feminine, and what is truly powerful is what adapts and adjusts."[70]

Comparing all of these religious traditions, there appears to be something unique in Jesus' physically embracing children—a very feminine gesture in his time—expressly pointing to a child as model for being human before God, and bluntly annunciating that to "receive" a child means to receive God. However, the vision of "becoming like a child" in order to be close to the divine can be found in various forms in other religions.

How, then, does this almost universal vision relate to the terrifying statistics of children as victims of poverty, hunger, abuse, homelessness, AIDS, prostitution, and war? Why are not people of faith the world over rallying to protect and defend the rights of children when thirty thousand of them, according to UNICEF, die daily of hunger and preventable diseases?[71] Philip Ariès has taught us that childhood is a social construct invented around the sixteenth century, and Neil Postman has suggested that childhood is now "disappearing."[72] But the UNICEF statistics about children as victims are not only a social construct. Children are suffering because their childhood is indeed disappearing, and we as grownups are not eager to "become like children," as Jesus and other divine messengers have asked us to do. Instead, "most of us are control freaks."[73] Becoming like children would mean turning the world upside down: giving up our craving for security, for success in the stock market and in war, our infatuation with technology, our exploitation of the environment, and the desire for everything to be more, faster, and bigger. It would mean giving up our fascination with "growing up" as model of maturity and to "grow down" instead to children's simplicity, trust, integrity of feeling, and ties to nature; their enduring spontaneity and ability to change, forgive, and forget, and their almost eschatological openness to an ever new, surprising future.

# RELATED ART

*We have to challenge
theology to listen to children
"for a change."*

— KRISTIN HERZOG

1. Emil Nolde, *Christus und die Kinder (Christ among the Children)*, 1910. Oil paint on linen, 34 ⅛ x 41 ⅞ in. Gift of Dr. W. R. Valentiner. Signed on the lower left "Emil Nolde." New York, Museum of Modern Art, Wvz Urban 350. Digital image © The Museum of Modern Art/Licensed by SCALA / Art Resource, N.Y., and Stiftung Seebüll Ada und Emil Nolde, Seebüll, Germany. Used by permission.

2. Lucas Cranach the Elder, *Let the Children Come Unto Me (Suffer Little Children)*, 1538. Photo: Elke Walford. Hamburger Kunsthalle, Hamburg, Germany. Photo credit: Bildarchiv Preussischer Kulturbesitz/ Art Resource, N.Y. Used by permission.

3. Edward Hicks, *The Peaceable Kingdom,* ca. 1840–45.
Oil on canvas, 45.8 x 61.2 cm. (18 x 24⅛ in.).
Photo credit and ©: Brooklyn Museum of Art,
Brooklyn, N.Y., 40.340, Dick S. Ramsay Fund.
Used by permission.

4. *The Good Shepherd,* first half of fourth century.
Museo Pio Cristiano, Vatican Museums,
Vatican State. Photo Credit: Scala, Art Resource, N.Y.
Used by permission.

5. *The Birth of the Buddha.* Woodcut.
From: Hans-Wolfgang Schumann, *Buddhistische
Bilderwelt: Ein ikonographisches Handbuch des
Mahāyāna- und Tantrayāna-Buddhismus.* Köln: Eugen
Diederichs Verlag, 1986, 51. Permission by Verlag
Heinrich Hugendubel, München, Germany.

6. *The Hindu Goddess Parvati Enthroned with the Infant Ganesa in her Arms.* Anonymous, ca. 1865. Watercolor, Kalighat style. Permission by Picture Library/ British Library, London.

7. *Pharaoh Akhenaten and His Family (with his wife*
*Nefertiti and their three daughters under the rays of Aton).*
Painted limestone relief (Tell-el-Amarna),
32.5 x 39 cm. Egypt, 18th dynasty, ca. 1345 B.C.E.
Ägyptisches Museum, Staatliche Museen zu Berlin,
Berlin, Germany. Photo credit: Bildarchiv Preussischer
Kulturbesitz/Art Resource, N.Y. Used by permission.

8. *Krishna the Butter Thief.* Calendar picture from
John Stratton Hawley, *Krishna the Butter Thief*
(Princeton: Princeton University Press, 1983).
Frontispiece. Permission by John Stratton Hawley.

9. The arhat Hvāsáng. Woodcut from
Hans-Wolfgang Schumann, *Buddhistische Bilderwelt:
Ein ikonographisches Handbuch des Mahāyāna- und
Tantrayāna-Buddhismus* (Köln: Eugen Diederichs
Verlag, 1986), 221. Undated. Permission by Verlag
Heinrich Hugendubel, München, Germany.

10. *Confucius Playing at Presenting a Sacrificial Vessel.*
Gu Yuan, *Shengji tu,* 1826; Beijing: Xianzhuang. From
*The Rivers of Paradise: Moses, Buddha, Confucius, Jesus
and Muhammad as Religious Founders,* ed. David Noel
Freedman and Michael J. McClymond
(Grand Rapids, Mich.: Eerdmans, 2001), 254.

11. *Sacrifice of Children in the Mountains in Honor of the Sun God.* Stirrup vase, Moche Culture, Peru, ca. 700 C.E. From the collection van der Zypen. Photo: Dietrich Graf. Ethnologisches Museum, Staatliche Museen zu Berlin, Berlin, Germany. Photo credit: Bildarchiv Preussischer Kulturbesitz/ Art Resource, N.Y. Used by permmission.

12. Joseph Beuys, *Familie (Family)*. 1961. Pencil, oil paint on drawing paper, 56 x 42 cm., sign. v. u. m.: Joseph Beuys/Beschr. v.u.m.: 1961 Familie. Stiftung Schloss Moyland, Bedburg-Hau, Germany. MSM00992. Photo credit ©: Dr. Maurice Dorren, Joseph Beuys Archiv, Stiftung Museum Schloss Moyland, Sammlung Van der Grinten. Permission by © 2005 Artists Rights Society (ARS), New York/VG Bild-Kunst, Bonn.

13. Walter Williams, *Roots*. Undated.
Mixed media, 48 x 61 in. © Fisk University Galleries,
Nashville, Tenn. Used by permission.

14. Oscar Kokoschka, *In Memory of the Children of Europe Who Have to Die of Cold and Hunger this Xmas.* 1946. Lithography. © 2005 Artists Rights Society/ Pro Litteris, Zürich. Used by permission.

There is no reason, however, to dream of the "good old days." The present-day victimization of children is not a modern phenomenon. We have earlier considered the "child abuse" among the Andean tribes of Peru in pre-Inca times (between 100 and 700 C.E.): they ritually sacrificed the most flawless, most beautiful children to the sun god, killing them on a mountain side, as is shown, for example, on a pottery vessel of the Mochica culture.[74] These victims were considered saviors. We may be horrified, but our Western modern world has sacrificed millions of the best young people by sending them to fight wars for grownups in the name of God and calling them heroes when they were forced to die for adult notions of honor and self-defense. As Bruce Feiler reminds us,

> The English poet Wilfrid Owen invoked Isaac's death in a vivid denunciation of fathers sending their sons off to die in World War I. An angel beseeches Abraham not to kill the lad, and even points to a ram to sacrifice instead. "But the old man would not so, but slew his son—/And half the seed of Europe, one by one."[75]

Moreover, our wars kill, maim, orphan, and make homeless countless infants and children who are simply considered collateral damage in the battles for some lofty goal like security, liberty, fatherland, or democracy. Our tax dollars contribute to this child abuse on a massive scale, and the world's religions have all too often supported wars that contradicted their founders' principles.[76] Yes, the use of military force can sometimes *save* countless children's lives and liberty, but these are rare exceptions, especially in the nuclear age.

Child abuse in our time may also take the seemingly innocuous form that the German artist Joseph Beuys has portrayed in his picture called "Family" (1961).[77] This is not a "religious" picture, but Beuys was a very unusual artist whose most abstract works still express his spiritual insights. The parents simply ignore the child. There is something wrong with the head of these parents—something is "cut off"—not only in the reproduction, but in the original. The child can only see what ground the parents are standing on. It has to step on their toes even to call attention to its presence. This child is not a savior, but a thoughtful victim. The challenge to repent from our society's callousness toward children is here stated in a secular way.

More hopeful is the outlook for the child in Walter Williams's painting "Roots."[78] Williams, born in 1920, is an African American painter from New York who became a well-known artist and citizen of Denmark. The child is still living in the shadow, but strong roots have caused the tree to burst the barbed wire; they have turned slave-time cotton fields into flower gardens and have given life to sunflowers, birds, and butterflies. Roots give hope for new freedom. The child as victim at the same time represents the saving future. Black liberation cannot be understood without the spiritual struggle behind it.

Williams's picture leads me back to Emil Nolde. Jesus bends down to the children, becoming himself, so to speak, a child and thereby acknowledging his own divine roots. It was not a matter of acquiring a new naiveté. It meant living a life rooted in trust like "the lilies of the field," and yet daring to lay it on the line for the sake of truth and compassion.

Isaiah, Krishna, the Buddha, Confucius, Lao Tsu, and Muhammad have not annunciated it as precisely as Jesus is reported to have done it, but they all knew that living like a child means true wisdom and power. It also means bending towards the suffering children of this world by looking down at our divine roots, forgetting grown-up notions of progress, domination, and control, *sharing* power instead of grabbing it, cherishing interdependence, not independence. Oscar Kokoschka has portrayed this "bending down to children" in an unsurpassed way when in 1946 he created a lithograph portraying Jesus as reaching down from the cross to a group of children, a cross on whose beam is written, "In memory of the children of Europe who have to die of cold and hunger this Xmas."[79]

Our own "bending down" happens only by grace, when a divine voice—like the irresistible cry of a newborn baby—awakens the child in us, lures us to places where children's joys and sufferings inspire us, and nudges us into action. Encountering other people of faith the world over may increase our sensibility for listening to that divine cry and help us to realize that the future of our globe may depend on our response.

# 4

# THE CHILD AS VICTIM AND AGENT AROUND THE WORLD

➤➤ ✴ ⬅⬅

## Child Workers and Child Soldiers[1]

Two hundred forty-six million children from
five to seventeen years work worldwide under conditions that hurt
their development. . . . 8.4 million children suffer from forced labor and
debt slavery, prostitution and pornography, recruitment as child soldiers
or other worst forms of exploitation.[2]

The future of our children is unavoidably tied to global forces. It does not only take a village to bring up a child, but every village and every city is determined by global market forces, global media, and global politics. Yet globalization is still being hotly contested: while promising improved commerce, communication, and living standards, it has been criticized for achieving the opposite—a greater gulf between rich and poor nations and an intensified hatred between religious and ethnic groups fearing a loss of identity and substance. A fifth of the world's population (1.2 billion people) have to live on less than a dollar a day. Half of them are children. The fifteen richest individuals of the world are worth more than the combined GDP (gross domestic product) of all of sub-Saharan Africa.[3] Some economists still contend that the increasing removal of trade barriers will bring more prosperity to hungry nations.

Whatever side we are on in this debate, September 11, 2001, has shown that globalization has furious enemies because it has been propelled by U.S. technology and politics and is considered a threat to less powerful countries and non-Western religions. Meanwhile globalization simply continues, and the only question is how it is managed and how we respond to it. Should it be any business of academics—especially in the field of religion—that countless children around the globe are laboring instead of going to school and learning to kill before they can even read or write? Pierre Bourdieu has called for a "scholarship with commitment" that breaks out of the ivory tower of an assumed neutrality that is "wrongly equated with scientific objectivity when it is in fact a scientifically unimpeachable form of escapism."[4]

In my research on the child in words and images of world religions I have tried to see things from interdisciplinary and global perspectives. Have Jews, Christians, Buddhists, Hindus, Muslims, and others always felt the same divine mandate to cherish, protect, and nurture children? Are there similarities in the different ways of envisioning a divine child or discovering "the child in us"? I then asked myself whether there is a "global" conviction that children should be able to play, go to school, learn responsibility by getting a job, and be trained to defend their country when they grow up. I soon realized that there are traps of globalization. Just as feminism in the seventies had to learn that sisterhood is not "universal," but comprises different ethnic, national, and religious women's movements, so the postmodern and postcolonial discourse on children has to take multiple forms depending on geography, culture, politics, gender, and religion.

> Invocations of the child . . . are historically and culturally specific. . . . The child accrues power and value across its multiple figurations, and . . . only by addressing this multiplicity can its cultural force be adequately addressed.[5]

Children's rights and wrongs are judged differently in different parts of the world, and we have to discern carefully where to draw the line between what is wrong in all times and places—like hunger, torture, or exploitation—and what may be justified under cultural circumstances completely different from our own.

There are people who would suggest that there is absolutely nothing that can be said to be wrong in all times and places. We have recently heard from defenders of torture who insist that in extreme cases it can help to prevent a terrorist attack—the famous ticking bomb scenario—or the life of an abducted child being at risk. I think any confession of a tortured person is bound to be unreliable, and even if it would not be, torture utterly destroys the humanity of the torturer and the dignity of his community or country.[6] We might remember that Amnesty International concluded in 2001—after three years of research—that children were being tortured in fifty countries.[7] For Christians and many others there are certain global claims of right and wrong, but they should not be used to feel superior or to dictate to others. The core of the Christian faith has always been a global claim: Jesus Christ as the light of the world. However, this basic tenet has often been misunderstood and used to dominate others. Christians traditionally illustrated it with stories from mission fields around the world. But now we ourselves have become a mission field, since Christianity is shrinking in the Western world and rapidly increasing in the Southern hemisphere, especially in Africa. Many—not all—churches have recognized this change, but Western economy and technology are still operating with a secularized, outdated "mission" concept: we will bring salvation to starving, oppressed, and illiterate masses, either by "development" or by military power.

Whether it can be called neocolonialism or neoliberalism, such a stance is the opposite of what Jesus called "becoming like children"; it is the grown-up version of saying to the rest of the world as we patronizingly say to children: if you do as I say, it will be for your own good. There is nothing intrinsically wrong with the global spread of commerce and technology. In fact, it can help countless children and adults to overcome poverty, sickness, and death if it is managed with consideration of the well-being of all people and the sustainability of the earth's resources. For this to happen the first group that must be taken seriously is the most vulnerable one: children. I will concentrate here on two global phenomena that are endangering the world's children in an unprecedented way: child workers and child soldiers. My point is that in respect to scholarship on these issues, globalization has to rhyme with differentiation. Only when we take particulars like culture, religion, social class, or gender into consideration can globalization be more than a cyberspace network or a commercial takeover. Responsible research on such matters can be a life-and-death issue for the children on our globe and even for ourselves.

## CHILD WORKERS

The term "child workers" evokes scenes of hungry children in the Two-Thirds-World carrying heavy burdens in order to earn a few pennies. But if we, like UNICEF and like the International Labor Organization (ILO), include in the term "children" all young people under the age of eighteen, then child labor is also a problem right here in the United States—and similarly in parts of Europe—where even rich families consider it a sacred right that their teenage children flip hamburgers at McDonald's or pack groceries to make money for their fancy tennis shoes or cars, even though their extended work hours might mean that the next day they return to school exhausted. Businesses want to keep the minimum wage low and are able to do so by hiring low-cost teenage employees; but what does that wage do to single parents who need to feed a family? The WalMart and Target Companies are both known for having illegally employed underage workers.[8] And what about the children of immigrant farm workers in the United States who often work alongside their parents? If we in our Western societies are ambiguous about child labor, how much more is that the case in so-called Third World nations?

During my annual visits to Peru over the past eighteen years I have learned that even in a country where almost 55 percent of the population or fourteen million people are living in poverty, opinions on child labor vary widely. One nongovernmental organization, called SEMILLA, that sponsors a wide variety of creative programs for mothers and children in some of the poorest districts of Lima, contends that children should never have to work, but simply go to school and have time to play. Another organization that has become famous in many Latin American countries for representing child laborers, called MANTHOC, opposes only exploitative labor and acknowledges the fact that countless families simply cannot survive without having the children bring in some money by selling fruit, candy, or newspapers; by polishing shoes, carrying water, selling bus tickets, or bringing up younger siblings.

A similar controversy prevails in India, where various organizations, especially the "Indian Campaign Against Child Labor" (CACL), are fighting hard against any work situation for children, because India—until 2002—had no law compelling children to go to school, and CACL estimates that fifty to seventy million Indian children who have not been attending school are mostly child workers. Very young Indian girls carry heavy bricks in some factory or work in quarries, in industries that polish precious stones, in households, garbage dumps, or agriculture. German television reported in September of 2003 that two-thirds of all gravestones in Germany are formed from granite blocks from India that have been worked on by children under miserable circumstances including tremendous noise, heavy machinery, constant dust, and minimal pay. While everybody knows that these youngsters usually have to work in order to help the family survive, Indian activists contend that lack of schooling increases poverty instead of easing it, because illiteracy worsens the chances of good employment.

Do children, however, have a legal right to work? In November 1989 the United Nations signed the International Convention on the Rights of the Child. It does not see children as objects to be nurtured and protected, but acknowledges their right as subjects to have a voice in matters that affect their lives. In article 32 it states that the participating nations acknowledge children's right to be protected from commercial exploitation and from work that is dangerous or that hinders their education, health, or physical, psychological, ethical, and social development. The article does not thereby prohibit all children's work, but challenges governments to prevent the worst forms of child labor. One hundred ninety-one countries have ratified the Convention, but the United States and Somalia have not. In Somalia's case the country has not had a functioning government since 1991. The transitional parliament and president still have to be recognized by various militias and warlords. In the case of the United States, the government signed the Convention in February of 1995, but Congress has not yet ratified it. Part of the problem is the fact that different U.S. states have different rights. For example, until March 2005 in some states the death penalty was in effect for persons who were under age when they committed a crime—which is against the Children's Rights Convention. Also, conservative U.S. groups oppose the Convention, arguing that it undermines the authority of parents.[9]

What the United States as well as more than a hundred other countries including Canada did sign is a treaty promoted by the International Labor Organization (ILO) banning the most dangerous types of child labor, like mining, prostitution, pornography, and drug trafficking.[10] But that treaty too needs ratification by the Senate, and it does not go far enough in light of the overwhelming statistics of ILO: 250 million children in the so-called developing countries work, almost half of them all day long. Of the total number, 110 million are girls and 140 million are boys. These statistics do not even include those girls and boys who work only in their own homes, bringing up younger siblings, nursing a disabled parent, or working in the fields instead of going to school.

There is hardly a type of labor that children do not perform, and most of their work happens in the informal sector where contracts or benefits are totally lacking: 70.7 percent work in agriculture or fisheries, often with their parents; 8.3 percent in businesses and small stores or restaurants; 8.3 percent in factories making rugs, clothing, shoes, and the like; 6.5 percent in social and personal services like housework; 3.8 percent in transportation and communication; 1.9 percent in construction, and 0.9 percent in mining and quarries.[11] Child labor often takes place under dangerous circumstances: for example, children in Nicaragua working with tobacco leaves suffer from the pesticides used to spray the plants. There are similar problems among children working in the flower industry.[12]

Much worse are the conditions of an estimated one million children who are annually forced into prostitution or the slave trade. The trade of women and girls from Eastern into Western Europe has in recent years been ten times as high as earlier. They are promised work or marriage and end up in prostitution.[13] Rita Nakashima Brock and Susan Thistlethwaite have pointed out that in Asia as well as in the United States certain religious and cultural traditions that downgrade women can contribute to the spread of prostitution, but poverty and sex tourism are still the special grounds on which it flourishes, especially since the fear of AIDS has dramatically increased the demand for young child prostitutes. In the United States, 80–90 percent of women in prostitution are estimated to have been sexually abused as children.[14]

Another troubling aspect of the type of work children are doing is the fact that about 10 percent of all child labor in the "developing world" supports the export of consumer goods, for example, in textile factories, the rug-making industry or the coffee and cocoa plantations. So the result of this work does not stay within the needy countries. Four out of five of these children do not receive a salary, either because they belong to the 70 percent who work within their families, or because they are actual slaves or forced laborers, paying off a loan that the parents needed in some emergency.[15] Many children who are secretly channeled into Western countries simply end up on the streets. For example, in the Vancouver, B.C., area, in the summer of 2000, about 250 Honduran children aged twelve to eighteen were involved in selling drugs on the streets.[16]

Whenever children work in their own countries, the scenes of their labor can be found in a wide variety of situations: a city garbage dump in Managua, where children look for items of worth in order to resell them; a home in Pakistan where a brother and sister sew footballs that need 690 stitches to be finished (it takes each child seven hours to finish three of them); a street in Potosi, Bolivia, where a thirteen-year-old shoeshine boy has to pay more than a quarter of his daily income for a can of shoe cream and is therefore eager to learn how to make his own shoe cream; a tin hut in Teheran where a twelve-year-old boy, who lives with his mother and four siblings, gets up before sunrise and pushes a self-made cart through the city to collect stale and often moldy bread from households and cafes that he sells for animal feed; a spinning factory in Bangkok where a twelve-year-old girl ended up doing slave labor after her parents could no longer feed their five children and entrusted her to a man who promised to find her a job in the city; a family in Bolivia that adopted an eight-year-old Aymara girl, used her as a maid and then mistreated and sexually harassed her; a factory in Indonesia where an eleven-year-old girl makes clothes for Barbie dolls, but cannot afford to buy a doll for herself.[17]

Some of the most terrible work conditions are found in the mines around the mountains of Peru, Bolivia, and Ecuador, where children haul ore on their backs or amalgamate it with (very poisonous) mercury using primitive grindstones. In the mines of the Republic of Congo children are exposed to highly radioactive cobalt, which is in high demand worldwide for the production of cell phones.[18] Even worse are the plantations of the Ivory Coast where boys from Mali are held as slaves, totally cut off from the surrounding world, to harvest cocoa, coffee, cotton, and bananas.[19] El Salvador is making progress in the elimination of an especially loathsome children's work: collecting mollusks in the mangrove swamps while smoking cigars in order to reduce mosquito and other bug bites and using amphetamines to stay awake during the seemingly endless workday.[20]

Any effort to abolish child labor or make it more humane has to take more than poverty into account. Contributing to the children's dilemma is, for example, the culture of machismo, says the Rev. Pete Byrne, a Maryknoll priest who for many years has been dedicated to various programs for children in Lima, Peru. "Because so many men flee the scene after their wives or girlfriends have children, household stability, including the economic component, starts to crumble. The man has taken off, so the mothers are placed in a position where they have no choice but to put their children to work."[21] Frequently the men can hardly be blamed, because the lack of jobs takes away their dignity, leads to desperate, violent assertions of masculinity in the home and finally to the search for work in another part of the country. Meanwhile overworked or battered spouses have to take even the smallest children along to the market to sell any trinket that enables them to survive.

Under these circumstances the complete abolition of child labor appears at best as a distant goal. Not only the above-mentioned activists in India and some groups in South America still work toward that end; also the ILO and Casa Alianza, the Latin American chapter of Covenant House, see this as a long-range solution.[22] But, as an ILO representative stated, immediate abolition is not necessarily the answer. "The relationship between labor and education is more complicated than expected."[23] MANTHOC, the most well-known Latin American organization of child workers, is convinced that a limited amount of nonexploitative work, leaving some daily hours for schooling and play, can contribute to responsibility, creativity, and personal development. UNICEF has found some evidence supporting this stance in Bolivia,

where employed students often outperform their nonworking counterparts in school.[24] Total and immediate abolition, involving, for example, the boycott of all child-made products, can be a global trap also
because it would throw countless families into deeper poverty.
Sensible organizations trying to help children will not close any factory that employs children without at the same time building schools,
opening training centers for unemployed teenagers, and lobbying governments for better healthcare.[25]

Along these lines a model program is "Rugmark," an initiative
against the exploitation of children in the rug-making industry.
Rugmark reported in 2003 that it had exposed two thousand cases of
illegal children's work in India, Nepal, and Pakistan. Numerous ex-
porters of rugs have agreed not to employ children. In exchange for
this promise they receive the Rugmark seal, a certificate of quality.
Even families where the children are helping with rug-making in the
home can qualify for Rugmark if the children also attend a school. By
2001, forty thousand rug looms were being inspected. If children were
found among the workers, the owner lost the Rugmark seal, and the
children were taken into a rehabilitation center where they learn a
trade. Rugmark also tries to reconnect the children with their parents
who sometimes have no idea where the children were brought after
they were given to some trader—posing as a job provider—in exchange for a loan. To make the controls of the looms possible, the rug
producers pay a small amount; and the rug importers pay one percent
of the import price to finance the rehabilitation of the children. By the
end of 2001, two million Rugmark rugs had been sold in Germany, the
Netherlands, Luxembourg, England, and the United States.[26] It should
be a signal to the rug industry that fairly made rugs do sell.

There are other factors besides profit-hungry producers, poverty,
and machismo that push children into working situations. There are
deep-seated cultural traditions that favor children's work. Indigenous
people in the Andean mountains, for example, have always seen it as
normal and natural that children help at a very early age with guarding
and feeding animals, gathering plants, driving birds out of cornfields,
or watching smaller siblings. During Inca and colonial times, children
had to help make the family's tribute to the state possible. Among
members of the Hamar tribe in Ethiopia it is still the custom to let

children help in grinding grains, carrying water, gathering wood, and cooking. The aborigines of Australia do not have words that indicate the difference between work and play; children enjoy imitating the work of adults. They learn early to distinguish the footprints of various animals and humans and help to gather food. The clear distinction between childhood and adulthood, play and work, is an invention of the European bourgeoisie.[27] However, the work of children today in most societies is fundamentally different from that in earlier centuries. ILO and UNICEF regard children's work as exploitative when it is done by too young children, continues for too many hours, demands physical or psychological stress, is unhealthy and dangerous, is not adequately paid, hinders schooling, or disregards the dignity of the child. Children themselves feel exploited when they are totally dependent on a boss who does not care about their rights, when they cannot keep any of the money they earn, when their work is considered "help" or "training" in order to avoid payment, or when they do not have any chance for education, relaxation, play, or other interests.[28]

We have to agree, then, with many of the laboring children that under certain circumstances they should have the right to work. Even some labor unions, which are traditionally in favor of abolishing children's work, are gradually changing their minds, and the children are organizing themselves in union-type movements. Groups as different as an Association of Shoe Cleaners in Bolivia and the Youth Branch of the German IG Metall union are working toward acceptance of children in adult unions. Since the late 1970s, movements of working children have organized in Latin America, Africa, and southern Asia. Since 1985, demands of the children of India have influenced Indian politics. In the mid-nineties, girls in West Africa who worked as maids founded a self-help organization that today has twenty-five thousand members in fifteen African countries.[29] In Latin America, MANTHOC began in 1978 in Lima, Peru, and was sponsored by the Catholic Young Worker's Movement. Similar initiatives arose in other parts of Peru. In 1996 the National Movement of Child Workers of Peru was founded. In 2003 it had fourteen thousand members. MANTHOC manages three houses in Lima where the children can meet during work breaks, where they can get help with school work, play, receive inexpensive meals, and participate in cultural events. Every child pays a small amount into a common fund to support children in times of sickness when they cannot work. Some children attend state schools in the morning and work in the afternoon; others attend a special MANTHOC school that is more geared to the needs of working children by emphasizing practical skills. Alejandro Cussianovich, a priest and pedagogue, has worked with MANTHOC since its earliest days. He explains that the movement is not trying to idealize the work of children, but where their work is unavoidable, the dignity of the children has to be respected and their concerns have to be listened to. When the children have larger meetings, he says, they do not talk as much about their work as about daily problems: the garbage in their neighborhood, violence and thefts in the street, a mosquito outbreak in some city district, or the continuing issue of family violence.[30]

All of these organizations demand the right to work. Out of their self-organizing arose special initiatives like street theater, meetings with ministers, mayors, or other authorities, or special fund-raising projects. Two international meetings have taken place, the first in Kundapur, India, in 1996, the second in Huampani, Peru, a year later, bringing together working children from Africa, Latin America, and Asia. These children formulated a program that included their rejection of any boycott of products made by children. They insisted on their right to work without discrimination and exploitation, their right to an education that corresponds to their daily life, their right to basic health care and to participation in the struggle for legislation that affects them.[31]

We have the difficult task, then, of distinguishing between, on the one hand, abstract attempts to close factories that employ children or to avoid any football or Barbie doll made by children and, on the other hand, serious projects like Rugmark that do not abolish or prohibit anything without providing a safety net for the affected families who might otherwise go more hungry than before. We must listen to those who see children's work under today's conditions in the Two-Thirds-World as damaging to their education and emotional health, because they have no chance to play and develop skills that will get them out of poverty. However, we also have to understand that sometimes work gives children a sense of self-worth and responsibility that the understaffed, underfinanced school in their neighborhood cannot give them, and that it enables them to help their families survive.

Schooling is not necessarily a cure-all. Whenever schools do not really relate their teaching to the children's daily lives, their administrators should not be surprised that children leave them for income-generating jobs. Also, when in some countries school teaching takes place in the language of the former colonists, which poor families do not speak, children will lose interest in learning. In Jamaica, for example, teaching is in Standard English, while children in most poor urban communities speak Creole. "Thus, for many children, schooling acts neither as a channel of upward mobility nor as an instrument of social change and personal development but as yet another medium of social control."[32] Peru has a similar problem with communities who speak the indigenous Quechua or Aymara languages while school is taught only in Spanish. Few countries want to spend money on a bilingual educational system, even though bilingualism is an enrichment for any child.

Thus governments and individuals have the double task of making schools more attractive and getting out the word about unfair labor practices and fair trade if they want to reduce or improve child labor. If conscientious citizens, churches, and civic groups make the public aware of companies that tolerate sweatshop conditions for children, the industries will increasingly participate in controls and in new creative projects, and consumers will more often prefer to buy fairly traded items. That this is realistically possible is proven by the growing success of campaigns to sell "fair trade" coffee.[33] Moreover, the Fair Trade Fair, held as an alternative to the Fifth Ministerial Meeting of the World Trade Organization, September 10–14, 2003, in Cancun, Mexico, promoted the concept of sustainable trade by offering goods from various countries and continents and found special benefits in ethical trading: "Small farmers and rural communities demonstrated that goods sold through fair trade can act as a powerful catalyst to revitalize local economies while protecting the environment."[34] Among the internationally established criteria for fair trade is always the avoidance of exploitative child labor. Churches in many countries have been in the forefront of selling fair trade products in special nonprofit, "One World" stores run mostly by volunteers.

Changing our buying practices, however, will in itself not suffice to help child workers throughout the world, and improving schools is not possible without increasing the allotment of funds for education.

Citizens will have to vote for the sensible spending of government money that takes children's needs into consideration. As *Latinamerica Press* reported in 1999, it would take only six billion dollars each year (in addition to current expenditures) to provide basic education for all people in developing nations, but $780 billion are spent each year on militaries worldwide.[35] Since then, things have gotten worse. World Bank president James Wolfenden declared in April 2004 that he was encouraged by the growing realization among wealthy nations that the $900 billion being spent annually on military budgets could not ensure a safer world as long as only $50 billion was being spent on foreign aid.[36] That brings me to another type of child labor that should simply be abolished.

## CHILD SOLDIERS

The number of child soldiers has increased the world over because the nature of wars has changed. The percentage of civilian deaths compared with military deaths has increased during the last decades from 5 percent to 90 percent. Through technological weaponry the moral and geographic distance between those that lead a war and the victims of war has grown steadily. Instead of wars between states there are chaotic wars in which the enemies as well as the political causes of war are hard to identify. Weapons are light and easy to handle. The longer a conflict lasts the more likely the fighting groups will try to recruit children, because they are cheap and can more easily be controlled.[37]

In many countries child soldiers are drawn into armed service after losing their parents and their home and therefore being hungry and without any livelihood. Others are conscripted into an army by guerillas or dictatorial governments. Currently, three hundred thousand child soldiers from seven to eighteen years of age are estimated to be involved in armed conflict in thirty countries, and several thousand more are members of armies, paramilitaries, and nongovernmental armed groups in eighty-five countries.[38] Child soldiers are favored by ruthless leaders because they are cheap and easily manipulated.[39] They work as spies, guards, carriers, sex slaves, human shields, and removers of mines. Under the influence of alcohol or drugs they can turn into cold-blooded murderers. Some become suicidal. They are not able to judge dangers correctly, and they often consider violent fighting a game, as a rebel leader in the Democratic Republic of Congo suggested.

When girls are recruited, they are usually kept as slaves and sexually abused, but many are also trained for armed struggle. Girl soldiers suffer even more than boys, because after an armed fight is over, their families and villages may not accept them again if they have been raped.[40] In Myanmar (Burma) many children have been used to clear minefields. In Sri Lanka, girls between eleven and fifteen years old, many of them orphans, have been recruited since the mid-eighties by the oppositional "Liberation Tigers" for *Tamil Eelam* (LTTE) in order to be trained as "Birds of Freedom," meaning suicide bombers. Girls are favored for this work because security forces cannot detect them as easily as young men. In October of 1999, forty-nine Tamil children, thirty-two of them girls age eleven to fifteen, were killed by government forces.[41]

The causes for a large number of child soldiers in a country and the reason they commit acts of cruelty vary widely. In the case of Colombia, the country has suffered forty years of civil war; twenty-six thousand people are murdered every year; more than a million people are refugees, and children grow up in a culture of violence, sometimes becoming armed fighters because they want to avenge the death of a loved one.[42] In the massacre around Bunia in the Congo, in May 2003, many of the hundreds of dead were killed by child soldiers between eight and fourteen years of age who had been drugged and appeared to act as if delirious.[43] In Sri Lanka the rebel organization Tamil Eelam not only offered a good salary to child soldiers, but also gave their parents a piece of land and regular donations of food.[44]

The Children's Rights Convention of 1989 stipulated that children under fifteen years old should not be "directly involved" in armed hostilities. But this later appeared to be insufficient, especially since many children on this globe do not know their exact age, and many would like to pretend a higher age or are forced to falsify their date of birth when they are illegally recruited. So in May of 2000 the United Nations added a special protocol to the Convention, declaring that children under eighteen years cannot be drafted. By May 2001, seventy-nine countries had signed this addition, including the United States, but only four had ratified it, namely Canada, Bangladesh, Sri Lanka, and Andorra.[45] By June 2005, 177 countries had signed and eighty-eight had ratified it, among them the United States on December 23, 2002.[46]

Meanwhile the horror of gun-toting children trained to kill and be killed goes on in places as far away as Burma, Mozambique, and Sierra Leone.[47] We should, however, also be aware of the way our Western world trains children in the martial arts. For example, the U.S. military increasingly uses Hollywood to help in recruiting very young soldiers. In the fall of 2002, the army brought out a computer game called "America's Army." Interested young people between thirteen(!) and thirty-four years of age were invited to order the software gratis from the Internet or pick it up at recruiting offices. Players can go through virtual basic training or advance to become rangers, sharpshooters, or electronic First Sergeants. In the "Action" part it is like in any ego-shooter game: kill the other guy before he kills you. It is well known that the teenage killer in Erfurt, Germany, who in April 2002 murdered sixteen people (mostly teachers) and himself, was an avid fan of violent computer games. But in this military game, players who shoot at their own cyber comrades are merely sent to "computer prison," which makes killing people appear as innocuous as killing time.[48]

There are many other types of cooperation between the Pentagon and Hollywood, for example, in popular war movies for which Hollywood gets the necessary tanks, airplanes, and other equipment only if the military decides that the army is shown in a positive light.[49] There are also serious efforts by the U.S. army to train children from the age of eight on for military service. In the "Young Marines" boys and girls of age eight to eighteen wear uniforms, have military grades, and take part in military exercises. This program had two hundred units throughout the United States and, in the spring of 2001, 14,865 children and young people participated. As to actual soldiering, Great Britain in 1999 had over sixty-six hundred soldiers of age sixteen and seventeen serving in its army, and, since 1982—until the beginning of the Iraq war—ninety-two underage soldiers died in armed struggles of the British army.[50] The United States has admitted that seventeen-year-old soldiers have participated in the Gulf War and in battles in Somalia and Bosnia.[51] Among the U.S. soldiers who died in the Iraq war since 2003 are many who were only eighteen years old or who signed up for the military when they were not even eighteen. In addition, continuing reports of illegal detainment and torture of Afghan and Iraqi child soldiers at Abu Ghraib and Guantanamo Bay are disturbing.[52]

While there is a big difference between recruitment of children in Colombia, Mozambique, or Burma, forced by hunger or dictatorship, and voluntary military service of young people in the United States or Great Britain, we have to realize that without the ratification of international conventions, the setting of age limits and other conditions, the brutalities in so-called Third-World countries as well as the increasing violence in our Western schools and neighborhoods will not be checked effectively. It is not only dictators who are teaching killing; "militainment made in Washingwood," as one newspaper called it, does so in a subtle, seemingly innocuous way.[53] However, in these matters the West is not worse than the rest: Russia is also intensively training very young boys for military service, taking advantage of the fact that those who come from backgrounds of great poverty have no other choice if they want to survive. In Petersburg a group of "soldier mothers" gets together regularly to protest against the use of very young, badly trained soldiers in the bloody fight against the rebels of Chechnya.[54]

It seems that everywhere the children of the poor are the first to be available for "service." The Junior Reserve Officer Training Corps (JROTC) ran three thousand programs in U.S. public schools in 2002, mostly in very poor school districts that find the programs attractive because they provide federal funds. While this kind of training can teach some wonderful discipline, endurance, and camaraderie, and can give some a new-found sense of dignity, the same could surely be accomplished by some tough "Outward Bound" wilderness programs or a strictly organized year of social service that would benefit the whole nation. As *Time* magazine stated, "JROTC teaches kids how to act and think like soldiers before they are old enough to know their own mind."[55]

I suggested earlier that globalization has to rhyme with differentiation. I think that in terms of child soldiering, which in some ways is the most dangerous type of child labor, the differentiation should reveal the various ways children are lured or forced into armed militias or militaries, learning to kill and be killed by open brutalities or "hidden persuaders." We do have to differentiate between hungry, orphaned children who drift into some armed group and children of well-to-do parents who sincerely believe in discipline, "manliness," and patriotism through early military training. In both cases, however, the use of arms by children teaches violence at an age when the child cannot fully understand its consequences. In all countries, soldiering is also a temptation for children because of the lure of adventure and the thrill of danger involved, the similarity to gang-related activities that lends a feeling of community, the desire to imitate adults, the attachment to some "Godfather" figure, and the rewards of prestige, glamour, and excitement.[56]

So what can be done about child soldiers all over the world? We can research and publicize some crucial facts. For example, children can handle only small weapons, and since worldwide some five hundred million small weapons are circulating—most of them leftovers from past wars that ended up on the black market—they will get into children's hands. In Uganda, a Russian AK-47 gun costs as little as a chicken, and in Angola one can buy it for a sack of corn. In the last decade of the twentieth century three million people, most of them women and children, are estimated to have died from pistols, guns, and other small weapons.[57] We can call for a stricter system of accounting for small weapons, which are abundant and superfluous since the end of the Cold War and are sold at random. The United States, Russia, and Germany are the three greatest weapon traders.[58] The president of Brazil, Luiz Inácio "Lula" da Silva, has called for a worldwide tax on all traded weapons in order to establish a fund to fight hunger and reduce debts.[59] I hope this proposal will find many supporters. The fact that even eight-year-olds can use these weapons often first comes to the attention of Westerners when our own soldiers are sent on peace mission in war zones where they might have to shoot children. It should seep into our consciences much earlier.[60]

The same pertains to the terror of landmines that kill and maim countless child soldiers and civilian children. The small bodies of children are easily destroyed by a mine, and children are less aware of dangers. In Cambodia hundreds of mines explode every month, and every fourth victim is a child.[61] The International Campaign to Ban Landmines, which received the Nobel Peace Prize in 1997, gives all of us a chance to donate money to clear a minefield.[62]

We can think globally and uncover some of the root causes of child labor and child soldiering in our Western countries and their intricate relationship with dilemmas "down south." Western families are often blind to the fact that "their purchases, their investments in arms, food, and manufacturing industries of their pension funds" contribute to child abuse in other corners of the world.[63] Amnesty International has traced the path of lovely bridal diamonds from tortured child laborers and ruthless rebel militias in Sierra Leone to Al Qaida arms merchants and finally Western bankers and jewelers.[64] Even on the very simple level of choosing toys for children, we have not been sufficiently aware of the damage done by ridiculous war toys that glamorize violence.

### What Can Be Done about Child Soldiering?

There are many admirable attempts to help children and young people to overcome the trauma of involvement in soldiering and at the same time to prevent future forced recruitment. In Guatemala, an indigenous youth movement, Movimiento de los Jóvenes Mayas, is lobbying for the right to conscientious objection and an alternative form of social service.[65] In Colombia, a Rap music group is inspiring young people to refuse participation in the state military, the guerillas, or the drug lords.[66] In Sierra Leone, UNICEF is trying to reintegrate former child combatants into society and to persuade parents to welcome them back, even if they fought on the "wrong" side or committed criminal acts.[67] In Uganda, the Roman Catholic Church has organized an intensive program to rehabilitate child soldiers. The diocese of Gulu among the Acholi people has engaged five hundred catechists who are being trained as community-based volunteer counselors. They know the culture and the villages to which the former child soldiers are returning. They help people see these children more as victims than as actors in order to further reconciliation. Since the children are considered impure because they have killed and have lived in the jungle among "evil spirits," a ritual is performed when they are reintegrated: the community greets the children at the border of the village; there are prayers and a sermon about forgiveness and understanding, the young people are sprinkled with holy water, and they step on an egg to symbolize the break with the past. Finally a congregational song expresses the joy of the reunion.[68]

Help for former child soldiers is not only needed in the countries where they fought wars. It is increasingly a challenge for Western countries that can grant or deny asylum to these young people. Germany, for example, still denies permanent residence to any person who cannot prove political persecution, thereby ignoring forced recruitment or the murder of a child's family as valid reasons for asylum.[69] Girls are in special danger of sexual abuse or total abandonment if they are returned to the country where they participated in armed struggle. The newly extended European Union also has to clarify the right to conscientious objection to military service; so far it leaves it up to the individual countries to interpret that basic right in very different and often limited ways.[70]

The UN Security Council has understood well that violations of children's rights are a matter of life and death not only for the children involved, but also for our own situation concerning international peace and security. If many years ago Russia and the United States had given the young people of Afghanistan good schools, perhaps they would not have been tempted to study hate and killing in Taliban schools. The neglected children of today are the homeless gang members, callous child soldiers, child prostitutes, AIDS patients, and terrorists of tomorrow. Whether we consider them as victims or agents, we can influence their future and thereby ours. The countless children who are dying in the Iraq war are rapidly increasing the hatred against Western powers. Palestinian children trained to become suicide bombers and young Israeli soldiers ordered to run their tanks over Palestinian homes are reminders that adults have failed to honor children and thereby to work toward a peaceful global future.[71]

While some of these issues seem far removed from our daily lives as scholars, church members, pastors, or teachers, we know from history that individuals and small groups that rise up, stand up, and speak up can have a tremendous influence. Private initiatives and nongovernmental organizations are playing an increasing role in world affairs. Some scholarly fields are discovering their global responsibility. For example, at the third World Congress of Psychotherapy in Vienna, July 2002, the prevailing message seems to have been an appeal to end the "egomania" of a dominant Western world and to be concerned for "the poorest against whom we lead wars."[72] Ken Dodge, a professor at Duke University, stated at a White House conference in July 2002, "It should not come as a surprise that we have so few solutions to [the] problem [of teenage violence], given how little our nation has invested in research . . . on education and children."[73] Children represent 36 percent of this globe's population, and a quarter of them live in miserable poverty, while the wealth of the four richest Americans could lift twelve million children out of poverty five times over.[74]

People of faith are called to learn again that God is the God of life—and that means protecting the growing life of children instead of teaching them to kill. As the Wisdom of Solomon says, "God did not make death, nor does God rejoice in the destruction of the living" (Wisdom 1:12–13). Whether we are poor or rich, pacifists or militarists, children younger than eighteen should not be trained to do the work of war and killing. There are better ways of teaching discipline, physical endurance, loyalty, altruism, and love of country.

Since child soldiering is a type of child labor, theology also has the serious task of thinking through the meaning of work. How does, for example, the Protestant work ethic affect our attitude toward child labor? How can theology respond to increasing unemployment—which often leads to reticent soldiering as the only way to get an education? Can we teach our children that we are not the sum of our work or actions, that *being* consists of more than *doing?* "Just to be is a blessing, just to live is holy," said Abraham Joshua Heschel, and that fits in with what Jesus told us about "becoming like a child." But there is the rub: just to be, a person has to eat, and as long as the world cannot share its resources more equitably around the globe, children will go on laboring and soldiering—"just to be." We have become so used to an atmosphere of violence that we do not even realize how the puzzle pieces fit together: our way of life, our treatment of the environment, our stumbling into preemptive wars, and our ignorance or callousness concerning the life of children in our poorest neighborhoods and in distant parts of the world. Our challenge is to see in every suffering child the body of Christ, broken, shared, crying out for us to become children again.

# 5

## VIOLENCE AGAINST CHILDREN AND BY CHILDREN

→→ ✴ ←←

### *A Global Environmental Issue*

A child born today in an industrialized country will add more
to consumption and pollution over his or her lifetime than 30–50 children
born in developing countries. The ecological "footprint" of the
more affluent is far deeper than that of the poor and, in many cases,
exceeds the regenerative capacity of the earth.[1]

Almost every day we learn from media reports that some child or youth
has committed a crime of violence, like shooting other children, teachers, or parents. *Time* magazine reported in December of 2003 that violence and "a wide range of explosive behaviors" have now become a
problem even in many kindergartens and among first-graders.[2] At the
same time we hear about child abuse by family members, priests, and
strangers. Above all, we know that children around the globe are victims of war, exploitative labor, prostitution, and AIDS on a massive
scale. How is this "mutuality of violence" to be understood? Could it be
related to the way we leave "footprints" on our environment, or the
way we regard creation and our children's—or our own—place in it?

Ivone Gebara sees the problem from a Latin American perspective:

> We have virtually forgotten what it means to "be like little children." Today we fear children, those who crowd the streets watching for the chance to violently snatch a crust of bread from us. We live in a society that is afraid of children! This is the most absurd of all absurdities![3]

Street children are among the foremost examples of violence by and against children. They do steal, sell drugs, and commit other crimes, but since they are so much weaker than the adult society that "breeds" them, the violence against them is indeed an absurdity. In various Latin American cities there are "death squads" that "clean up" the city, targeting children who are a nuisance, and some of them have the hidden support of the police and the business sector.

> Impoverished children, some of whom are perpetrators of the violent crime that has swept the region, have come to be vilified to such an extent as to prompt one anthropologist to liken them to "folk devils."[4]

As a Uruguayan journalist stated already in 1991, "Until recently, the image of the abandoned Latin American child was of a ragged child sleeping in a doorway. Today the image is of a body, lacerated and dumped in a city slum."[5] Since then the problem has grown worse in spite of many wonderful programs to help street children. How could it be getting better when every fourth child of the 2.1 billion children worldwide grows up in a family that has less than a dollar per day to live on?[6] UNICEF estimates that there are a hundred million street children worldwide.[7] Some live alternately at home and in the streets, often expected by their parents to bring in some money. Others never return home because of broken families or the lure of the street where adults promise them work or food while frequently exploiting them in the process. Some of these children develop an uncanny ingenuity of surviving heat and cold, hunger and beatings, sexual advances and thefts within their groups and from outside, but many others die violent deaths.

## OUR OWN INVOLVEMENT

What is easily overlooked is the intricate relationship between the "First" and "Third" world concerning hidden triggers of violence. There is, for example, the impact that Western corporations can have on the lives of street children. A leading manufacturer of industrial glues, coatings, and paints finally stopped selling one type of shoe glue in Latin America because child advocates like Casa Alianza (Covenant House) as well as a large California stockholder of the company had complained for years that the glue is sniffed by street children who get addicted to the fumes that relieve hunger and psychological distress. The U.S.-based H.B. Fuller Company, whose sales worldwide totaled U.S. $1.35 billion in 1998, sold hot-melt glues and water-based glues in Europe, but solvent-based glues in Latin America. While critics are happy that the glue "Resistol" is no longer sold over the counter in Central America, it is appalling that the company did not right away substitute water-based glue in these countries when it became available but continued to sell solvent-based products in Chile. In previous years it has sold the products to large industries when it stopped over-the-counter sales. So critics continued to monitor the situation.[8]

Another obvious tie between the northern and southern parts of the globe is our conspicuous consumption of goods and foods imported from "developing countries." There is an outrageous irony in the fact that among U.S. children obesity has more than doubled since 1980 while at least a billion people in this world are starving or malnourished, and half the world's population is subsisting on less than two dollars per day.

> One in four American children is clinically obese, with corresponding increases in diabetes, hypertension and cardiac arrest among young adults. Americans are literally as well as figuratively eating the earth . . . .
>
> Unless our political machinery disentangles itself from benighted pressure groups and ravenous conglomerates—faint hope indeed—the planet we leave to our inflated children will be so hot, crowded, polluted and barren that no living creature would dwell here by choice.[9]

Increasingly children from well-to-do U.S. families elect to have surgery for obesity, having the size of their stomachs reduced.[10] While obesity frequently is a medical and not an ethical problem, we might ponder the fact that "Americans spend five billion dollars each year on special diets to lower their calorie consumption, while 400 million people around the world are so undernourished, their bodies and minds are deteriorating."[11]

Global market conditions determine not only what the children of this world eat, but what they play with or whether they have time for play. The gorgeous evening dresses and sporty tennis outfits of Barbie dolls are partly sewn by children, some of them as young as thirteen years old (pretending to be older in order to fit the official regulations) in well-guarded factories of Sumatra, often supporting a whole family with their meager salary. They can be hired and fired at will.[12]

## THE VIOLENCE OF THE MARKET AND OF ECOLOGICAL CARELESSNESS

Pablo Richard has observed that in the neoliberal system that countries of the Two-Thirds-World have to live by, the law of the market is seen like a messiah who will save humankind.[13] So the messiah is no longer a child, an image of fragility and need of care, and the freedom of the individual is no longer, as in the apostle Paul's message, tied to the faithful community of all children of God, but it is a private freedom built on efficiency, not vitality, on exact predictions of productivity, not the constant surprise that a newborn child represents, demanding special, not universal, care.[14] If U.S. schools are lacking the most necessary facilities because state funds have been curtailed, they will put soft drink and candy machines into their cafeterias in order to make ends meet. While the children's health is thereby endangered, some companies will make huge profits by simply following the law of the market.

The market, however, is not the only force exerting a hidden violence against children. The way we treat our environment contributes to hunger and diseases, which always devastate the weakest members of society first. The Genesis mandate to "have dominion" over creation has been misinterpreted for generations, and the masculine rhetoric of conquest, control, and utility, represented, for example, by Bacon or Descartes, has aggravated a Western history of disregard for the environment that nurtures us.[15] We have overlooked the fact that "creation is a series of delicately calibrated interrelations and interactions in which the abuse or destruction of any single element in the 'system' will disrupt and impede each of its parts."[16] Children are much more susceptible than adults to environmental pollution or poor diets, and by impacting children, future generations are affected.

For example, twenty-five years after the Vietnam War ended, millions of Vietnamese have continued to suffer the toxic consequences of America's devastating chemical weapon, Agent Orange. According to Vietnamese estimates, five hundred thousand children were born with birth defects on account of Agent Orange, a herbicide of which the U.S. military is said to have used 11.2 million gallons to defoliate hardwood forests, mangrove jungles, and crop lands to deny food and cover to enemy forces. Traces of Agent Orange could still be found in the ground in Vietnam in 2000, but the expense and the political consequences of a thorough investigation make an exact fact-finding impossible at this point.[17] In January of 2003 we learned from the media that an Institute of Medicine study has found a link between chronic lymphocytic leukemia and Vietnam soldiers exposed to herbicides like Agent Orange. Birth defects in veterans' children are only one of the symptoms that have led to this research.[18] While the implicated veterans are now receiving extra benefits, that is little comfort for the children who got hurt for a lifetime even before they were born.

Not only veterans are worrying about the possibility of having children with disabilities on account of environmental pollution. Even average mothers in the United States are anxious about the chemical contents of drinking water, the effects of lead paint, and the hazards of agricultural pesticides on the children they bear.[19] In December 2003 the U.S. government proposed to ease—rather than tighten—restrictions on mercury emissions from coal burning power plants, even though mercury is highly dangerous for pregnant women because of the developmental effects on fetuses.[20] The *New York Times* reported recently that 26 percent of children in central Harlem have asthma, caused by urban pollutants from trucks and buses, home heating systems using cheap oil, and lead poisoning from deteriorating old school buildings.[21] While the federal effort to eliminate lead poisoning has made progress, more than four hundred thousand children from one to five years of age still have blood levels above that considered toxic by the Centers for Disease Control, leading to permanent and debilitating health, learning, and behavioral problems.[22] The demoralizing effect of such environmental problems was recognized as early as the nineteenth century, when the Beecher sisters declared that a little boy's bad behavior was not due to innate sin, but to his small, badly ventilated bedroom where his brain was all night being "fed by poison," inducing "a mild state of moral insanity."[23]

There is also the danger from nuclear plants. The genetic damage done to children by the Chernobyl disaster has been proven to occur even with low radioactive impact.[24] Another type of devastation takes place in Latin America. It is widely known that representatives of the U.S. "War on Drugs" are still fumigating vast areas of Colombia in order to eradicate coca plants, thereby erasing the livelihood of countless families who have used coca leaves since ancient times to fight hunger and to heal diseases, and today they do not know how to survive without selling this crop. The spraying is aggravating the pollution caused by those coca farmers who use pesticides that make plants more resistant, and those who are involved in the refining process, which causes "thousands of barrels of sulfuric acid and kerosene" to be dumped into creeks and streams."[25] The U.S. spraying program has been, according to the writer and human rights advocate Robin Kirk, not only a "spectacular failure," but fuel for the war itself, so that drug-fighting and military action are hard to distinguish.[26] However, Kirk also stresses that any U.S. military action in Colombia is by far not as destructive as drug use in the United States and other Western countries, which keeps all the warring parties financially afloat because drug money seeps into the economy at large.[27] Children and young people are hurt in both hemispheres: drug use destroys the lives of U.S. teenagers, and the fumigation in Colombia causes fever, diarrhea, and eczema in children and an increase of babies born with birth defects, in addition to making thousands homeless because families are fleeing the areas being sprayed.[28]

Even more violent, of course, has been the environmental effect of bombs. The Vietnamese woman who as a nine-year-old girl was photographed fleeing naked and screaming during a 1972 napalm attack, says she wants the picture to be used as a protest against war. "With this photo, I want to tell people how horrible a war can be," said thirty-seven-year-old Kim Phuc, currently president of a humanitarian foundation that helps young victims of war.[29] The bomb dropped on Hiroshima on August 6, 1945, killed one hundred and forty thousand men, women, and children instantly and another sixty thousand more slowly by the deadly after-effects. Three days later the bomb on Nagasaki killed 35,000 people. Regarding these events, Dorothy Day wrote in *The Catholic Worker*:

> (President) Truman was jubilant. He went from table to table on the cruiser that was bringing him home from the Big Three Conference, telling the great news. "Jubilant," newspapers said. *Jubilate Deo*. Regarding the number of Japanese dead, the *Herald Tribune* stated that the figure was not known for certain. The effect is hoped for, not known. It is hoped they are vaporized, our Japanese brothers, scattered, men, women and babies, to the four winds, over the seven seas. Perhaps we will breathe their dust into our nostrils, feel them in the fog of New York, feel them in the rain on the hills of Easton.[30]

## INDIVIDUAL, CORPORATE, AND STATE RESPONSIBILITY

Pointing a finger at any government, however, does not let the average citizen of the "First World" off the hook. Our responsibility begins with as mundane a matter as our daily food. A study by Brown University in the 1980s stated that with a record food harvest of 1985, a minimal vegetarian diet could be provided for all people on the planet (at that time the world population in 2000 was projected to be six billion). But when grain is diverted to livestock or poultry, only 2.5 billion people could be adequately fed.[31] Vegetarianism is increasing in Western countries, but mostly for reasons of health or love for animals. Few people realize that eating no meat or less meat could on a global scale feed more hungry people and especially hungry children who are in greater need of energy for growing.

There are other delicate questions about the impact of our most cherished foods on the children in the world. If we are considering a triple chocolate layer cake after dinner, we might consider that there is a good chance the chocolate beans were harvested by child slaves in the Ivory Coast.

> Purchased from their destitute parents, forced to work twelve hours a day, regularly beaten, inadequately fed, and locked up at night, these children, some as young as 9 years old, help this West African country supply 43% of the world's cocoa.[32]

We can shrug this off as beyond our control, or we can try to buy chocolate from manufacturers who "keep a sharp eye on their suppliers' labor practices," like companies offering organic or "Fair Trade" chocolate.[33]

These are only some examples of the often invisible connections between north and south, between Western daily life and the violence in "Third World" countries that we easily attribute solely to other cultures and nations and not to our own. The same dynamic can be observed where the "Third World" is present within the United States and within European countries. The Children's Defense Fund reported in 2001:

> Just four wealthy Americans possess greater wealth than the GNP of the 34 least developed nations in the world with over 650 million people. *Harper's* magazine estimated in 1997 that 240,183 people could be fed for one year with the food we Americans waste in one *day*. The gaping divide between rich and poor nations is mirrored in the gap between rich and poor in our own country.[34]

The report also emphasizes that the United States has an

> arms export business that exceeds $50 billion a year. A military budget five times that of Russia, eight times that of China, twice that of all the other NATO countries combined, and twenty times the combined spending of the seven "Rogue States" (Cuba, Iran, Iraq, Libya, North Korea, Sudan, and Syria) we have designated as our principal enemies in a post-cold-war era.
>
> We've sent humans to the moon, spaceships to Mars, cracked the genetic code, amassed tens of billions of dollars from a tiny microchip, and discovered cures for diseases which give hope to millions if they can access treatment. We can transmit information faster than we can digest it and buy anything we desire instantly on-line in our global shopping arcade. Why can't we teach all our children to read by fourth grade?[35]

We might add: and why can't we teach children nonviolent ways of solving conflicts? Children model the behavior of adults, says

Barbara Kingsolver in response to the high school killings in Littleton, Colorado.

> Ours are growing up in a nation whose most important, influential men—from presidents to film heroes—solve problems by killing people. It's utterly predictable that some boys who are desperate for admiration and influence will reach for guns and bombs. And it's not surprising that it happened in a middle-class neighborhood; institutional violence is right at home in the suburbs. Don't point too hard at the gangsta-rap in your brother's house until you've examined the Pentagon in our own. The tragedy in Littleton grew straight out of a culture that is loudly and proudly rooting for the global shootout. That culture is us.[36]

Popular opinion seems to confirm that view. When *Time* magazine and CNN polled the U.S. public after the war on Iraq had started, people were asked whether they would still support the war if it would result in the death of five thousand U.S. troops, and 34 percent answered yes. The question whether they would support it if as many as five thousand *Iraqi civilians* died, was answered affirmatively by 40 percent.[37] No child is being sensitized to value life if grownups callously calculate how many friends and foes are expendable. But probably the same people giving these answers would react very differently if their own lives or that of their children would be at risk. Since they are far removed from the reality of war, they simply react abstractly to an abstraction. We have to reawaken our consciousness of real bodies, real blood, and real life—ours and that of "the other."

## THE COSMIC WEB OF LIFE AND "VIRTUAL" REALITY

Since wealth and poverty, north and south, "First World" and "Third World" are inextricably bound and indebted to each other, how can violence be mitigated—if not overcome? How can the wisdom of the world's religions, emphasizing that mature human beings will strive to "become like children," turn us toward nonviolence in a world that is afraid of its violent children? In order to dig up the roots of violence, theology has to teach not only that we are responsible for the children of this earth, but that we are linked with every creature on this globe, every star in space, and every wave of the world's oceans. All beings are threads in the same fabric. This awareness of our being a tiny link in the order of the cosmos in which every atom is filled with the same ungraspable Spirit can help us check our instinctive urge to define enemies and to oppose them violently.

> The ingredients are the same for everything that lives; we are cousins to sequoias, and slugs—one life, one creation . . . .
>
> Like a vaccine against pride, the sublime achievement of the human intellect reveals that we have only twice as many genes as a roundworm, about three times as many as a fruit fly, only six times as many as bakers' yeast. . . . Our DNA provides a history book of where we come from and how we evolved. It is a family Bible that connects us all; every human being on the planet is 99.9% the same.[38]

We have lost the sense of the sacredness of our bodies and of all "matter," because Western philosophy has separated theology and science, nature and culture, body and soul, reason and emotion. The Bible does not support such a separation. In the Psalms, beasts and trees, kings and young people praise God (Ps. 148); hills, valleys, meadows, and trees "sing together for joy" (Ps. 65:12–13; 96:12), and floods can lift up their voice or even "clap their hands" (Ps. 93:3; 98:8). For the apostle Paul creation is like a woman in labor (Rom. 8:22), and Jesus understood the psalmist's conviction that "out of the mouth of babes" can sound the praise of God (Ps. 8:2; Matt. 21:16). Psalm 104 is a hymn teeming with animals, winds, fire, waters, thunder, trees, and mountains that are part of God's power and wisdom, with the human being just one item on the list of divine creations (v. 23). Jesus' message is always connected with lilies of the field, sparrows in God's care, the mother hen gathering her children, and the "wild beasts" accompanying him in the desert (Mark 1:13). His healings affect body and mind.

The Koran sends the same message of the unity of creation.

> All the beasts that roam the earth and all the birds that soar on high are but communities like your own. (Sura 6:38)
>
> Behold! In the creation of the heavens and the earth; in the alternation of the night and the day; in the sailing of the ships

through the ocean for the profit of humankind; in the rain which Allah sends down from the skies, and the life which he gives therewith, to an earth that is dead; in the beasts of all kinds that he scatters through the earth, in the change of the winds, and the clouds which they trail like their slaves between the sky and the earth; here indeed are signs for people who are wise. (Sura 2:164)[39]

"For Christians and Muslims the theological foundation for protecting the natural world is grounded in a shared view of creation."[40] This union of nature and the divine is also found in Asian religions. Kwok Pui-lan points out that Western anthropocentrism

thinks of God in terms of the image of human beings: God is king, father, judge, and warrior. . . . Oriental people and indigenous people who are tied to the soil imagine the divine, the Tao, as silent and non-intrusive. They speak of the earth with respect and reverence as the mother who is sustaining and life-affirming. A shift from anthropocentrism to biocentrism necessitates a change in our way of thinking and speaking about God.[41]

Children, however, do not yet separate human beings and nature. For the child the border between animate and inanimate objects is fluid. It can converse with a wooden toy or feed a stuffed doll. In the spirit of a child William Blake could write:

To see a World in a Grain of Sand
And Heaven in a Wild Flower,
Hold Infinity in the palm of your hand
And Eternity in an hour.[42]

For a playing child there is no difference between creation and re-creation, art and work, visions and re-visions of the world around it. Children thrive on relationships in which physical and psychological contacts are inseparable; they could not survive without them. Psychologists have found that even newborn babies respond to eye contact, smiles, touch, sound, and movement to establish a "conversation" with their caretaker.[43] In a thoroughly technological society, however, the relationship to the physical world easily gets lost in favor of a "virtual" world. A recent survey has shown that, while children in earlier times knew how to play about a hundred games, in Western societies today they know an average of four or five.[44] As Elise Boulding states,

> Humans developed as a species with nature as our teacher and partner. The trees and plants interacted with us and taught us. The winged and the four-legged and the swimmers and crawlers interacted with us and taught us, and all of our senses were involved in the learning partnership.[45]

But our children to a large extent live in a virtual universe: driving or being driven in cars keeps them from walking around the neighborhood to meet people of different ages, classes, and occupations; in front of the television no dialogue is learned; with pushbutton toys no creativity is nurtured; credit cards lead to enormous debts because they do not concretely show that actual money is being spent; computer games turn virtual killing into entertainment, because there is no experience of real blood and real pain.

> Online communication does not carry the cues of human feelings that can be read in facial expressions and body language. And television images do not convey the intimate multisensorial realities of the natural world. "Virtual reality" is the most isolating reality of all.[46]

The immensely popular science fiction film *Matrix Reloaded,* which on the surface shows a group of righteous cyber rebels fighting against the enslavement by a powerful supercomputer, in the end projects only humans determined by programs. The film appears like a free-floating video game and lacks any sense of real bodily existence. *Matrix Revolutions* continues the trend toward fantastic action scenes in which humans cannot think of anything better than fighting against machines by climbing into more machines,

> so their muscles control more powerful muscles made of steel and cybernetics. Each of their surrogate arms ends in a mighty machine gun that sprays limitless streams of ammo at the

enemy. . . . The first *Matrix* was the best because it really did toy with the conflict between illusion and reality—between the world we think we inhabit and its underlying nature. The problem of *The Matrix Reloaded* and *The Matrix Revolutions* is that they are action pictures that are forced to exist in a world that undercuts the reality of the action.[47]

It is not surprising that Lee Malvo, responsible for at least a part of the cold-blooded murders in the Washington, D.C., area in 2002, loved the Matrix series. He was fourteen years old when the first of the films appeared in the movie theaters. Other criminals have testified to their obsession of being controlled by *The Matrix*.[48] Dylan Klebold, one of the two killers in the infamous Columbine massacre, named his sawed-off shotgun Arlene, after a favorite character in the gory Doom video games and books that he particularly liked.[49] My point is not to say that films like *The Matrix* lead to crime, but that children who live too much in a "virtual" world may never get a feeling for the sanctity of bodily existence. The fact that *The Matrix Revolutions* opened simultaneously worldwide in forty-three languages and on more than ten thousand screens suggests that it will have some global impact.[50] Sociologists have in recent years debated whether the technological, virtual violence of video games, films, and television programs is gender specific; whether girls find violence offensive or boring.[51] While girls seem to be drawn to computer games like "Barbie Fashion Designer" and "Let's Talk About Me," nothing is gained if the game industry keeps falling into the old trap of violent action and "Mortal Kombat" for boys and home and secret gardens for girls. What counts is overcoming the traditional pattern of games that privilege "victory over justice, competition over collaboration, speed over flexibility, transcendence over empathy, control over communication, force over facilitation."[52]

James T. Hamilton has compared the risk assessment of pollution from hazardous waste sites to the study of a possible increase in crime from "Action Adventure Programming" on television with violent content. He states that "television violence is fundamentally a problem of pollution." Tests have shown that watching violent movies in a lab setting increased blood pressure if the victim was of the same gender as the viewer. Stress hormone levels generally increased, especially in female subjects.[53]

Young children are more likely to be affected by media violence, according to Hamilton, if the perpetrator of a violent act is attractive, if he or she is being rewarded, and if there is no punishment. Not only the content of a program is influential, but the impact of reduced attention span and the lack of beneficial activities that are excluded by the time spent on watching television is mind-boggling. Children know more about famous media personalities than about their grandparents.[54]

It is not surprising, then, that some parents have found ways to set strict limits to the "one-eyed monster" television, as Barbara Kingsolver calls it in a witty autobiographical essay on the subject.[55] Also, letting children listen to a story on a cassette recorder is not a good substitute for reading to them personally, because it is not interactive; it does not give children the chance to ask questions and the adult to add some personal remarks or interpretations. Viewing a "Survivor" program on TV fails to give a child an insight into the way millions of people on our planet are daily struggling courageously for survival in actuality. While the electronic media have a legitimate value when they are used sensibly for education and entertainment, they often contribute to a loss of connection with the bodily world and the animal world, thereby desensitizing children toward living creatures, including other human beings.

## ABUSE OF ANIMALS AND CHILDREN

Carol Adams has shown the intimate relationship between the abuse of animals, women, and children. Battering, rape, and abuse of a child or woman often occur after an animal has been abused or killed. The common notion of anything physical as weaker, less rational, or without "soul" in comparison with rational male power leads to the urge to dominate and exploit.

> Finally, our growing understanding of the commodification of bodies in conjunction with militarism can benefit from insights into the commodification of animals' bodies. Dismantling somatophobia involves respecting the bodily integrity of all who have been equated with bodies.[56]

Temple Grandin, the gifted animal scientist who has designed one third of all the livestock-handling facilities in the United States, was able, in spite of—or because of—her autism, to describe in her books and lectures the sensibilities of animals. She is neither a pacifist nor a vegetarian, and she does not consider herself religious. However, she thinks that slaughtering an animal is a sacred act because life is taken in order to sustain other life, and so it should be done with respect and minimal pain. She suggests that callousness in the killing of animals can lead to the same callousness toward the life of human beings.[57] Feminists who propose an "ethic of care" point to the serious implications of eating animals.

> One becomes violent by taking part in violent food practices. . . . Much of the effect of the eating practices of persons in industrialized countries is felt in oppressed countries. Land owned by the wealthy that was once used to grow inexpensive crops for local people has been converted to the production of expensive products (beef) for export. Increased trade of food products with these countries is consistently the cause of increased starvation. . . . One need not be aware of the fact that one's food practices oppress others in order to be an oppressor.[58]

Carol Adams has presented fascinating examples of images and texts that reveal the relationship between pornography and meat consumption. Countless advertisements have subtly or drastically, humorously or outrageously, mingled images of women's (or blacks'!) bodies with images of animals to be cut up and consumed.[59] This game of power (men over women over other races over animals that can be objectified and consumed) also involves power over children, as Adams shows in relationship to child abusers, who blur the difference between women and girls, and to commercial items like a deep sea fishing lure in the shape of a mermaid type of hula girl.[60] Children, however, tend to see animals as their peers, frequently dream of animals, and sometimes refuse to eat the meat of animals of which they are fond.[61]

## LEARNING FROM NATIVE AMERICANS

Representatives of an "ethic of care" challenge our treatment of animals and take positions that may remind us of Native Americans who traditionally would not take the life of an animal without a prayer and who feel that in taking a life something has to be given back to the cosmos, even if it is only an expression of thanks, a song, or an offering of tobacco.

> The necessity for reciprocity becomes most apparent where violence is concerned, especially when such violence is an apparent necessity as in hunting or harvesting. Violence cannot be perpetrated, a life taken, in a Native American society, without some spiritual act of reciprocation. I am so much a part of the whole of creation and its balance, anything I do to perpetrate an act of violence, even when it is necessary for the survival of our families and our communities, must be accompanied by an act of spiritual reciprocation intended to restore the balance of existence.[62]

That does not mean every act of violence can be compensated for by adding a ceremony.

> American technological and economic development cannot embody the Indian ethic of reciprocity. It is not enough to plant a few trees or to add nutrients to the soil. These are superficial acts to treat the negative symptoms of development. The value of reciprocity which is a hallmark of Indian ceremonies goes to the heart of issues of sustainability, which is maintaining a balance and tempering the negative effects of basic human survival techniques. There is no ceremony among any people for clear-cutting an entire forest.[63]

There is no reason to romanticize Native Americans, but we might keep them in mind when we are looking for people who traditionally have not become as widely removed from nature and communal living as the average North American or European city dweller. We know about the misery of alcoholism, diabetes, unemployment, and bingo palaces of some reservations where the ancient wisdom of communal living seems to have been obliterated; but Native American theologians remind us that this wisdom is not lost. We can still find it among indigenous groups the world over that are struggling to keep technology and neocolonialism at bay.[64] As long as we adults fail to model for children a "Native" respect for everything that is alive—whether people, animals, plants or soil—we should not be surprised if they turn to violence. As long as we teach them only individualism, independence, and material success we cannot expect them to be concerned with the well-being of the human community, with those of its members who are dependent on our care, and with all of creation. We can learn from Native Americans that "all of one's so-called possessions are ultimately not possessions but relatives that live with someone."[65]

> The Lakota and Dakota peoples have a phrase used in all their prayers that aptly illustrates the Native American sense of the centrality of creation. The phrase, *mitakuye oyasin,* functions somewhat like the word "amen" in European and American Christianity. As such, it is used to end every prayer. . . . The usual translation offered is: "For all my relations." . . . "Relations" must also be understood as fellow tribal members or even all Indian people. At the same time, the phrase includes all the nations of Two-Leggeds in the world and, in the ever-expanding circle, all the nations other than Two-Leggeds —the Four-Leggeds, the Wingeds and all the Living-Moving Things of the Earth.[66]

Native Americans know the power and wisdom of animals that play a large part in their rituals. Their masks of animal heads indicate their identification with revered animal ancestors. Our society, however, sees animals largely as resources or pets. Whenever a virus affects them— often because of the way they are commercially caged and fattened— thousands end up as garbage. While there is widespread resistance to stem cell research, few people object to the use of countless primates, dogs, cats, and mice in painful experiments that routinely include burning, electrocution, paralysis, and dismemberment, often done without anesthesia or painkillers. New research has shown that even fish that have few ways to express pain can actually feel pain and stress.[67] Some animals show a sense of cooperation, and dogs and dolphins seem to know empathy.[68] But we respect their gifts only when we can use them to our profit as, for example, in the Iraq war where pigeons and chickens were used for detecting chemicals in the air (the chemicals make them fall off their perches), where dolphins were trained to detect sea mines, and sea lions learned to capture enemy divers.[69] As the Rev. Holmes Rolston III commented after receiving the "Templeton Prize for Progress Toward Research or Discoveries about Spiritual Realities": what a society does to its "fauna, flora, species, ecosystems, and land-scapes" reveals its character as much as how it treats minorities, women, or children."[70] When we consider humankind's worst atroci-ties, animals appear sometimes more "humane" than people:

> Surely mankind has yet to be born. Surely this is true! For only something blind and uncomprehending could exist in such a mean conjunction with its own flesh, its own kind. How else account for such faltering, clumsy, hateful cruelty? Even the possums and skunks know better! Even the weasels and the meadow mice have a natural regard for their own blood and kin. . . . Yes, it could be that mankind has yet to be born. Ah, what bitter tears God must weep at the sight of the things that men do to other men![71]

There are other aspects of Native American as well as black tradi-tions that correspond to what we can learn from children in trying to create an environment of nonviolent communities. There is, for exam-ple, the importance of orality instead of a narrow focus on literacy. We know how delightful and helpful storytelling is for children. Native Americans have passed on the wisdom of their elders orally from one generation to the next, and writers like Leslie Marmon Silko have proven in their art how the oral heritage still empowers the literate works of today.[72] The same pertains to the best black literature of this century. Orality is important because it creates community, whereas reading and writing can be done in isolation. The virtual orality that children grow up with today is based on television images, and it is a lonely affair. But when, for example, Jewish children learn about their tradition through the biblically ordered conversation at the annual Seder, community is established. When parents, grandparents, or teachers pass on stories that have given meaning to their lives, the physical presence of these adults creates human ties that no written or televised story could provide.

When I compare Native Americans and children, I am of course not suggesting that Native Americans are "childlike" in the sense of lacking the sophistication of European American adults. That would be a bad throwback to colonial times when, for example, the Spaniard José de Acosta, S.J., declared in 1588 that "the Indians have an intelligence that is little and childish like that of children and women, or better still beasts."[73] Acosta admitted that the Indians were not subhuman, but he assumed that their savage customs had suffocated their inherent rationality. A merely peaceful approach at missionizing would therefore not be effective. They had to be compelled by force "to enter salvation." By contrast we must emphasize that the countless different Native American patterns of thought are extremely complex. They cannot be fitted into an abstract dogmatic system. It is very difficult even to translate words like "God" or "worship" from their languages into English, because the Spirit present in every part of creation and in the ceremonies, testifying to this web of relationships, cannot be straightjacketed into such terms.[74] In a similar way, a child will sense God as a power that protects and connects, but is not clearly circumscribed, and a child's prayer or song is not necessarily something separate from everyday play. Many Native Americans do not have an abstract notion of "salvation," but they are well aware of the power of "healing."[75] It is the same with children.

Moreover, Native tribes are tied to their land in a way that European Americans can hardly understand. Children too have a special relationship to place. Recent research in "children's geographies" has shown that "children use, experience and value space differently from adults . . . children appropriate public space for themselves and give names to their favorite places." They construct "their own secret places and dens within 'public' space."[76] The struggle for space has fueled the problem of Brazil's street children.

> Underlying the crisis of the "dangerous" and endangered street child is a deep national preoccupation with the future of Brazil, the causes and effects of violent crime, and the uses of public space. . . . With the gradual dismantling of the military police state, the former authoritarian structures that had kept the social classes "safely" apart . . . weakened. And suddenly . . . the favelas ruptured, and poor, mostly black, and aggressively needy children descended from hillside slums and seemed to

be everywhere, occupying boulevards, plazas, and parks that more affluent citizens once thought of as their own.[77]

Whether the problem is a lack of space for impoverished masses of children or the commercialization of play spaces in Western countries, we have to learn again that for children, place matters and can be related to violence. That does not mean domestic space more effectively keeps children away from violence than public space. Both can breed violence against and by children, but depriving children of a place of their own is as unjust as depriving Native Americans of their inherited land. Artificially constructed reservations can be as damaging as the cyberspace in which children are commercially exploited, or as restrictive as the life of children who are without any space for playing.[78]

Since place matters so much to children, any refugee existence does enormous damage to a child's development and easily breeds violence. UNICEF estimates that half of the world's refugees are children.[79] Patricia Marín has described what displacement means for Salvadoran children. She states that half of all refugees in El Salvador were under the age of fourteen in 1988. Education, healthcare, nutrition, economic stability, and physical and mental health are affected by displacement and can lead to "insomnia, personality changes, and psychosomatic reactions such as headaches, as well as severe psychosis, such as schizophrenia."[80]

## LEARNING ENVIRONMENTAL PEACE

As we try to dig up the roots of violence in our natural and cultural environment and to catch glimpses of cultures that can help us rediscover what makes for peace, we should beware of idealizing any culture. Native Americans or other aborigines are as violent and as peaceful as any other people on earth, but their sacred traditions have survived extreme victimization and can be helpful, along with the Hebrew and Christian Scriptures, in unlearning violence. Children are not innocent either, and yet Jesus pointed to children as human beings who can lead us in the right direction. Likewise we can point to Native Americans—and to the native people of other countries and continents—to find traces of ancient human instincts for taming violence that got lost in the process of "civilization" and technological development. Indigenous people, like many adherents of Asian religions, do not emphasize certain beliefs as much as the practices growing out of them. It is the same with children: they love rituals, but do not have a set of dogmatic beliefs. Their faith will change as the children grow up. Likewise our beliefs have to change and grow as we learn from the Scriptures, from life experiences, and from prayer and searching. That does not mean giving up basic convictions or valuable traditions. It does mean the humble insight that we do not own divine truth. All churches and religions—including indigenous traditions—have to be constantly self-critical, correcting and renewing themselves by learning from each other and from their own histories with all their saints and sinners.

Above all, we simply must learn peaceful ways in relating to our environment. Children in the "First" and all other worlds need models of nonviolence. Examples of peaceful conflict resolution are hard to come by when the most powerful men of the world threaten other nations with preemptive nuclear strikes, and the media fictions continue to depict killers as heroes. The difference between cultures lies in what children "breathe in" from birth on. "Children begin at birth to internalize all aspects of their society, including evaluations and legitimizations of war and violent behavior."[81] They can quickly become protagonists of war if they lose the protective shield of early childhood.

It is up to us as adults, then, to rekindle ancient wisdom and to shape and sustain the environment that we pass on to our children. If we abandon them to the virtual world in which they observe multiple murders every hour of viewing television; if we expect society accurately to register cars and dogs, but not handguns; if we elect officials who go to war for oil and power, but do not subscribe to international agreements on reducing greenhouse gas emissions or bringing war criminals to trial, then we cannot expect children to act nonviolently. If we do not pay attention to the fact that landmines continue to kill or cripple thousands of people annually, about a third of them children, we should not be surprised if some young people in faraway countries react violently to the fact that the United States refuses to sign an international ban on these devilish weapons.[82]

The brutality of child soldiers in the Congo massacres of the summer of 2003 should remind us again of another kind of pollution: the existence and circulation of millions of small weapons that help to turn children into killers. There is ample evidence that ruthless rebel leaders force children to use these weapons, which are the only ones they can easily handle. Small arms are the weapons of mass destruction for the poor of this world, and they kill more people than any other kind of weapon. The United Nations needs every possible support for international controls of weapon traders as, for example, through an indelible marking of weapons in their production so their origin can be traced, and an international system of certification for small arms.

Another issue has forced itself into public consciousness during the recent Congo violence. How are peacekeepers or military personnel supposed to fight against children who have been drugged and compelled to commit the worst atrocities? How can soldiers learn and teach peace when children are serious perpetrators of crimes and not only victims? In the year 2000 in Sierra Leone an officer of the Royal Irish regiment refused to shoot armed children with the result that the child soldiers managed to lure the Irish soldiers into their camp, keeping them hostage. Sixteen days later, after fruitless attempts to free the prisoners, British fire power was finally used to free them, and many of the armed children died.[83] Western soldiers are neither tactically nor psychologically trained to fight against soldiers that might be younger than their own children at home. Research has established that the fighting morale of the average soldier is weakened after a fight against very young enemies because the situation causes particular trauma. Also, children react differently from adults during battles: they are likely to give up fighting very quickly if adults do not force them to continue, and they are scared of heavy weapons, explosions, airplanes, and armed helicopters. That means peacekeeping troops have to be especially trained to take these circumstances into consideration. In order to save as many lives as possible, heavy weapons have to be shown in order to scare the children into giving up the fight.[84]

Even more important, however, is making the public aware that the war in the Congo and many similar wars are not just ethnic rivalries, but power struggles for environmental riches. The Congo has treasures of gold, diamonds, copper, and cobalt under its soil. It contains the minerals needed for producing millions of cell phones. The brutal warlords are using child soldiers in order to bring precious mines under their control. Nobody should doubt that violence is here an environmental issue. Where children are used as workers or slaves in gold mines, diamond mines, and pits of ore, they will be so worn out that they would rather join some militia and take up arms in the service of whoever owns these riches in the soil. In the Sudan it is oil that children are supposed to help defend; ethnic and religious differences are not the only reason for continued civil war.[85] The global environment is suffused with violence to an extent that we hardly realize in our comfortable Western niche. Our cyber world and our markets are consuming our interest and our time, and real bodies and places have lost their spirit and their sacredness. Even where life appears peaceful, the care of the environment is neglected because we have not yet realized how every fiber of our existence is touched by lives and events as far away as Angola or Indonesia. Our treatment of environmental resources can influence people and places at the other end of the world by seemingly insignificant ideas and actions. If we did not learn this from the Christian faith, we could have learned it from science.

## LEARNING FROM SCIENCE

For decades scientists have told us that the seventeenth-century Newtonian worldview is no longer valid. The cosmos is not a mechanism that can be dissected into its parts, observed objectively, and directed toward certain goals. Today physicists know that the universe is immensely complex, unpredictable, chaotic, and yet in amazing ways self-organizing; that the smallest current of air or water on one side of the globe can have tremendous consequences on the other side.[86] If we embrace this "new science," we can come a little closer to "becoming like children," because we are constantly awed by new discoveries, and we are not overwhelmed by what seems chaotic, because we trust that our daily life still follows an invisible order and care. We are not tied down to the prediction of a future fate, because life consists of ever new surprises. "We inhabit a world that is always subjective and shaped by our interactions with it."[87]

> It is a world where *relationship* is the key determiner of what is observed and of how particles manifest themselves. Particles come into being and are observed only in relationship to something else. They do not exist as independent "things."

Quantum physics paints a strange yet enticing view of a world that, as Heisenberg characterized it, "appears as a complicated tissue of events, in which connections of different kinds alternate or overlap or combine and thereby determine the texture of the whole." . . . These unseen *connections* between what were previously thought to be separate entities are the fundamental elements of all creation.[88]

Children exist only in relationship; they cannot survive without it. What science teaches us is lived by children every day. Margaret Wheatley has observed this in terms of children's daring energy in relating to their environment:

> I sit now in a small playground, watching my youngest son run from one activity to another. He has climbed, swung and jumped, whirled around on a spinning platform, and wobbled along a rolling log until, laughing, he loses his balance. Now he is perched on a teeter-totter, waiting to be bumped high in the air when his partner crashes to the ground. Everywhere I look, there are bodies in motion, energies in search of adventure.
>
> It seems that the very experiences these children seek out are the ones we avoid: disequilibrium, novelty, loss of control, surprise.[89]

There is uncertainty in children's lives, and, as the quantum physicist Werner Heisenberg has taught us, there is uncertainty in the universe. "All measurable quantities are subject to unpredictable fluctuations, and hence to uncertainty in their values."[90] For our interaction with children that means the continued openness to their ability to change and grow instead of dividing them into "good" and "bad," violent and nonviolent beings. The universe cannot be totally understood by scientific reason; we can only observe and experience patterns that repeat themselves in beautiful or fearful changing rhythms. Likewise the child explores the world not just by reasoning about it, but by interacting with it emotionally and physically and discovering patterns that are pleasing or frightening. We can learn from children as well as from the "new science" that reason alone does not lead to understanding. In fact, it might lead to the illusion of control and domination, to hierarchy and patriarchy. The Romantic poets and philosophers of the nineteenth century have sensed this without knowing the science of the twentieth century, and it is not by chance that they discovered the importance of the child for our adult life, the power and beauty of nature, and the mystery and dignity of all creatures.

> *Our childhood sits,*
> *Our simple childhood, sits upon a throne*
> *That hath more power than all the elements.*[91]

## SOCIAL AND DOMESTIC ABUSE

Meanwhile in more recent times "our childhood" has been abused. Our churches have not paid much attention to the overwhelming influence of rationalistic and hierarchical Western traditions that ignored nature and unwittingly or intentionally supported systems of domination and submission. The many revelations concerning the abuse of children in Christian institutions or by priests and the continuing domestic child abuses bear witness to a lack of sensitivity for the sacredness of life and of bodies. Many of these abuses arose out of an urge to wield power, and this instinct has been aggravated by ancient patriarchal notions of domination: human beings over nature, men over women, parents over children, clerics over lay people.[92] At the same time these notions involve a low estimate of everything sexual, emotional, natural, weak, and nonrational. Child abuse too is an issue of ecology, because it involves the way humans relate to their environment, in this case the social environment. Whereas ecology originally was concerned with science, from the 1930s to the 1950s anthropology, psychology, economics, and other disciplines used ecological perspectives, and "as of the 1970s a social ecology begins to develop that seeks to overcome the break between the natural and the human sciences."[93] The family household and the household of the universe are closely related. Domestic child abuse grows out of the same disregard for the eco-logy, the rules (*logos*) of the house (*oikos*) of the universe as the exploitation of the natural environment. The degradation of a human body results in a chain reaction: wife-beating will lead to child-beating, and beaten children are more likely to end up with social and psychological problems or violent acts. More than a third of the women in state prisons and jails say they were physically or sexually abused as children, roughly twice the rate of child abuse reported by women overall. The figures for male inmates who suffered child abuse, while far smaller, also are about double that of the overall male population.[94]

How closely domestic and environmental problems are interwoven becomes clear from Latin American statistics: about eighty thousand children die annually in Latin America and the Caribbean as a result of violence in the home, a phenomenon that affects about six million of the region's minors, according to a UNICEF report on family violence.[95] There is no doubt that the often extreme poverty of the region with all its environmental and psychological consequences plays a large part in this phenomenon. Men who are without work and income or who are being degraded by their superiors in exploitative jobs will come home frustrated and will let their rage out on the family. Women who cannot feed and nurture their children adequately are likely to stay with an abusive husband in order to hang on to a semblance of normalcy, especially if the church encourages them to do so. They may be unable to limit the number of their children because of their husbands' and the church's demands, and because of the fear that in their old age the couple will have no social security or health insurance except for the care provided by their children.

In other areas of the world, poverty, often caused by environmental degradation or exploitative labor through Western corporations or by the lure of Western consumer goods, leads to massive child prostitution and trade of children. The organization *terre des hommes,* for example, cares for children in Cambodia and Mozambique who have been sold by their parents or caretakers into job situations that promised a good income and that ended up being hard adult labor or sexual abuse.[96] The environment of child abuse, however, can just as easily be a wealthy suburb in a Western city where technology, individualism, and the relentless drive for success may prompt parents to push their children into an early adulthood through beauty pageants or TV advertisements. The tragic and short life of JonBenét Ramsey is just the most dramatic example. It has ironically spawned a whole industry of police officials, detectives, journalists, lawyers, and psychologists who are likely to make their fortune in the process.[97]

There are also violent disasters of social and natural ecology for which we cannot easily push the blame on individuals or institutions. The enormous global AIDS crisis that has orphaned millions of children is another example of the intricate relationship between animals and humans, nature and social conditions. While AIDS seems to have simply originated from a virus that was transferred from animals to humans, its consequences and treatments have vast ecological implications, especially in Africa, in terms of the cost and availability of medications developed and controlled in Western countries, the unraveling of families due to the death of parents, the deterioration of schools due to dying teachers, and the overburdening of children who have to care for themselves as well as for surviving family members. Fourteen million children who in 2003 were under fifteen years of age have lost one or both parents to AIDS.[98] Every day two thousand children under fifteen years old are newly infected with AIDS.[99] In many regions the income of a family affected by HIV will tend to fall about 80 percent and food consumption between 15 and 30 percent.[100] All of these factors will harm children and can lead to violence, thereby disrupting the natural and social environments.

## OVERCOMING FATALISM AND DISCOVERING PEACE TRADITIONS

Violence, then, does not spare any continent, race, or social class. But whether it is related to the natural or the social environment, whether children are its victims or perpetrators, it is not a fate to which we have to submit. It can be tamed, and nonviolence can be learned. The World Health Organization, under the direction of Dr. Gro Harlem Brundtland, in October of 2002 released a report on violence around the world. It concluded that "violence kills more than 1.6 million people each year, and suicide claims almost as many lives as war and homicide combined." Violence is often tied to income: "the vast majority of violence-related deaths occurred in low-income countries." It also has a gender aspect: "men account for more than three-quarters of all homicides, with the highest rates among men ages 15–29." "Violence against women by their male partners occurs in all countries, regardless of economic class and religion." Above all, the study found that "violence, particularly war, seems to beget more violence." There is evidence that after wars the levels of assault and violence remain higher than before, in part because there are more guns available, and young men have been trained to fight. The report's main premise is that violence can be studied as a health problem and prevented in much the same way as disease. "Violence is predictable, and therefore preventable. We can study it, just like a disease, understand the causes, and act on these causes."[101]

It takes imagination and courage to act on these causes at a time when the billions of dollars for military expenditures are constantly being increased and the modest allotments for environmental health and social services are increasingly curtailed. Christians are not innocent partners in this development, nor are members of other world religions, because their actions and nonactions, their statements and silences, always have political consequences. And yet it is possible to discover in the roots of various religions the power to transform the human condition and to mitigate violence. I will mention here only Judaism and Christianity.

Arthur Waskow has convincingly described how biblical Israel did not always counsel the use of military conquest against cultures it deemed evil. There is another Jewish tradition that counseled the use of nonviolent resistance against unaccountable power. Examples range from the midwives who refused to obey Pharaoh's order to murder Hebrew boy babies, to the prophet Jeremiah, who in a kind of street theater wore a yoke as he walked in public, embodying the yoke of God that the king had shrugged off, as well as the yoke of Babylonian captivity that the king was bringing on the people. "Jeremiah warns against using violence and military alliances to oppose the Babylonian Conquest, and argues instead that God will protect the people if Judah acts in accord with the ethical demands of Torah—*freeing slaves, letting the land rest.*"[102] Waskow pleads for an assertive nonviolence based on Jewish traditions, not a "universal," passive pacifism. Murray Polner and Naomi Goodman have edited a volume of essays that make the same claim as Waskow: there is a strong Jewish tradition of peacemaking, and it is not unrelated to environmental concerns.[103]

The Christian tradition of peacemaking starts with the beatitudes. We might easily believe that peacemakers are blessed and shall be children of God, but that the meek shall inherit the earth goes against all our notions of power struggles for the riches of the land. Military might seems to be in charge of the most precious real estate in any nation. But even here ancient Israel already set an example: "the meek shall inherit the land," says Psalm 37:11. God is at work in the most inconspicuous or downtrodden creatures and in the most bloodstained soil. Jesus of Nazareth keeps challenging us to tap into this divine activity by speaking the truth as unabashedly as a child, cherishing our interdependence with other human beings as happily as a child, and relating to people who are different from us as naturally as a child. We might then learn to forget fights and quarrels as fast as children and anticipate each new day with the trust, energy, and curiosity of children who have not yet been damaged by violence, war, and poverty. We might once again learn to use all our senses, to cherish the soil we walk on and the plants and animals it nurtures along with us. We will then realize with the German eighteenth-century theologian Friedrich Christoph Oetinger that "bodiliness is the end of God's ways."[104] Christians do not have a monopoly on living such a holistic life, nor do Muslims or any other religious group. "When a religious language shows claims of imperialist universality and struggles to impose itself and eliminate others, it is guilty of obstructing the flow of biodiversity. It closes itself off within its own truth and can become destructive," says Ivone Gebara. Her call for a "biodiversity of religions" does not mean that "anything at all is acceptable or that we should give up our struggle against the powers of destruction that make themselves manifest in the religious domain."[105] It means instead realizing our limited understanding of truth; our growing awareness of being small links in a universe we can only regard with awe and reverence; our childlike dependence on a power beyond our control, and our incredible strength in living with each other interdependently. Thomas Merton understood all of this:

> The more I am able to affirm others, to say "yes" to them in myself, by discovering them in myself and myself in them, the more real I am. I am fully real if my own heart says *yes* to *everyone*.
>
> I will be a better Catholic, not if I can *refute* every shade of Protestantism, but if I can affirm the truth in it and still go further.
>
> So too with the Muslims, the Hindus, the Buddhists, etc. This does not mean syncretism, indifferentism, the vapid and

careless friendliness that accepts everything by thinking of nothing. There is much that one cannot "affirm" and "accept," but first one must say "yes" where one really can.[106]

Merton also knew that this is an openness we can learn from children:

The hope of the Christian must be, like the hope of a child, pure and full of trust. The child is totally available in the present because he has relatively little to remember, his experience of evil is as yet brief, and his anticipation of the future does not extend far. The Christian, in his humility and faith, must be as totally available to his brother, to his world, in the present, as the child is. But he cannot see the world with childlike innocence and simplicity unless his memory is cleared of past evils by forgiveness, and his anticipation of the future is hopefully free of craft and calculation. For this reason the humility of Christian nonviolence is at once patient and uncalculating. The chief difference between nonviolence and violence is that the latter depends entirely on its own calculations. The former depends entirely on God and on His word.[107]

Moses received the commandment "Thou shalt not kill," and he also was given many instructions concerning justice for the environment. The year of Jubilee, for example, was to keep the peace and guarantee basic rights to land, animals, and human beings (Lev. 25). The psalmists speak of a time when justice and peace "will kiss each other" (Ps. 85:10f.), and they knew that creation and liberation are intimately related (Ps. 136). Jesus asked his disciples to love their enemies, and his images of God's reign and care are those of sparrows and lilies, fields ready for harvest, shepherds and sheep, "living water," bread and wine. Nonviolence between human beings is impossible without also embracing nonviolence toward nature. To understand that, we have to reawaken our sensibilities for the sacredness of bodies, soil, water, air, trees, and flowers, exploring and cherishing them like little children. By grace we can "mature into childhood" and teach our children not only justice and peace, but also the integrity of creation.[108] That is the task of the churches in the twenty-first century.

**6**

# THE TASK OF THE CHURCHES

*Converting Adults by Welcoming Children*

> The reign of God can only happen when
> In all the schools of the country
> We become like children.[1]

These words from a poem by Dorothee Soelle could pertain to churches as much as to schools. The purpose of this chapter is not to give detailed practical suggestions concerning the care and spiritual nurture of children in our churches, for there are many excellent books that serve this purpose. The focus here will be on adults and on the basic "change of mind" we all need in order to welcome children and to share our faith with them. That will involve some reflection on the history of what we call "Sunday school" and "Christian education" and an emphasis on learning today from children and with children how to trust God's presence in our individual and social lives, how to be good stewards of creation, and how to be peacemakers.

Every church knows that to be a vital congregation it has to give children special attention. Even in the secular realm, child advocacy has become an important challenge in social circles and human rights groups. As such, however, it does not fulfill the demand of Jesus of Nazareth to welcome children and to become like children, for Jesus did not promote a social action program. Consider that whenever we "welcome" a guest, we might have to rearrange our house, our meals, and our time in order to make room and to honor the guest by allowing for another person's special needs and idiosyncrasies.[2] When we talk about somebody's hospitality, the term popularly evokes images of "tea parties, bland conversation, and a general atmosphere of coziness."[3] The epistle to the Hebrews, however, takes hospitality seriously by stating that in welcoming strangers we might "have entertained angels without knowing it" (Heb. 13:2). Chrysostom emphasized the importance of showing our guests that we are not conferring a favor on them, but receiving one.[4] Welcoming children in Jesus' name means rearranging our hearts and minds, our consumption, and our time to make room for those who can teach us how to be children of God. Only in receiving the grace of this conversion have we really "welcomed" a child. In fact, Jesus' words are even more radical: he says that by hosting a child we are hosting God (Mark 9:37).

The churches' task, then, cannot simply be a special emphasis on children's programs in addition to the usual care for the adults. By lovingly putting a child *among* us (Matt. 18:2) or *by our side* (Luke 9:46)—the way Jesus did it concretely when he wanted to teach his disciples a lesson—we as adults will be nurtured and changed. We ourselves will be the learners. The result might be called a deeper "faith," but it might more precisely be understood as a spiritual knowing, a sensitized conscience, a *con-sciencia* (knowing together with God).[5] Welcoming a child and thereby learning to be a child of God can teach us endless hope, unquestioning commitment, and a boundless love of life. Nevertheless, this process of *learning* from children of course also involves the *teaching* of children, whether by pastors, lay workers of the church, or parents and other family members. While we know that faith is often "more caught than taught,"[6] passing on the faith from one generation to the next will always involve continual teaching. It might be helpful to consider how this teaching within the church has traditionally been understood.

"Sunday school" has usually meant, especially in the Protestant churches, appealing to children's rational faculties in terms of teaching texts like Bible stories, hymns, and prayers, because Christianity is, like Judaism and Islam, a religion of the Book, and it has played a large role in the history of education through monasteries, universities, and support of public schools.[7] In addition, Christian education, especially in the United States, traditionally has been considered a means of forming well-behaved, well-adjusted, happy children in "God-fearing homes." Horace Bushnell, for example,

> emphasized the importance of outward, physical practices as a means of grace. Thus, he advocated regular family devotions, recitations of the catechism, and Bible memorization as well as careful attention to a child's dress and diet. . . . Good table manners and high-minded dinner conversation similarly prepared a soul for God, as did personal cleanliness and tasteful clothing.[8]

In the mid-nineteenth century, "Christian child rearing dovetailed with the developing canons of middle-class behavior."[9] By the turn of the century, however, the emphasis was less on transmitting knowledge and ethical rules than on child-centeredness. "The new goal of religious education was self-realization."[10] Family-centered religious practices turned into a more individualistic personal faith development, which was heavily criticized by neo-orthodoxy.

World War II brought drastic changes and a sense of insecurity to American families; so the more peaceful fifties reawakened a desire for blissful domesticity, dismissed by Peter Berger as "a surrealistic blend of Horace Bushnell, John Dewey, and an emasculated Freud."[11] Meanwhile church attendance dropped as rapidly as family devotions. From the seventies on, feminism led many female Sunday school teachers back into jobs or university training, leaving them little time to do what women had been expected to do for generations: keep the church programs going. Racism divided liberal from conservative churches; families broke apart and were then newly blended, and television indoctrinated children more heavily than the churches had ever managed in their more doctrinal eras. Secularism crept into daily life as well as into the churches, keeping producers of Sunday school materials eagerly searching for what might still attract the young crowd. Matters of divorce, premarital sex, and homosexuality came to the forefront of

Protestant denominational discussions so that the issue of how to teach children slipped into the background. The Roman Catholic Church was intensely preoccupied with the struggle against abortion and, like liberal Protestants, not enough with the nurturing of born children.

Certainly the development was different in African American churches. Here, there continued to be more emphasis on traditional Bible learning, powerful choirs for children and young people, and a social life that was centered in church activities. Fancy church school materials were too expensive for many black congregations—as for not-so-affluent white ones. Besides, children were included in the adult worship service and were supposed to learn simply by participation. Nobody expected them to need childlike bulletins and crayons in order to be occupied during worship and to be kept completely quiet. For black teenagers, the church frequently provided the type of music that their nonchurched friends found in clubs and bars. Socially conscious African American churches would teach black history by letting children present to the congregation the stories of famous civil rights leaders. As in daily black life, so also in the black church, children could count on various members of the extended family as mentors.[12]

In the new millennium, many Protestant as well as Roman Catholic churches have continued to promote the family as the most important place of Christian nurture. Government pronouncements and regulations have supported this emphasis. While parental example and a stable family situation are doubtless extremely important in the life of a child, there is no biblical or theological reason to see the family as some "haven in a heartless world"—usually understood in the traditional way as consisting of father, mother, and children—where faith can *always* be more successfully transmitted than in a church or among peers. Reinhold Niebuhr even suggested that the family "is easily tempted to gain its advantage at the expense of other families" or to cling excessively to private property instead of serving the needs of the world at large.[13] The present-day popular notion that even very wealthy parents should have the right to bequeath all their assets to their children without having the state tax the inheritance points in the same direction.

Bonnie Miller-McLemore mentions the "typical U.S. prayer—'I just want my child to be happy'"—and suggests that we might seek a deeper conviction and cause than the alternatives of happiness and un-happiness."[14] While the Roman Catholic Christian Family Movement, within the larger framework of the Catholic Action movement that emerged after World War II, did not fall into this trap, but successfully fought the consumerism and individualization of U.S. society, Protestants today will need new models and concepts.[15] Since the family today often fails to provide Christian nurture, how are churches supposed to pass on the faith to the next generation? We also have to ask the question the other way around: how can children teach grownups about God? Certainly the Spirit works in both directions. Mutuality is at the core of any faith relationship.[16]

As to passing on the faith, we first of all have to realize, whether as parents or as church members, that there is no sure way to be success-ful in this enterprise. One of the critics of Bushnell observed that even the most famous biblical parents, like Abraham, Isaac, Jacob, Aaron, Samuel, and David, have seen their children go astray.[17] We might add that some biblical parents have made horrible or foolish mistakes, like Jephthah (Judg. 11:29–40), Eli (1 Sam. 3:13) or the mother of the sons of Zebedee (Matt. 20:20f.). Teachers, like parents, will always be tempted to neglect their responsibility toward children, abuse their power over them, or act out of their own ambition for them, even if they are unaware of it.

Ralph Koerrenz has raised the problem of power in any educa-tional relationship. Part of being human is the right to a measure of freedom, and every education sets limits to that freedom. Even the best-intentioned attempt to educate a child from a child's perspective, letting his or her gifts and insights determine the process and not some adult, objective program, still represents a trespass on the child's freedom.[18] We may consider this to be unavoidable, but since the child is always the weaker partner in the relationship, the intrinsic principle of domination and submission should cause some reflection.[19] Any in-trusion into the freedom of another human being is an ethical prob-lem. Koerrenz points to the German pedagogue Johann Friedrich Herbart who at the beginning of the nineteenth century suggested that parents or teachers take on a temporary debt toward their children from which the children will some day release them or not, depending on how they will critically look back on the adults' efforts.[20] This observation is not supposed to give adult educators a *bad* conscience, but it is indeed supposed to awaken their conscience, and the church can alert parents and teachers to this "temporary debt" concerning a process for which the young generation will later thank or reproach them, rightly or wrongly. Biblically and theologically, says Koerrenz, this can only mean that "education is a business that is based on grace and lives by grace."[21] We are not supposed to feel guilty in guiding and shaping a child's view of God and the world, but to remain aware of the child's independent dignity as a full human being. We can only be Socratic midwives, eliciting thoughts and actions from the child's own heart and mind by telling stories, asking questions, and arousing interest, never talking the talk without walking the walk (1 Cor. 4:20).[22]

The process also works the other way around because the child also teaches us lessons about God. In Italy in 1954, Sofia Cavalletti started a unique program for children aged three to twelve called the Catechesis of the Good Shepherd. She thinks that children communicate to us their own way to God by the deep joy overwhelming them when they learn to trust the Good Shepherd Jesus and the love and light of God. They do not see God as the one who, in Bonhoeffer's words, stops the holes that indicate the limits of human understanding or the one who is grasped only in suffering and weakness. It is instead the God who dwells in the center of life, in strength and joy.[23] Children's first prayers are not petitions, unless adults have taught them to ask for something, but they are praise and thankfulness, according to Cavalletti. It was the children's deep enjoyment of God that inspired the Catechesis of the Good Shepherd, a program that now exists in twenty countries, from Europe to North and South America and Australia, among children from rich and poor families, ethnic groups, indigenous mountain people, and various denominations as well as atheists. Environment did not seem to change the basic religious receptivity of the small child, which is "something that cannot be taught."[24] Cavalletti makes us aware of the mystery inherent in the child. She suggests that understanding the spirituality of children demands the same abilities as those used by ethnologists who research a distant culture.[25] Dorothee Soelle speaks of the mysticism of childhood and quotes Ernst Bloch, who called the mystical experience "something that shines into the childhood of all and in which no one has yet been: homeland."[26]

The most important trait of a good catechist is therefore the ability to stand back, to let the good news do the work, to be willing to say like Jesus, "My teaching is not mine, but his who sent me" (John 7:16). The humility before the child, the refusal to overpower the child, is at the same time the humility before God, the readiness to make room for the Other—like the *tzimtzum* God whom I mentioned in the second chapter.[27] Friedrich Schleiermacher had already noted that humility is the greatest virtue of a teaching pastor. It has nothing to do with self-abasement, but indicates the joy of feeling like a child. As Schleiermacher lets Joseph say in *The Celebration of Christmas,* "I myself am become a child again, luckily for me."[28] Christmas celebrates the humility of God, getting down to the *humus* (earth). Becoming again like children, we are getting "down to earth." "You cannot reach heaven if you do not touch the earth."[29] Setting aside our power over children, we can learn from them, from their fears, their hopes, and their intuitive knowledge of our adult ways. How can they know about us?

Sociologists and philosophers since the time of Hegel have known that in any unequal relationship of power the underdog knows more about the superior than vice versa. Slaves know more about their masters and mistresses for whom they have to manage the most intimate services than the masters know about the slaves whose private lives they share rarely or never.[30] Similarly, children know or sense more about the adult on whom they are totally dependent than the adult knows about the inner life of the child. Children are constant "border crossers," a term Latinas use to describe their daily need to cross cultural, social, and racial borders, because children need to negotiate between their own world and the adult world, whereas adults can afford to ignore the children's world to a large extent. Churches can challenge adults to share the children's world more intimately by listening to their fears and hopes and their thoughts about God.

This listening is a difficult job if it is done with adolescents, especially when they live in very poor urban communities. Some African American theologians have been on the forefront of caring for these youths whom the middle-class churches of all colors easily ignore. Evelyn Parker suggests that such young people have an "emancipatory hope" and the capacity to redefine their lives if one does not expect them to conform to certain norms of the dominant society.

> Metaphorically, African American adolescent spirituality is a *kente* cloth of Ghana, with brilliant threads of poetry, prose, prance, praise, petition, protest, all of who black adolescents are, human and divine, woven together.[31]

Elizabeth J. Walker has described pastoral counseling with African American male youth offenders, and Bridgett Hector has shown how middle-class black women can relate to inner-city black female youth.[32] Certainly affluent black as well as white churches can learn to break down class and ethnic barriers to listen to children and adolescents on the margins of our society. The rapid growth of Hispanic communities needs special attention in this regard. While Roman Catholic churches have an easier time reaching out to the mostly Catholic Hispanics, any church can offer services like tutoring of children or English classes for their parents. Reaching out to children of a different faith, class, and culture can "convert" any adult to a different view of life.

Jonathan Kozol has proven this as a Jew in a most remarkable way. He has movingly described what even the poorest and most neglected children in the South Bronx can teach us about life, death, trust, and resurrection. He quotes a teacher in Massachusetts as saying, "There are some children who are like windows. When you look into those windows you see something more than the kids themselves—more than innocence. . . . You see the deep, inextinguishable goodness at the core of creation."[33] When Kozol regularly visited in an Episcopalian parish, he was surprised how much the children wanted to pray and how it quieted them. One of his young friends told him that his father might soon "graduate" from prison.

> "I've been giving my prayers to God," he said with a shy smile.
>
> As he said this, he did something that I'd never seen him do before. He held his hands, with palms up, right in front of him, his elbows curled, and lifted his forearms in a sort of "rowing" motion, coaxingly, and did it several times, the way my father's mother used to do when she said Hebrew prayers on Friday nights. I may have revealed by my expression that this motion of his hands and arms had puzzled me, or stirred

something in me, because he said, in an explanatory way, "I open my hand—like *this*—and then I close it"—and he closed it as he spoke—"like *that*."

"Why do you open it?" I asked.

"To *catch* something," he said.

"Catch what?" I asked.

"God's answer," he replied, as if this should be obvious.[34]

Even communion is not taken lightly by some of these children, who mostly come from marginal black or Hispanic families in an area of up to 75 percent unemployment. One boy noticed that Kozol did not take part in communion and told him repeatedly, "The bread is good!" "Try it!" "You'll like it!"

> Leonardo, like the other children, knows that I am Jewish, so I asked if he was trying to convert me through my appetite. He said no but kept on coaxing me for several days whenever he ran into me downstairs. "The bread is *good!*" he'd say with teasing laughter in his eyes. He sounded like a salesman for communion—or a bakery . . .
>
> Even the teenage boys who slip into the church after the service has begun and slouch in one of the back rows, with baseball hats still on their heads, as if this were a boring duty or a sullen favor for their mother, don't look sullen in the least when they kneel down to take the wafer on their tongue at the communion rail.[35]

The eucharist speaks to the senses. If the church wants to welcome children, it has to awaken their senses and not just address their rationality. Sofia Cavalletti, in describing the simple crafts that the children use to represent the Good Shepherd and the sheep, points out what Maria Montessori taught us, that "one learns not only with the mind, but also with the sense of touch."[36] In addition, children learn with eyes, ears, nose, taste, and emotion. Brett Webb-Mitchell speaks of "Christly gestures" that we practice in learning to be members of the body of Christ.[37] Praying and taking sacraments can be such gestures, or singing and making music, worshipping or healing the sick. Some gestures might seem like mere formalities, like parts of the liturgy that are always repeated. But Goethe was right when he observed,

In every new situation we must start all over again like children, cultivate a passionate interest in things and events, and begin by taking delight in externals, until we have the good fortune to grasp the substance.[38]

Children learn by bodily imitating adult gestures.

Imitation is such an effective way of educating in Christly gestures for young and old, rich and poor, intellectually brilliant and developmentally disabled, and across ethnic cultures, simply because imitative learning begins with the body and the senses. Pierre Bourdieu says that the body, like a living memory pad, remembers everything that happens to it.

The gestures learned by the body are no longer actions, according to Bourdieu, but they mark who we are.[39]

The emphasis on bodily gestures, however, should never mean that we do not through the senses also try to reach the children's mind. Children think in mythic images, but they are capable of serious reasoning. They have been called philosophers, because they ask questions that indicate the need to explore the world and their life.[40] Frequently adults are not able to answer these questions. Helmut Hanisch quotes an example from Christa Wolf's work, *Der Störfall*, in which she describes how her grandson, while sitting on the toilet, asks his daddy how the big door of the toilet gets into his small eye. The father then draws for him the door, the eye, the rays of light, and the way the crossing beams reach a certain center in the brain which turns the image in the consciousness of the viewer back to the right size. So the child answers: How can I be sure that my brain shows the door the right size?[41] This type of question, says Hanisch, cannot always be answered, but it might lead to the Socratic insight that human thinking has to be constantly probed concerning its truth claims, because even the wise can be ignorant. So we should never discourage even those children's questions that appear somewhat absurd to us. We want them to become critical thinkers, and they can remind us that matters are not always as self-evident as we assume.

Children's reasoning, however, should not lead to a dualistic modern thought that values only formal, abstract logic. This kind of thinking is produced when a teacher attempts to simplify complex circumstances and to reduce them to what is right or wrong, true or false. Such a trivialization excludes anything that is numinous, awe-inspiring, extraordinary, and vulnerable. Any question that can be answered by the simple label "true" or "false" presupposes that what is true or false has been predetermined.[42] There are of course situations where especially small children have to be told that something is definitely right or wrong, but we have to make children aware that "good" and "bad" can appear in wolf's or in sheep's clothing. Even the Harry Potter story lets us know by volume 5 that the bad can sometimes hide behind the good. If politicians divide the world in good and bad countries and leaders, the church is all the more challenged to teach children that individual people and nations do not fit into such compartments. Certainly some of the most well-known Bible stories show people who are a dubious blend of admirable and deplorable traits, and children will therefore have no problem relating to people like Joseph, a vain yet abused child and a wonderfully wise and forgiving adult, or Jephthah, a military hero and a thoughtless gang leader in pursuit of honor.[43]

To let children explore what is real and truthful, we have to appeal, then, to their whole being by images, sounds, tastes, smells, touch, emotion, and thought. Only in this way can their spirituality express the deep joy that Cavalletti finds in children who sense God's loving presence. Traditionally Protestantism has shown a deficit in reaching children's senses and emotions, since—in reaction against popular Roman Catholic practices—it has emphasized thought more than anything that can be seen, touched, or felt. From its roots, however, Protestantism knows about "enjoying God forever," as the answer to the first question of the Heidelberg Catechism phrases it, and Luther's hymns as well as Bach's music or Lucas Cranach's Reformation art certainly appeal to our hearts and senses. Nevertheless, we are still too much shaped by Descartes' view of the mind as a kind of reasoning machine separated from the body, and we forget the critical role of emotions in all our thinking.

The important contribution that feelings make to our thought processes have been emphasized recently by the neurologist Antonio Damasio who thinks that Spinoza was in this regard much closer to the truth than the rationalistic Descartes.[44] Since children in our time are daily bombarded with images and sounds, we have even less of a chance than previous centuries to reach them solely by way of their minds. As Marshall McLuhan has taught us, the medium is not only the message, but also the massage; that is, it shapes the message and the receiving person. McLuhan saw the media as extensions of the human body—printed books as extension of eyes, radios as extensions of ears. Each new technological advance reshapes humanity and traumatizes it. "We shape our tools and our tools shape us."[45]

Thus it makes no sense to hinder this development. But we can use it sensibly and learn from indigenous patterns of thought how pretechnological cultures have assumed the unity of mind and body, science and art, reason and emotion. Jeanette Rodríguez has described the pre-Columbian Nahuatl philosophical thought. It is

> an aesthetic conception of the universe; to know the truth is to understand the hidden meaning of things through flower and song (flor y canto) . . . . Understanding the language and affectivity of the heart is paramount to this worldview.[46]

Such an intuitive thinking, which is, according to Rodríguez, "dynamic, fluid, open, creative, and searching," is also appropriate for Christian education. We have, however, lost the connection to art as much as to nature, and both appear remote from compassion. They are not part of our daily affairs, but are often relegated to museum visits, vacation trips, and volunteer projects.

Edward Farley has described how in the history of humankind we have lost the unity of arts and life, beauty and compassion, "living as we do in a desacralized time in which a thousand things are inserted between us and the immediacies of nature. And clearly it is the desacralization of nature that separated the arts from life."[47] Art should not be something elitist, sophisticated, or expensive. Art can be part of Christian education in a very simple way: in the beauty of a sanctuary or Sunday school room, in music, dance, or crafts, and in a variety of biblical illustrations that inspire the imagination of a child, without leaving the impression that this is exactly the way Moses or Jesus or Saint Paul looked. Children's drawings can often give adults a deeper insight into a child's faith and thought than their words. "It is clear that being human is not really separable from the aesthetic."[48]

Not all of us are artists in a formal way, but working with children helps us to be creative, to shape those pieces of clay into Noah's ark, to act out that Jonah story in a way that makes us all rise from the terror of the whale, or to draw a picture of the Good Samaritan that stirs us to compassion. "We share certain sensibilities with the artists. We, too, have antennae that quiver with wonder, interest, perplexity, and sometimes even astonishment and awe that certain things can happen, that the world can be as amazing as it is."[49] A German story describes how the experience of beauty creates community. A mother takes her little daughter to see the Caribbean Sea for the first time. The child runs ahead of the mother out of the car and discovers the vast, brilliant, green-blue-golden ocean behind the palm trees. Excitedly she runs back and calls out: "Mother, come help me see!"[50]

Children coax us to share with them what is beautiful and to be artists in our daily lives, embodying God's love in tangible, visible ways that any child can understand. After all, this is what Jesus did:

Christ . . . was the greatest artist of all, disdaining marble, clay or colour, working with living flesh. That is to say that this unbelievable artist, one who is scarcely conceivable to such an obtuse instrument as the modern neurotic, worn-out brain, made neither statues, nor pictures, nor books; indeed, he said clearly enough what he was doing—fashioning living men, immortal beings . . . .

Christ, this great artist, though he disdained books written about ideas . . . never . . . disdained the spoken word . . . .

These spoken words, which, like a great prodigal lord, he did not even deign to write down, are one of the highest peaks, the highest in fact ever reached by art, which there becomes a creative force, a pure creative force.

Such considerations as these . . . take us a long way, a very long way: they raise us even beyond art. They enable one to catch a glimpse of the art of creating life, the art of living immortality.[51]

If we teach children the art of living that took shape in Jesus' life, they will teach us the art of living like a child, open to the future, changing and growing, exploring the mysteries of life with curiosity and imagination.

Teaching and learning by using our five senses and our creative imagination will include an exploration of our environment, our place in the universe, and our need to make peace with all other creatures. By teaching children of all ages their connectedness with even the smallest parts of creation, the wonders of scientific discovery, and the awe of the universe, they will teach us their love for animals, flowers, rivers, mountains, stars, and a faith that is not an unnatural or supernatural straining for a future paradise, but first of all a witness to God's presence within this creation. The children will also show us their easy acceptance of people who have a different skin color. They will not always act nonviolently, but they will teach us that they more easily than adults forgive, forget, and start anew. If nonviolence is taught as a law, it will not succeed. But we can learn it together with the children as something that St. Paul calls "a still more excellent way" (1 Cor. 12:31); not as passivity, but as an imaginative alternative solution in personal, national, or international conflicts. Learning to make peace will be easier if we bring together Christian children from different racial, economic, and ethnic backgrounds and welcome members of other faiths or atheists whenever they are near. That does not mean looking for the lowest common denominator among religions and cultures; it does mean searching together for truth and respecting the dignity of those who think and act differently.

Making peace can also start with something as basic as gender justice, because patriarchal attitudes will lead to domination, oppression, and violence. A congregation can model equality between men and women in its organization and practices. Pastors and teachers will call attention to feminine images for God in the Bible and to the fact that Jesus asked his male disciples to do "feminine" services like hugging children, washing feet, caring for the sick, and feeding the hungry. Concern for gender justice will also include frank discussions of sexuality in all its forms and an "open and affirming" congregational life in which people of all sexual orientations feel welcomed. Children will observe whether God's faithfulness to us is mirrored in the faithfulness of our sexual relations.

As important as gender justice is justice for the disabled and differently abled. When children and adults with disabilities take part in the liturgy and other activities of the church, the other children will learn to respect them. We know that children can be very cruel to disabled people, but they are frank and open about it, whereas adults hide their cruelty behind politeness, pity, or embarrassment.[52] Together we can learn that we are all handicapped in one way or another, even without any physical impairment, even if only by getting old. We can all, however, be coworkers with God (1 Cor. 3:9), whatever our level of physical or mental agility.

Learning to be peacemakers also has to involve learning to be thoughtful users of the media and of money, discerning the traps of commercials, evaluating movies and music with the children, and being aware that even our hard-earned money is not ours, but God's. Violence and wars start with propaganda and with greed, and it is adults who plant such devastating seeds into a child's mind. The church can teach a critical distance to popular temptations. What makes boys eager to fight in a war, and what makes girls eager admirers of "heroic" fighters? All of this has to be learned *together* with children and young people, not figured out *for* them.

Above all, the churches together with children will practice prayer and praise, singing and quiet reflection. In a time when attention deficit disorder affects children and adults alike; when teenagers and grownups never have time because our lives are filled to the brim with "appointments," children can teach us the kind of timing that is still prevalent in nontechnological societies: a timing that is ordered like the seasons, like sunup and sundown, going to sleep and waking up. It is regular, but not based on mechanic clockwork. It is alive with surprises, delays, and sudden jumps. It is the time of children. "Receiving one's first watch is a kind of introduction to adulthood, though kids usually don't know it."[53] Children can liberate us from captivity to the clock if their very presence nudges us to give time to God in prayer and praise, singing and silence.

> The passage of hours is either an invitation to despair or a ladder to eternity. This little time in our hands melts away ere it can be formed. . . . However, there are hours that perish and hours that join the everlasting. Prayer is a crucible in which time is cast in the likeness of the eternal.[54]

In the process of praying with children and teaching children, adults can rediscover the child in themselves, and Jesus' life and death may appear in a new light, with a focus on his birth, his simple, courageous, vulnerable life, and the continuing power of this life in connecting us to each other.

> To understand the meaning of Christ, we must be willing to acknowledge the Child in ourselves and in each other and we must acknowledge our interdependence. In those moments of acknowledgement the tomb of death becomes the womb of life.[55]

Realizing our interdependence with God and with all vulnerable children of God can lead us, together with the children of our congregations, to those with whom we are usually not connected, like the homeless, the prisoners, the refugees, or the undocumented immigrants. We can take children and youth to places where they will meet people who are different from them in various ways, and occasionally to places of worship of other denominations and religions. They often go to school with black Muslims, Jews, Hindus, or Buddhists, and may understand their own religious "home" much better if they also get to know other traditions. While many adults find it impossible for one person to worship according to different faiths, there are religiously blended families who regularly visit Roman Catholic as well as Protestant churches and even those who alternate between a Christian church and a Jewish synagogue.[56] There is a "growing number of persons who claim a dual religious identity as both Muslim and Christian,"[57] especially in Black families in the United States. We may approve of such practice or oppose it—it will be fruitful only if distinctions are upheld and not blurred. The point is that children will usually not find anything wrong with it, as Yann Martel has shown in such an inimitable—although fictional—way in his book, *The Life of Pi*.[58] In New York, Jewish and Roman Catholic high schools have cooperated in exchanging rabbis and priests to converse with teenagers about the "other faith."[59] Conversations between children of different faiths are not intellectual exercises, but training for peace. They should, however, be proceded by a thorough grounding in one tradition.

Learning from our own children and from those in our surroundings is one thing, but meeting those in other countries opens a whole new world. Teenagers can be encouraged to take "mission trips" with parents, pastors, or teachers to countries of the Two-Thirds-World, not just as "outreach" activities in terms of "helping the poor"—although that should be included—but as "inreach" to discover our own past and present Western involvement in the condition of suffering countries and our own spiritual drought.[60] If that sounds like Christian education "becoming political," we have to remember that the church needs to teach two things: to be "subject to the governing authorities" (Rom. 13:1) and to be critical of the state when it usurps power over the conscience of its citizens or when it commits acts of injustice (Acts 5:29). Martin Luther King Jr. gave us a good example when he said,

> The church must be reminded that it is not the master or the servant of the state, but rather the conscience of the state. It must be the guide and the critic of the state, and never its tool. If the church does not recapture its prophetic zeal, it will become an irrelevant social club without moral or spiritual authority.[61]

Any church that does not teach its children such wisdom is just as "political" as those that do, because it might produce citizens who tolerate injustices and who lack the insight or courage to stand up for truth. Silence can be a powerful political statement. Children do not have the power of lobbying for their rights, so churches should be their first advocates.

The World Council of Churches in 1990 announced the program of "Justice, Peace, and the Integrity of Creation," and congregations will do well if also in the new millennium they teach these three basics on all levels of Christian education. Justice is not just a Christian virtue. It is so commonsensical that Ralph Waldo Emerson could say, "Perfect-paired as eagle's wings, / Justice is the rhyme of things."[62]

The Hebrew prophet declared, "The LORD of hosts is exalted by justice"(Isa. 5:16), and the psalmist is certain that "righteousness and peace shall kiss" (Ps. 85:10). Justice, or righteousness, is often misunderstood as legalism or as lacking love and grace, but it simply means sharing God's good creation in fairness to all. While different cultures have different understandings of what is just, some human communities consider justice as so sacred that linguistically it cannot be separated from "law," "religion," or "peace." That is the case for the Hebrew *shalom* as well as for many Native American concepts of wholeness and blessing. Within the ethical totality of *shalom*, usually called "peace" or "wholeness," all other human virtues and values are subsumed.[63] Peace is not the absence of war, and it is not a state of affairs. It is an activity: making peace. "The effect of righteousness is peace" (Isa. 32:17).[64] Making peace is as unending, tiring, creative, and essential as mothering.[65] It is like the continued fitting together of small puzzle pieces that will some day make a beautiful picture not yet quite known to us. It demands all our imagination, effort, and courage on a daily basis.

> To say that we shall achieve greater peace by making more war
> is no less a *contradictio in adjecto* than to assert that we would
> achieve greater justice by causing more injustice.[66]

Whether we are absolute pacifists or condone some necessary violence in emergencies, our teaching of peace will only be effective if we act on it in our homes and churches and in public life. Children cannot be forced to be nonviolent, but they can be trained in common-sense sessions of conflict resolution and "lured" by examples of great peacemakers, past and present. We can teach them the absurdity of war toys and violent videos by together exploring the hidden ties between a profit-hungry toy industry and overly eager military recruiters, between war games and the brutal reality of violence and war. We can support organizations that bring together children and young people from "enemy nations" to spend a few weeks getting to know "the others" in work and play.[67] Children can also be made aware of the ecological devastation wrought by wars and the need for a just distribution of environmental resources to prevent armed conflicts.

Besides justice and peace, how then can we teach the "integrity of creation"? It would be foolish to think that environmental responsibility can be taught only when a child has developed critical thinking. Ardys Dunn has described how at every stage of the child's development the trust in the goodness and wonder of creation, the relatedness to every smallest part of it, and the care for its continuation can be taught.[68] It does not happen by simply teaching "facts." As Maria Montessori has emphasized, children have to be given hands-on opportunities. These can come in many forms, from planting a tree or sowing seeds to observing animals—in the wild as well as in commercial "factories" of animals to be fattened and slaughtered for the most profitable sale. Children can pick up litter during a hike or recycle household containers for crafts. Ardys Dunn distinguishes various ways in which children react to environmental dilemmas. They may simply observe that throwing garbage into a river or on a street hurts other people, or they may discover that nature has an intrinsic value apart from serving people and that animals have a right to live. They may also feel that animals fulfill the psychological needs of people, especially children. Finally, the older child can understand that everybody's quality of life depends on a healthy environment.[69]

The point is that inner-city children, who often learn about nature mainly from television, have to be introduced to natural environments, learn about where meat and fruit come from, and find out about scarcity and abundance of resources and how the two are related. Meals at the church can become occasions to teach about hunger in our world and the careful use of resources. In general, the teaching of environmental responsibility within the church is of course not only an effort in civic duty or cultural enrichment. It means taking part, together with children, in God's continuing creative activity.

> Spiritual maturity seeks to achieve a unified balance of this ecological system—in essence to realize the Reign of God in which all creation is restored and renewed. Implicit in this notion is that relationality is both social and physical in nature; the self relates to others but also to the physical environment.[70]

A recent study by the Commission on Children at Risk sees a lack of relationship as the main reason for problems like major depression, suicide attempts, alcohol abuse, and a variety of physical ailments, not to mention crime, delinquency, and the drop-out problem. The authors of the study, many of them physicians and mental health professionals, believe that human beings have an inborn need for connections, first with their parents and families, then with larger communities. The research suggests that human beings may be hardwired for transcendent connections as well—for an interest in ultimate meaning.

> It is, they say, the weakening of the connections between children and their extended families and communities that is producing a virtual epidemic of emotional and behavioral problems. . . . The relationships are the source of the thing we call

conscience, without which rules are only as strong as the ability of rule makers to enforce them. Relationships are key.[71]

Here lies the churches' responsibility, especially in extending this consciousness and nurture of relationships to all of creation.

Teaching children forces adults to clarify their own convictions or doubts. In trying to pass on what is important we get "converted" to realize our total dependence on grace: we are unable to control our own doubts and shortcomings as well as the child's receptivity. All we can rely on is the power inherent in a community of faith, struggling together to share creation justly and to make peace possible.

We might ask why the churches have been so slow in teaching children about the integrity of creation or about "body, nature, and place," the three entities that, for example, Charlene Spretnak regards as seriously neglected in the modern worldview. She sees the Reformation as coresponsible for the development of a mechanistic, dualistic view that permeates modern life.

> Luther and Calvin asserted the theological doctrine of radical sovereignty, the belief that God's sovereignty excluded the contribution of lesser beings to his work. No "natural revelation" was possible by human apprehension of the natural world. . . . The passivity of nature, argued by the Reformation in order to protect the glory of God, was subsequently adopted by the mechanistic philosophers and became central to the Scientific Revolution.[72]

The Reformation also contributed to modern individualism (the individual standing alone before God), to rationalism (rejection of some sacraments, of saints and miracles), and to a worldly asceticism that turned into utilitarianism and the rigid business order of modern capitalism. I am here simplifying Spretnak's thesis. I agree with her basic outline of the various developments (including the Reformation) that led to "modernity" with all its negative consequences, the assumed "passivity of nature" being especially problematic. But there are other, positive aspects to the Reformation heritage that Christian education today can tie into. Every age reacts against the shortcomings of the previous era, and no historical movement will represent all facets of the faith in a balanced way. While our age certainly has the task of calling attention to body, nature, and place—all three being of great importance to children—they are not completely lacking in the history of Protestantism. The Reformers' fight against monasticism and enforced celibacy certainly gave new dignity to male and female bodies. As to nature, there is a wealth of Reformation hymns that praise creation in all its manifestations. Place gained a new importance when Luther declared that the maid sweeping the kitchen honored God as greatly as any cleric working in the church. Places like kindergartens had their origin in the imaginative work of Protestant educators.[73]

Nevertheless, we are all products of Western technological society and of an academic tradition built on iron-clad Newtonian or Cartesian science. Ironically, it is the new science that has gotten ahead of theology in discerning a constantly changing, chaotic, yet self-organizing universe.[74] If we can transmit to our children a fascination with the constant creativity of the cosmos and an awe of its fluid order, they might together with us believe also in human—personal and social—transformation, in spite of the violence of our age. As Larry Rasmussen has observed, quoting Michael Lerner, there is a "double helix" genetic ribbon of faith: "Celebration of the grandeur of creation goes hand in hand with transformation of the social world."[75]

It is the task of the churches to teach this double helix, and welcoming children can bring about the conversion of adults that makes such teaching possible. The child represents in a nutshell both the grandeur of creation and the hopeful vision of social transformation. Ralph Waldo Emerson knew how much we need the presence of children: "Infancy is the perpetual Messiah, which comes into the arms of fallen men, and pleads with them to return to paradise."[76]

Our society has tried in various ways to return us now and then to an imagined paradise of childhood, Disneyland having been the foremost grandiose attempt in this regard. I mentioned in my introduction that I got the idea of working on "the child" in theology during a theological conference in Disney World. What struck me then was the difference between the childlike "paradise" that the church is called to envision and the small world that Disney created.

The adventures of Disneyland are packaged and stage-managed illusions that take place in an undemanding and reassuring setting. Here in the company of other relatively prosperous, well-adjusted, adequately conformist members of society a pleasurable sense of belonging is engendered (!). . . . The potential challenge posed by youthful and other cultural imaginations of beneficial anarchy is tamed and regulated and only then, and that temporarily, joined in pseudo-nirvanic togetherness by the romanticized, sentimentalized, nostalgic myths of their progenitors.[77]

The church, however, needs in its life the "beneficial anarchy" of all kinds of children, from all walks of life and all corners of the globe, in order to break through the barriers of "pre-programmed, pre-packaged togetherness"[78] and to struggle for the new creation that we can only glimpse in watching children and becoming like them. Meeting children from a completely different culture can be especially helpful in this process. That is why I would like to indicate in the next chapter how the children of Peru made a difference in my life.

# 7

# CHALLENGING
# ENCOUNTERS WITH
# "THIRD-WORLD"
# CHILDREN

➤ ✦ ◄

## Peru as Case Study

A gospel of personal wealth meets the gospel of commonwealth.[1]

In all these things we are more than conquerors (Rom. 8:37)

Any time people from the northern hemisphere are sufficiently well off to fly for a visit "down south," they are confronted with the "great chasm" between riches and poverty that may appear almost as insurmountable as the chasm in the Lazarus story (Luke 16:26). However, welcoming the children of the "Two-Thirds-World" who are in greatest need is just as important as caring for those more closely around us. No news article, letter, or television program can have the same effect as a visit.

## MY PERSONAL EXPERIENCE

When I was reading a newspaper in July of 2003, I found in one little corner a report stating that around sixty children died recently of extreme cold in the district of Puno, high in the Andean mountains of Peru, near Lake Titicaca. No explanation was given, but I could imagine how they died, for in 2001 I accompanied a group of Methodists from North Carolina on a trip to Puno. We had been asked to lead a Christian education workshop for Aymara and Quechua Indian Methodists. For three days we met in a Roman Catholic retreat center high above Puno. The area is a rough, stony countryside and yet beautiful in its austerity and wide view. Indigenous Methodist pastors and lay people had come from far away, eager to learn how to teach the Christian faith to the children entrusted to them, grateful for every shred of material we provided for studying or crafts, happy about every meal, every presentation. Many worked in agriculture, nursing, or teaching, but none could afford to be just a pastor, because the small Methodist Church of Peru could not pay them a salary. Many lived far away from doctors or medical centers. Some wanted to study at the university but did not have the money to fulfill their dreams. It is in this situation of extreme poverty that children die young from "preventable diseases," as the UNICEF statistics phrase it, and a harsh winter is sometimes more than they can take. The adults attending the workshop would sacrifice a few days of work and income and put up with tiring trips in ramshackle buses because they wanted to learn more about welcoming children in their congregations. While we were still sleeping at five o'clock in the morning, they would break into song, grateful for having come together from distant, lonely places where normally nobody has money for traveling.

While this was a meeting with adults concerned about children, I have met with children in Peru almost every year since 1987, and I have learned much from them as well as from those who care for them. I would like to share here how many of these children who are obviously victims—of a terrifying guerilla war,[2] of poverty and hunger, of torn-up families—have become agents, living an active, meaningful life because some adults welcomed them. They became agents of their own lives, but also of reconciliation, inspiring common projects among divided people.

How did I first go to Peru? In 1987, my husband, Frederick Herzog, who died suddenly in 1995, started a theological exchange program between Duke University Divinity School and various institutions and churches in Peru. Since our United Church of Christ did not have a branch in Peru, and since Duke University is Methodist-related, the exchange began with the Methodist Seminary, the Comunidad Bíblico Teológica in Lima, but it was conceived as an ecumenical project with ties to the highly respected Pontificia Universidad Católica del Perú, to Roman Catholic priests, and to various other denominations through the ecumenical diversity of the Methodist Seminary's instructors. Students from Duke were to combine studying and social work, and an exchange of churches, directed by a former student of my husband's, the Rev. Dr. Mark Wethington, was related to the academic exchange. The terrifying guerilla war soon interrupted the program, making it too dangerous for Duke University to send students to Peru. So my husband established a similar program in Cochabamba, Bolivia. But the short-term exchange of professors and church members continued with Peru throughout the most difficult years of the war between guerillas and government forces (1980 to 1992), and the mutual visits of Methodist pastors and lay people from North Carolina and Peru have continued without interruption until today. I have annually joined one of the groups. Unfortunately the Methodist Seminary in Lima closed in 1996 for lack of money, leadership, and theological consensus, but after some years without any formal Methodist theological training center, one interdenominational and one small Methodist seminary are now operating in Huancayo in the mountains of Peru. Both are directed by a Methodist theologian, the Rev. César Llanco.

## THE ROLE OF CHILDREN IN THE RELATIONSHIP
## WITH PERUVIAN METHODISTS

The Methodist Church of Peru has barely five thousand members and suffers from internal tensions between "liberals" and "conservatives," urban and rural, mestizo and indigenous congregations, but all of these problems are aggravated by lack of money and educational opportunity, which in turn leads to massive emigration of potential leaders. In recent years there have been valiant attempts to overcome the disagreements, with some success. The average salary of a pastor is between $140 and $200 monthly in 2004, but countless pastors do not receive any salary at all and have very little formal education. They subsist on more or less informal side jobs and on small donations by their parishioners. Sometimes the church provides nothing but housing for them.

Children were not originally meant to be in the forefront of the North Carolina exchange program, but they continued to "erupt" into it in surprising ways. I will describe different ways in which children are being cared for under the most difficult circumstances, and how in the process they changed our adult notions of "academic exchange" or "mission" and brought unity where there was tension.

First of all there are admirable attempts by congregations to care for the children among them. In every Methodist congregation we visited, children seemed to appear out of nowhere to assert their presence, often poorly dressed and nourished, but full of vitality, curiosity, and affection. In the community soup kitchens, frequently established by church women during the most difficult guerilla times, the older children would line up, hold a pot, and receive a meal to carry home to the family, a banana or other fruit being a cherished dessert. Many children would receive no other adequate meal for the rest of the day. We learned that of a thousand live births in Peru, thirty-nine children will die before the age of five, and thirty will die before the age of one year. Ten percent of infants are born with low birth weight.[3] According to Peruvian government statistics of June 2002, 24.4 percent of Peruvians live in extreme poverty, meaning they subsist on less than a dollar a day.[4] The situation has not improved since then. Poverty hits children the hardest because they cannot grow without adequate physical, emotional, and intellectual resources.

When Methodists from North Carolina and Peru had first established a formal covenant with each other in the early eighties, financial support from the U.S. friends was of course extremely important. But North Carolinians were never sure that the money they donated went to the causes for which it was designated because the Peruvians had so many urgent needs that they sometimes "borrowed from Peter to pay Paul." Also, the Methodist Board of Global Ministries in New York, through which the money was channeled, changed personnel and procedures frequently, so that accounting was difficult in both countries.

In the end the children's presence made the difference: both sides agreed that a program for a nourishing daily meal for children should

always have priority and be established in several districts. The result-
ing so-called "Breakfast of Love" consisted usually of a fortified oat-
meal breakfast and sometimes of a noon meal provided by volunteers.
The program has functioned with several interruptions, caused in part
by an irregular flow of money from the north and in part by disagreements among Peruvian Methodist leaders concerning the way it was to
be used: should the children in the metropolitan area of Lima—a city
of about eight million—be the main recipients? Are not the rural areas
much more in need? Should congregations distribute it only in combi-
nation with religious instruction? North Carolinians visiting Peru in
2003 continued to discuss these issues with the Peruvians without
coming to clear agreements and without getting a detailed report on
the distribution of the funds, but the very presence of the children
continues to set the agenda, and is leading to action: the program has
once again flourished in 2004 in seven congregations.

Various groups from North Carolina Methodist churches continue
to visit Peruvian congregations every year, and Peruvian leaders are
often invited for annual conferences in North Carolina. In March of
2004, a congregational group from Southern Pines, Northern Carolina,
led by the Rev. Dr. Mark Wethington, included a retired pediatrician
who treated over two hundred children during a short visit to a congregation on the outskirts of Lima. During the same month, Mark
Wethington and I led some Duke Divinity School students and some
pastors in team-teaching a three-day course, "Women, Children, and
the Bible," in the Methodist Seminary in Huancayo, twelve thousand
feet up in the Andean mountains, because the seminary has a hard time
paying for instructors. We conducted a similar project in March 2005
in Ica, several hours south of Lima, where the seminary runs an extension program.

Apart from the North Carolina support, Peruvians have tried to
find other funding to give basic care to children. A project we visited in
2003 was initiated by an urban Methodist congregation in Lima with
the support of a donation by the Latin American Council of Churches.
The lay woman in charge, with the help of her husband, employs two
or three trained teachers to gather children from the most difficult
home situations of the neighborhood, who come for a few hours on
workdays to learn, play, and get a meal. I was apprehensive when I

learned that "accepting Christ" seemed to be the goal for which these children were being trained. I asked myself whether they would have received help and care just because they were in need. Did the teachers pressure them to swell the ranks of the congregation? But the children themselves were soon to dispel my misgivings. The "discourse" of their leaders may be different from our mainline North American language, but these children had fun playing games, engaging in friendly conversation with the visiting U.S. strangers, receiving help with homework, and performing a play about biblical texts that would have impressed any North American congregation. For us North Carolinians, meeting these children was in fact like "accepting Christ."

A unique approach was taken by a young pastor who was unable to finish his theological studies when the Methodist Seminary in Lima closed. He was invited to study at Duke Divinity School for a semester in the context of the exchange. Later, as a pastor of a small congregation at the outskirts of Lima, he learned of an abandoned church building in an extremely poor district, high on a hill and difficult to access by car. He started gathering children there by going from house to house, inviting them for play and worship. The result was amazing. Soon a congregation of thirty to thirty-five children was filling the little church three times a week in the afternoon, participating in Bible study, singing, crafts, games, and refreshments. Some adults began to join in. When members of a North Carolina church, who had "adopted" this congregation of children earlier, visited the place in March of 2003, they helped to furnish and paint the building. When at the end of the fantastic musical and biblical program for the visitors the children held out their hands to receive a little roll and a drink, a visiting theology student was moved by their attitude: they took a simple refreshment as though it were a eucharist, a great thanksgiving, she remarked later. It appeared that here a congregation was being born from children.

New birth, however, is painful as well as beautiful. Some neighbors of the church had been stealing water from its precious faucet, since water is scarce or only available at some distance in this poor neighborhood. The young pastor, together with the children, then started visiting the neighbors, offering the church's water in exchange for the promise that the community would work hard to lobby the city for its own water source in the future. By grace the children became the "living water" reconciling the neighborhood. By 2004 the Methodist leadership moved the young pastor to a different congregation where he is again working with children. Such work can be an inspiration for U.S. or European churches to build up new congregations literally from the bottom up: by gathering children.

Besides various congregational projects, there are countless individual initiatives in Peru. In Chincha, several hours south of Lima, where Peru's most famous Pisco is brewed, an eighty-year-old man, Tadeo Rojas, runs a "Casa de los Niños" ("House for Children"). He is a retired city worker and lay pastor who in the early 1990s used to go through the extremely poor settlement of his neighborhood to tutor children. Realizing that many of them had no place to play, do their homework, get a decent meal, or earn a few pennies as they grew up, he managed to buy a very simple house, which gradually he turned into the Methodist Church and Social Center of the settlement. He organized the children and invited to the Center many of them who worked in the local cemetery, carrying water and flowers and getting only a few dimes for their work though being exposed to many dangers. The destitute parents of the children appreciated the efforts of Tadeo and supported his work. When a visiting missionary saw that the Casa still lacked some walls and extensions and was constantly in danger of being "invaded" by poor neighbors,[5] he donated enough money to improve and enlarge the building. The Latin American Council of Churches, the Methodist Church of Peru, the United Methodist Church of the U.S.A., and a congregation in North Carolina also contributed funds, so that finally the Casa de los Niños could provide tutoring, meals, recreation, and training in crafts for a hundred children. They attend only during the day and are not exactly homeless, but come from situations of extreme poverty, sickness, drug abuse, or neglect. Tadeo taught the older ones to cook and care for the little ones. He provided a room with small desks where he supervises their homework. He managed to get some inexpensive materials to teach the children how to make toy animals and sandals that they sell in order to pay for their meals whenever support from individuals and churches fails—which still happens often, so that the project is always "at risk." Recently some computers were donated so that basic computer training can be offered. Around sixty children come on Sundays to gather for worship. The Casa de los Niños is another example of victims becoming agents because somebody welcomed them.

In the same city of Chincha a most amazing children's project has come into being. In 1995, Josué, the eight-year-old son of a Methodist couple—the wife being an ordained minister and the husband a lay preacher—started a radio program for children with the help of his cousin Carol and some advice and monetary contributions from adult family members. Every Saturday, when children were out of school, they offered a program at eight o'clock in the morning and called it "Dejad los niños venir a mi" ("Let the children come to me"). They offered Bible stories, poems or riddles, Christian music, "Advice for Children," and dialogues about school or home problems from the past or the following week, according to the time of year. After three years the radio station made it possible for children to call in and ask questions, make comments, or ask for special music. It became a very popular program for children from different churches and from the community at large. By 2000, when Josué was thirteen, he started directing the program toward teenagers, and his ten-year-old sister Jemima together with another cousin, Karen, continued the part for younger children. In 2001 they had to give up the program because of problems arising in the radio station. They do not know whether they will be able to resume the project some day. Meanwhile Josué is a leader of the youth group in his church.

Radio programs strengthen communities, especially in places where televisions are not affordable. In 1997, Peru had only 126 television sets per thousand households, but 273 radios.[6] The children's radio program was an enjoyable project, but also a unique Methodist way to teach Christian education to a wider public, from children for children. It does indeed offer some simple lessons to Western visitors.

In the overall situation of the Methodist church of Peru and its connection with North Carolina Christians, children have made a difference when theological tensions were at an all-time high. The ecumenically oriented seminary in Lima, with its close ties to North Carolina, was regarded by some Peruvians as having emphasized social and political issues at the expense of true pastoral training, a spiritual focus, and a clearer Methodist identity. After the closing of the seminary and the death of Frederick Herzog, the academic relationship with Duke Divinity School for several years consisted only in giving some Peruvian students the chance to study a semester at Duke. The congregational exchange, however, under the leadership of Dr. Mark Wethington and later of the Rev. Para Drake, continued intensively, and it was decided to concentrate on the needs of children instead of quarreling about "conservative" or "liberal" theology. The Peruvians asked the North Carolinians to join them in special conferences on Christian education, and three such workshops have taken place in 2000, 2001, and 2002, the first near Lima, the second one—mentioned previously—in the Andean district of Puno where the indigenous population is mostly Aymara, and the third one in Cusco, near Machu Picchu, where the Quechua people predominate. Four Duke Divinity School students participated in leading the meeting in Puno. In all these conferences, theological differences largely melted away as we tried in three languages, Spanish, English, and Quechua, with several translators, to focus on children's needs and expectations, on understanding biblical stories, crafting colorful felt banners for every represented district of Peru, creating paper mobiles, painting stones, and singing in different tongues.

At the Cusco conference children again brought about an important change. The Peruvian Methodists were divided between those who supported baptism as being exclusively for adults and those who believed—with the North Carolinians—that children's baptism was as valid as that of adults because it witnessed to God's claim on a human life. When at the end of the workshop a baptism of new adult believers was to take place by immersion in the swimming pool of the retreat center where we met, a Quechua family simply decided to bring along their children for baptism. While the older children bravely suffered being dunked into the ice-cold water together with adults and I was asked to become a godmother and to hold a one-year-old child for her baptism by sprinkling, all quarrels about what was theologically correct also took a plunge, and the sacrament ended with singing and a common celebration of the eucharist. Even the former Quechua bishop, an outspoken advocate of adult baptism as the only valid form, participated in the service.

## A MODEL VILLAGE FOR TRAUMATIZED CHILDREN

One of the highlights of nearly every North Carolina–Peru exchange since 1989 has always been a visit to a Children's Village in Cieneguilla, two hours southeast of Lima. The Aldea Infantil/Westfalia Kinderdorf was founded in the early 1980s by a Peruvian-German family who wanted to help Peruvian children traumatized by the guerilla war and by poverty and hunger. The director, Liselotte Schrader Woyke, received help from her parents, her brother, and later from her husband, in establishing an amazing oasis in the desert. The Peruvian government gave them a stony, mountainous desert terrain with a little river at the bottom. A German nongovernmental organization in Westfalia that had already established one Children's Village in Ghana and another one in India offered to sponsor the project. The original plan of having at least ten houses, each with a Peruvian foster parent couple that would not have more than two children of their own and would care for eight foster children, is now, after little more than twenty years, a reality. From year to year more children were gathered through various social service agencies. Some were so undernourished that they needed years of special treatments; some were found in a park and did not know their own names; some had seen their parents or other relatives being murdered by guerillas or government troops, and still others had only a single alcoholic or sick parent who could not take care of them. The houses were built one at a time, depending on how money could be found from organizations or individual sponsors. Besides money worries, there were countless other problems to tackle. Finding foster parents in a Roman Catholic country who promise not to have more than two children of their own, who have to live in a tiny village two hours away from the city, and who are willing to be trained in hygienic, psychological, and educational matters, is not easy. In addition, every bag of concrete, every brick, wooden beam, or sack of potatoes had to be brought to the village over a dangerous hanging bridge without railings that would sometimes be carried away by the river water underneath it. One time, in 1996, still traumatized by my husband's death, I was so scared of crossing that bridge that I could only manage it face down on my belly, slowly pushing myself forward while trying not to look at the water rushing over the rocks underneath.

The beginning of the project had been extremely difficult. It took expensive, giant machines to shatter the huge rocks in order to clear the area for building the first house and to make the planting of trees, flowers, and vegetables possible. Water from the river had to be pumped up the stony mountain to irrigate the vegetation in the relentless heat of the Peruvian summer. A psychiatrist had to come twice a week to counsel children with special traumas. Tutors and a nursery school were needed to prepare the children for being able to attend the regular village school. The Aldea Infantil has no formal religious ties. The director grew up in the Lutheran church and has one Catholic and one Protestant parent. Since most of the children come from Roman Catholic families, they attend mass and religious instruction in the near village, but if, for example, Methodists provide Bible study, it is gratefully accepted. Common meals in each of the houses start with saying grace, and prayers written by children decorate some of the living rooms. A friendly interchange with nearby peasants extends also to the use of a medical station that the Village was able to build with the help of the Peruvian and the German governments.

The Village is an ecological model: fertilizer is produced from wastewater, and a wind wheel and solar equipment provide electricity. Vegetables, flowers, and bushes are grown on terraces of the kind the Incas used for better irrigation. Cactus plants are constantly added to cover the rocky desert surroundings. By now the Village includes many animals, from guinea pigs to llamas, for petting, eating, and selling. As the children have grown older, occupational training has been needed for the teenagers. They can now learn carpentry, shoe repair, drilling, drafting, animal care, doll and puppet production, needlework, and other skills within the Village; training in car repair, bakery work, and other jobs is possible in Lima. A children's band practices music on traditional Peruvian instruments. Sports teams compete in games at nearby schools. Young and old volunteers come for weeks or months from Europe or the United States to work and play with the children or help in the construction of another home. In fact, the first big fundraiser was done by a German teenager who with a friend bicycled from the southern tip of Europe to the north of Scandinavia, gathering money from friends for every mile of cycling, the way we do it in the States for the CROP Walks. In 2003, special care was provided in the

Village for two seriously disabled children, one who cannot move out of a small carriage, and another one who fell from the hanging bridge onto the rocks and water below. The Aldea Infantil is quite simply a model of welcoming children who have had traumatic experiences and need special care. It challenges visitors to "go and do likewise."

## UNIQUE CIVIC AND CHURCH-RELATED INITIATIVES

I could describe countless other Peruvian projects, many of which are church-related and inspire visitors to befriend the children they serve. There are, for example, the Roman-Catholic Maryknoll priests who support homes for former street children and who initiated a public school program to prevent teenage pregnancy by providing better training for young girls and improving their self-esteem. The Maryknoll Order is always interested in letting Peruvians run these projects as much as possible. The Roman-Catholic MANTHOC program I mentioned in chapter 4 tutors working children and makes them aware of their rights. The *Semilla* project, initiated by a Methodist lay woman, teaches children in some of the poorest districts of the country to learn creative writing, drawing, and painting, and produces from the work of the children a superb journal, *El Periodiquito. Semilla* is a nongovernmental organization founded in 1982 that focuses on women, young adults, and children together; it also offers educational radio programs, job training for teenagers, and ecological projects like community gardens. Another program, organized by a Methodist woman pastor, teaches children—using hand puppets and stuffed animals—how to avoid sexual abuse.[7] In addition, there are innumerable foreign nongovernmental organizations like *terre des hommes* who employ Peruvians in their programs, but are funded by foreign money.

There are attempts by city governments to get children off the streets into meaningful work. During the years of the guerilla war Lima looked sad and bare, with garbage piling up in the streets. But for years now flower beds and trees are again flourishing, and parks are kept cleaner than before. A small part of this improvement happened through children. The city decided to implement a program for *niños jardinieros* (child gardeners), who worked for four hours daily in the parks and streets for a small salary. They also received psychological counseling. More privately organized are the "tomb tenders," children who clean and polish tombstones or bring flowers to the niches of various columbaria. A famous Peruvian film of 1990, "Juliana," movingly describes the life of these children. *Latinamerica Press* reported in 2003 that in La Paz, Bolivia, about fifty children from five to fifteen years work for about $0.60 (five bolivianos) per day or $2.40 (twenty bolivianos) on weekends by shining headstones, hauling water, and fetching ladders to reach the higher niches. Some children get paid by visitors to the cemetery for saying special prayers for a deceased person. One little boy said he charges only half price for the soul of infants, "because it takes [adults] longer to get to heaven."[8] Apparently he understands Jesus' word that the reign of God belongs to children!

## WHAT CAN WE LEARN BY CONNECTING WITH "THIRD-WORLD" CHILDREN?

For people going on a "mission trip" the temptation is to see the children as victims who need our dollars and our visits and who make us feel good if we respond this way. But they can also be our "saviors" by holding up a mirror to our adult Western ways and our various colonial histories. Who are we to deserve the luxury of our malls and supermarkets? Are we voting for politicians who give us the biggest tax break and promise the biggest military for our safety, or for those who provide foreign aid to countries like Peru, and who sign international agreements that are beacons lighting the way to a worldwide recognition of children's rights? Are we eager to buy the least expensive clothes without thinking about their possible origin in factories using child labor? Do we throw pennies to street children instead of supporting institutions and individuals who are really helping them to help themselves?

We may resent the relentless stubborn begging of children in the streets of cities like Lima, following us to our comfortable hotels (comfortable even though we make sure every time that we take a very modest one); but do we realize the suffering behind this terrible habit? I remember an evening in Cusco during our workshop in 2002. It had grown dark, and two little girls had followed us from restaurant to store to hotel, begging and simply bothering us. We were completely overtired after a day of hard work with translations in three languages in a room that was very cold and not rain-proof so that we were dripped on occasionally. We were eager to get to bed at our hotel, a place where the water did not always function but overall conditions were good enough. Two pastors of our group, however, did not go to bed. They had started a conversation with the two girls who were perhaps about ten years old. They invited them into the lobby of the hotel for a soft drink and listened until late into the night to their stories about what "home" was like for them. When I learned about this the next morning, I was embarrassed that I had felt annoyed by the presence of these children. Jesus did not tell us to welcome *good* children only. The next evening I bought some picture postcards from two well-behaved little boys who even were able to talk some English, and minutes later I noticed that they had cheated me badly in the exchange of money. When I remembered the girls from the previous evening, my momentary irritation vanished. I realized again that we simply have to change our middle-class notions of "missions" and a well-ordered "academic exchange" and "helping the poor," and to see that the "transcendence and immanence of evil" (as Ivone Gebara calls it from her Brazilian experience) is present in all of us as much as the image of God.

> When I see a young mother with four children, abandoned by her husband and having to leave her youngsters in a tiny room facing the street, with bars almost like a prison, so she can go to work; when I see that there are no schools for children; when I see children brawling in the streets, committing little thefts and sometimes crimes, easy prey for drug traffickers; when I surprise myself by being afraid of children, of their violence . . . when I see my neighbor, who beats his wife and abuses her in public . . . when I feel powerless and ignorant as to how to use my own abilities in my neighborhood, suffering becomes my daily bread, and I feel in my own skin the transcendence and immanence of evil.[9]

## DISCOVERING THE WEB OF LIFE

Besides this gut feeling, which traditional theologians trace back to "original sin," there is also another possible experience: I can discover that fragile web of life that connects me with every creature on earth, angelic, normal, or criminal. I can celebrate the incredible mystery and splendor of the universe in which no creature is a clone of the other, but the lives and fates of all, good and bad and in between, are intricately interwoven. The genes of the chimpanzee are only by 1.6 percent different from those of human beings.[10]

> We, and all else, are variations on exactly the same thing—star dust. The atoms in our bodies, and all atoms everywhere, were born in the supernova explosions of early stars. Everything is thus radically "kin" from the very beginning. When you look at the Southern Cross, Orion or the Big Dipper, the gnat on your arm, the flower near your path or the food on your plate, you are gazing at a neighbour who shares with you what is most basic of all—common matter together, as old and venerable as time and space themselves.[11]

Jesus of Nazareth knew that he was related to the lilies of the field as well as to the criminal crucified beside him to whom he said, according to one Gospel writer, "Truly I tell you, today you will be with me in Paradise" (Luke 23:43). Criminal street children might be hunted down by policemen and merchants who regard them as the pests of their city, but Christians and other people who know that we have to "mature into childhood" can learn from these children that we, like them, live by grace and not by merit, that we, like them, are caught in systems of evil from which we cannot extricate ourselves, like the system of military recklessness that we support by our taxes, or the system of using massive amounts of energy that contribute to the deterioration of our environment. We can learn from the children close to us that we are dependent on the care, goodwill, and forgiveness of others, but the lesson becomes so much more alive if we try to bridge the "chasm" to reach the suffering children south of the equator, especially since their countries contain many more children and young citizens than Europe or the United States.

## LEARNING THE "GOSPEL OF COMMONWEALTH"

"Mission" trips into the "Third World" can be covert neocolonialism, exhibiting our charity and our cultural, financial, or religious power. The gospel of personal wealth was not unrelated to early Methodist missions in Peru, since Methodist schools were to provide well-trained employees to the newly rising middle class and successful corporations.[12] However, during our visits we can also opt to learn the gospel of "commonwealth," to use David Batstone's phrase, especially when we focus on the dignity, needs, and rights of children. North American and European teenagers will then, for example, be compelled to compare their average huge pocket money with the empty pockets of young Peruvians. German youngsters aged six to nineteen years had a combined purchasing power of 20 billion Euros in 2003,[13] and their U.S. counterparts are likely even better off. If such considerations in connecting with the "Third World" lead to individual charity or to support from one church to another, that is great. But a much more complex response is needed if we have the commonweal and commonwealth of all countries in mind: people of insight and conscience can influence public opinion and government policy in order to effect change.

For example, Peru, along with Colombia, for years has been drawn into the U.S. war on drugs. Some political analysts think that this war is producing more terror instead of less, because interdiction drives up the price of drugs so that drug lords can have even larger profits, and these profits get into the hands of terrorists. I have mentioned earlier the environmental damage from spraying coca fields that takes a heavy toll on children's health and stability while their families flee the sprayed regions. "The war on drugs might possibly go down in history as the worst domestic policy blunder in American history."[14] If we are concerned for the children "south of the border," we should worry about the wisdom of spending more millions on aid for eradication efforts. But can this truly be a task for Christians and people of other faiths?

Gayatri Spivak has contended that the great religions of the world cannot be of help in solving a global crisis because "the history of their greatness is too deeply imbricated in the narrative of the ebb and flow of power." "We must learn from the original practical ecological philosophies of the world," and the collective effort has to be supplemented by "love."[15] But there is no reason why the religions cannot themselves learn from these philosophies and practice "love," regardless of their deplorable histories of violent power struggles. In connecting with "developing" countries, Christians can "become like children" by putting aside their Western cultural synthesis based on individualism, rationalism, scientism, and belief in progress, and can instead learn from indigenous or Eastern cultures that communal rights are just as important as individual rights, and that communal modes of experience are just as viable as the abstract "rules" Westerners live by. "The expansionist dynamic inherent in the Western economic model may eventually come to destroy the very civilization built on that dynamic."[16] One way of life is not necessarily "better" than the other, but both have to influence and interpenetrate each other in the age of globalization. Westerners have become too much the "adults" who would like to educate the world in terms of liberal democracy, but especially the United States is experiencing raw opposition.

> We seem to enter the stage of a new pax Romana—but now on an unprecedented scale: a world order or world civilization, basically of Western design, encircling the globe with a network of universal, uniform ideas and practices. Among these ideas, easily the most prominent and influential is that of liberal democracy. But [the irony is that] the blessings of pax Americana are bound to be resented and resisted precisely in the name of popular self-determination.[17]

If we "become like children" in our relationship with "Third World" countries, we will resist the struggle for domination and expansion and work for cooperation. As Jesus told his disciples,

> You know that among the Gentiles those whom they recognize as their rulers lord it over them, and their great ones are tyrants over them. But it is not so among you; but whoever wishes to become great among you must be your servant, and whoever wishes to be first among you must be slave of all. (Mark 10:42–44)

These words are found in the same chapter in which Jesus urges his disciples to welcome children, and they follow the story of James and John asking for the best places, "one at your right hand and one at your left, in your glory," while these disciples are overconfident that they will be able to "drink the cup" of suffering. Mark's gospel had told us earlier that Jesus responds to the quarrel among the disciples as to who might be the greatest by putting a child among them (Mark 9:36; cf. Luke 9:47).

So our "mission" is to listen to both the joyful and the painful cries of "babes and infants" praising God (Ps. 8:2; Matt. 21:16) and to live in solidarity with them. No theological "academic" exchange should screen out the cries of those who live on a $1.00 a day. No church group should just "help the poor"; instead, such groups can learn from children to live in loving relation with all creatures around us, thankful for the "commonwealth" of all. "Becoming like children" we will be, in St. Paul's words, "stewards of God's mysteries" (1 Cor. 4:1) and certainly "more than conquerors" (Rom. 8:37). The future of the globe will depend on it.

# 8

# THE CHILD AS
# (GOD'S) AGENT OF
# GLOBAL CHANGE

➤➤ ✦ ◄◄

Like women, [children] have a hidden history
of remarkable achievements.[1]

Whenever we challenge theology to take the child seriously, both
within biblical and theological scholarship and in our global situation
today, we have to cross over into other academic fields. In many ways
the research process is similar to the beginnings of feminist scholarship in theology. Just as women have for centuries been seen in the
contrasting images of goddess and temptress, so children in the popular mind have predominantly been regarded as either saviors or victims, but not as human agents. Women's and children's historical and
future significance as actors on the global stage has traditionally been
ignored. Since ancient times sons have been needed to save a royal tradition, a family name, business, or honor. Children were needed for a

woman to be saved from the "curse" of infertility and for a tribe or nation to be saved from extinction. It is therefore not surprising that in many religions a divine child was seen as a savior. Yet at the same time children have always been victims in secular as well as religious ways, from the Pharaoh's or King Herod's baby killing to the drug lords' forced recruiting of child soldiers or religiously tolerated child abuse in our time.

How can the contrasting images of the child as savior and as victim be overcome today? How can the fragile future of this globe be strengthened by recognizing the child as agent? We all know about victimized children throughout the world and close to home, because the media bombards us with images of AIDS orphans, child soldiers, street children, child workers, child prostitutes, undocumented immigrant teenagers, and hungry inner-city preschool children. These television images, however, usually just float on by before our eyes while we eat a hurried supper. Although we know about the child as savior, for the average Christian that knowledge is limited to the Christmas story. We have gradually awakened to the fact that children can be agents of terror when they shoot their schoolmates or teachers and when they become suicide bombers or practice legal or illegal killing in some official or shadowy army; but usually we have not recognized that they can also be agents of liberation and "salvation" in a new way, although we could have learned this from the Bible.

Theology has paid scant attention to Jesus' radical words about our "becoming like children" and so becoming part of the reign of God. In fact, understood in the context of Jesus' day these words were probably a "conscious poetic as well as theological provocation, not at all something self-evident, probably even something offensive."[2] While the Hebrew prophet celebrated a newborn prince as the deliverer of his people and the New Testament saw the Christ child as the promised savior, the reported words of Jesus also indicate that "regular" children can save us if we "welcome" them, take to heart their way of being in the world and in so doing follow Christ in becoming God's children. The Hebrew Bible, fully aware of children as victims of power politics, poverty, or exile, continually calls for special attention to orphans. The same is true of the Koran. The New Testament describes the child Jesus as a victim from the time of his birth, a poor refugee child persecuted by a tyrant. Jesus tells his disciples to side with all the "little ones" who are victimized, whether children being pushed away by overly zealous disciples or simple, faithful followers of his who were easily made to "stumble" (Luke 17:2).

Victimized children in Israel, however, could also become powerful agents, like Moses or Joseph, and Jesus sees all children, who were nobodies in his time, not as objects of pity, but as agents of life and salvation. This is why his metaphor of "becoming like children" is relevant for our time and why it has nothing to do with self-deprecation, naiveté, or anti-intellectualism. Indeed, Jesus wanted us to be "wise as serpents." We have learned from other fields of knowledge that children can be agents of change. They can be so either by making actual decisions, contributing to their own life and to that of adults—if we give them the chance—or by their mere being.

## NURTURING CHILDREN AS AGENTS IN PRAXIS

Riane Eisler, who was a refugee child from Nazi-ruled Vienna, urges us to exchange the traditional "dominator model" of our society with the "partnership model" in bringing up children. She wants education to cultivate empathy and cooperation instead of praising the violent "heroes" of classical myths and of our day or teaching science as a ruthless competing of genes for survival of the fittest. Even in the work of Darwin she finds an emphasis on conscience, moral responsibility, and cooperation—depending on habit, reason, instruction, and religion—and not only on natural selection.[3] Partnership models to be taught and learned are not unstructured, she insists, but they inspire rather than coerce and empower rather than restrain, using the knowledge and skills of all members.[4] Likewise Elise Boulding calls for a peace education that gives children the responsibility and dignity of agents.

> Where are the . . . stories of the creativity, inventiveness, and determined action for change on the part of children and youth —the six-to-eight- to eighteen-year-olds? Who even notices them? Like women, they also have a hidden history of remarkable achievements in private spaces. Unlike women, their entry into public spaces in recent decades has been neither recognized nor acclaimed. The heavy hand of patriarchy still weighs on them. They are minors by law and voiceless by custom.[5]

Especially children of minorities have been stereotyped as essentially childlike and incapable of rational judgment and action. Though African American young people led the civil rights movement, bringing about both desegregation and voting rights in the 1960s, it took whites many years to acknowledge the power of "children."[6] When the Poles revolted against the brutal Nazi occupation in 1944, children were among those who fought and died.[7] Children's achievements can be found in all corners of the world. A Jesuit priest in southern India, along with local Jesuit school students, has launched an AIDS-awareness campaign conducted mostly by children orphaned by the disease. A sixteen-member theater group is traveling with a play promoting prevention as the only cure for AIDS. "People in this area commit suicide when they get to know they have contracted AIDS," said theater group member Kunda Deepthi, age ten. "I plead with all so that such people may live." The program is a joint venture by the students of the local Jesuit school and two Hindu doctors.[8]

Realizing that young students can understand and take action much more than previously assumed, since 2002 some German universities have been offering special classes for children in which famous professors explain the mysteries of our world to very young students.[9] The U.S. journalist Elizabeth Rusch has published a book based on interviews of children from eight to sixteen years of age who made some remarkable suggestions when asked what they would do to solve social problems like poverty, pollution, or crime.[10] In my local church a teenage girl regularly organizes the congregation's participation in the Interfaith Hospitality Network for homeless families, and other young members are working in the Community Kitchen feeding people coming in from the street. We simply have to overcome the dichotomy of children as victims or saviors and see them as agents—for good or for ill—while providing them with opportunities for involvement in a meaningful communal life. They are able to participate in decision making not least because our technological culture has given them enormous power.[11] They are growing up faster because they have to cope early with problems caused mainly by adults.

We can see this process mirrored in children's literature. Books for children these days are not about a child's romantic adventures or "fighting foes in slightly enchanted realms" as in *A Wrinkle in Time,* but about children who have to "come to terms with" or "work through" harsh realities because of missing or irresponsible parents with complex characters.[12] Even responsible parents, however, have children struggling with grown-up problems because young and old are caught in systems of relentless "progress" and competition, demanding constant involvement that includes the children. While French literary theorists are debating whether Harry Potter's world is driven only by capitalism—forcing children to acquire high-tech magical objects to survive—or whether Harry is an antiglobalism crusader, he is in any case a child who has to act in a forceful way.[13]

In real life, children have begun to manage their fates as well as they can, especially in the so-called developing countries. War, poverty, and AIDS have forced them to grow up at an early age and to act as adults in taking care of younger siblings, fighting in government or guerilla armies, and doing work that children in the Western world would hardly ever do. We easily overlook children as agents in everyday life because we have grown up with the Western notion that they have to be shaped and protected before they can act responsibly.[14] The line between childhood and adulthood is fluid and varies from culture to culture, but certainly in our society children are agents much earlier than before.

So what will happen when children act like criminals or at least in ways that harm families or communities? Of course we cannot say that a child becomes an agent of evil and violence at a specific age, and the term "original sin" does not effectively express our present-day instinct for what ails this world.[15] Human beings are born into a good creation that appears to have some inexplicable cracks in even its smallest parts and its very foundation (see Ps. 51:5). God's good news is that these cracks, even if we continually fail to heal them, do not determine our fate, but by grace can be overcome in constant conversion and renewal. Like adults, children have the potential for evil, but in their early years their dependence on love and care keeps them open to an ever new and surprising future, to the vitality and enjoyment of life itself, and to trusting relationships. Their necessarily close ties to body, place, and nature limit their desire to dominate, deceive, or hurt others. They can be cruel, for example, toward children with disabilities or peers who simply do not "fit in," but that happens partly out of ignorance or a lack of nurturing community and family ties. In situations of war, displacement, and extreme poverty, children are not just acted upon, but they can themselves become brutal victimizers.[16] However, they are not responsible for having created the circumstances in which they find themselves.

In our environment of relative peace, as we give children and young people responsibility in making decisions affecting their own lives and ours, we can learn from their needs and their mistakes just as they learn from ours. As we set limits in our own lives, we urge them to accept their limits. If they go astray, we can only lovingly wait and hope like the father in Jesus' parable of the prodigal son (Luke 15:11–32). If we take the New Testament message seriously, we cannot ever give up on a young person who has committed a crime. As Isaac Bashevis Singer emphasized in his works about Yiddish-speaking people: every human life is sacred, singular, irreplaceable—and this is particularly true when a person has not yet had the chance to grow up. Even if fifteen-year-old youths are murderers or terrorists, we have no right to take their lives, to judge them like adults, or to let them rot in prison without trying to rehabilitate them.[17] Letting children and young people be agents in their own right means risking that they make wrong choices—like adults. Each culture has different notions concerning the age at which a person becomes accountable, but we should certainly not expect teenagers to be as ethically mature as adults before they are even allowed to vote.

Concerning vote and voice, many marginal groups of our society have some representation, like the elderly and people with disabilities; but children have never had their own vote or lobby, so politicians easily overlook them. The media must share the blame for this neglect. A nongovernmental organization in Brazil did a study of some large newspapers of their country and found that only thirty-one of eight hundred news items dealt with the situation of children. In reports on violence more than two-thirds described the children as victims and almost one-third characterized them as "aggressors." What was prevalent in these reports was terms for children like "minors," meant to indicate some deficiency, and "child prostitutes," which overlooks the fact that adults initiate the prostitution. "Children and adolescents who are protagonists of civic action are rarely heard of."[18]

However, there is progress on the international level. The United Nations historic General Assembly Special Session on Children, held in May 2002, for the first time included large numbers of children as official members of delegations, representing governments and non-governmental organizations. As Kofi Annan stated,

> The children's presence transformed the atmosphere of the United Nations. Into our usually measured and diplomatic discussions, they introduced their passions, questions, fears, challenges, enthusiasm and optimism. They brought us their ideas, hopes and dreams. They gave life to the values of the Convention on the Rights of the Child. And they contributed something only they could know: the experience of being young in the 21st century . . . [19]

In 2001 the annual report of UNICEF concentrated on leadership of and for children around the world. What is done on the international level can also be done locally: giving children a voice and giving them models of leadership. Letting them speak up can make things messy and time-consuming, but democracy has always been that way, and yet we still believe in it. Showing them models of leadership does not mean creating heroes and heroines, for even the best leaders are flawed human beings; rather it means learning from people who have made courageous decisions under the most difficult circumstances. We find these people in the Bible as well as in real life, and they are children as well as adults.

The biblical writers already knew that children could be agents of transformation. Samuel initiated change in Israel's history as a young child, and so did the shepherd boy David. Jeremiah thought he was too young to preach, but he became a powerful prophet. The twelve-year-old Jesus in the temple, obviously breaking the boundaries of his parents' traditional expectations, must have challenged some old theologians' ways of thinking.[20]

The children of our time can learn to be agents of justice, not justice as a legalistic demand, but as "love under the conditions of conflict," as Catherine Keller calls it.[21] When about six hundred million children in the developing countries must attempt to live on less than a dollar a day, our well-to-do children must be made aware of it in order to become responsible agents of a more just global society.[22] Technology can be helpful in raising awareness in children as well as giving them a voice, as Justine Cassell has shown in describing a children's online forum that connected and empowered children from various parts of the world and different levels of society.[23]

## CHILDREN AS AGENTS BY THEIR MERE BEING

Just as important as the transformation that results from certain actions by children and young people is the change of heart and circumstances that can happen by a child's mere being and an adult's simply "becoming like a child." The very presence of a helpless baby in a reed basket moved the Pharaoh's daughter. The mere presence of the child Jesus transformed the lives of shepherds and wise men. The suffering of sick children in Jesus' surroundings intensified the faith of those who pleaded for their health (Luke 7:9; Mark 9:24; Matt. 15:28). It is the presence of Godself in a vulnerable child that makes human transformation possible and opens a new future.

Children can remind us that our worth lies not in the achievements of our work, but in our mere being: not only in what we do, but in what we are. Any human agency is a gift representing God's agency. In a time of increasing joblessness and obsession with work, small children are beautiful examples of constant activity and attentiveness without the compulsion to compete for success. They can inspire us to create "alternative" work and to remember that "success is not one of the names of God."[24] It is play that makes us truly human, whether in a job or outside of it. Playing was what *sophia* did at the creation in cooperation with God (Prov. 8:22–31). "Play and childhood make the world bearable and actually are its foundation," said the writer Ilse Aichinger, who survived a traumatic childhood during the Nazi holocaust and in whose work children play an important role.[25]

At a time when "spending on luxury goods is climbing at four times the rate of overall spending," various studies have pointed out that "acceptance of a lower standard of living can mean more freedom and less stress with no real decline in the quality of life."[26] However, today unemployment is an even greater problem than stress and overwork. While joblessness is a traumatic experience for many North American or European people, it can remind us of its pervasiveness in the southern part of the globe. After all, the mere notion that young adults can choose what type of work they want to do for the rest of their lives is a completely unrealistic concept for most of humanity. In the age of technological globalization where machines make many workers superfluous, jobless people in all parts of our world need the imagination, energy, and constant activity of a child in order to create something new out of whatever is at hand, to be cocreators with God in sustaining life and giving it meaning.[27]

When we work like children, we are not involved in what the apostle Paul and Martin Luther warned us about: trying to accumulate merit in order to earn salvation. That would be the equivalent of today's market economy, eliminating everything that does not show a profit at the bottom line. A child's work is intensive play; it gives pleasure and pain through winning and losing. But above all it gives strength through growing and participating in the work of the universe. Native Americans are aware of this mystery when they pray in the morning to help the sun come up or to keep the wheels of life turning. Saint Paul wanted us to have faith in God's activity and not in our merit, but he also saw himself as a "co-worker" for God's reign on earth (Col. 4:11). Luther did not want us to buy our salvation through some "indulgences," but he reminded us that the work of a maid is as godly a work as that of a preacher. Justification through faith alone is, then, not an invitation to passivity. It is instead an invitation to become like a small child: to be active without obsession and without calculating the benefits.

Agency through mere being can especially be observed in children with disability. For example, scientists have recently suggested that autistic children, whose number has increased drastically, may be important agents in giving us deeper insight into environmental problems. Many of these children cannot tolerate gluten or dairy products; many show high levels of mercury and other poisons in their system. Some seem to have been harmed by overuse of antibiotics or unsafe vaccines. These children might cause us

> to embrace new dietary patterns and a radical rethinking of all our policies concerning industrial waste disposal, agricultural practices, the preparation and use of vaccines, . . . and the manufacture of consumer goods.[28]

Other disabilities can also result in new knowledge.

> Reading methods developed to work with dyslexic children
> have proven useful for helping "normal" children to read more
> effectively.
>
> . . . . . . . . . . . . . . . . . . . . .
>
> It's the marginal elements of the student population that often
> stimulate out-of-the-box educational thinking.[29]

## CHILDREN AS AGENTS OF RECONCILIATION

Besides alerting us to our lack of care for the environment, small children can be agents of reconciliation. They are models of peacemakers
because they do not carry grudges very long and do not construct elab-
orate images of the enemy as adults do. If we learn from them, our theology will be a "theology of becoming," and even our politics will be a
"politics of becoming," as William Connolly phrased it.[30] Children are
constantly becoming, that is, growing and changing. In the midst of
the seeming chaos of this world, some stability always asserts itself,
sometimes gradually, sometimes suddenly and unpredictably. This
discovery of physicists can be observed in something as simple as a
child singing in the dark.

> A child in the dark, gripped with fear, comforts himself by
> singing under his breath . . . by singing quietly in the dark. . . .
> The song is like a rough sketch of a calming and stabilizing,
> calm and stable, center in the heart of chaos. . . . Perhaps the
> child skips as he sings, hastens or slows his pace. But the song
> itself is already a skip: it jumps from chaos to the beginnings
> of order in chaos . . .[31]

Any attempt at reconciliation in our warring world might look as
useless as a child's song in the dark, but it can also be such a stabilizing
force. A recent discussion in the German media illustrates the point.
Eva Moses Kor, a woman who in her childhood underwent cruel medical experiments in a concentration camp together with her twin sister, felt the need to forgive her tormentor in order to free herself from
a lifelong trauma. The guilty doctor was no longer alive, but she met
another physician who had participated in similar atrocities. She went

to visit him, and after the meeting she decided to forgive him. After five decades she refused to remain trapped in the role of a victim, and she sensed a new feeling of power and liberation.

Her action has been criticized by people who knew that the forgiven doctor had not really repented and still was making inexcusable statements. The sociologist Natan Sznaider of Tel Aviv, for example, pointed out that personal forgiveness has nothing to do with political reconciliation. He refers to Hannah Arendt, who considered a new beginning in politics to be a matter of respect and not of emotions like guilt or personal forgiving. She thought that crimes that cannot be punished also cannot be forgiven. Certainly forgiveness is not a way for nations and ethnic groups to cope with crimes of the past, but when Eva Moses Kor insists that her life has totally changed, that she now feels free, her public witness can have a tremendous effect. She becomes, so to speak, a child again, who senses that life is energized by an ever new future, not by a past trauma.[32]

Forgiveness is not a norm or a political principle, but whenever it happens in personal, social, or international relations, adults become children again, making up after a fight, trusting without demanding proof, and sensing their own inability to live without honest relationships. In the Hebrew Bible that happened to Jacob and Esau (Gen. 33) and to Joseph and his brothers (Gen. 50). It often happens when adults have been as hard hit as Jacob after his struggle at the Jabbok that left him limping (Gen. 32:25). Jesus of Nazareth became a child again when in the face of death he asked his father to show motherly mercy to those who did not know what they were doing (Luke 23:34). People like Martin Luther King Jr. or Oscar Romero understood this lesson taught by a "marginal Jew."[33] They acted like courageous children singing in the dark when they risked their lives. They blurted out the truth like the child in "The Emperor's New Clothes" while the crowds were constrained by adult conventions and fears. Victims can become *God's* agents and thereby saviors. It takes nothing more or less than to open oneself to grace and become a child again.

# CONCLUSION

∗

"A little child shall lead them"? (Isa. 11:6)

*What's wrong with our children, Lord?*
*Adults are what's wrong with our children.*[1]

This book is a plea to give children their rightful place in theology and in our daily life. For most of the twentieth century, theology has ignored the child except for treating it in Practical Theology and in Christian Education. However, the picture has changed in recent years. In different countries and cultural contexts, theologians are discovering the challenge of our scriptural heritage regarding children as well as the dilemma of their contemporary situation the world over. If we see children the way the Bible does, we will take them into account in our spiritual as well as our social and political life.

While perhaps nobody has enunciated and embodied as radically as Jesus of Nazareth the need for adults to enter the realm of God by becoming like children and caring for children, many religions have emphasized the need to "mature into childhood," because in the process of growing older human beings seem to forget a childlike life, dependent yet interacting with others, vulnerable, yet full of vitality, growing and changing, yet remaining centered in trusting relationships.

For many of us, childhood evokes images of an irretrievable past, something precious that got lost. However, as Karl Rahner stated,

> Childhood does not constitute past time, time that has eroded away, but rather that which remains, that which is coming to meet us . . .
>
> Childhood is valuable in itself, . . . it is to be discovered anew in the ineffable future which is coming to meet us.[2]

So how can we get ready for this future or even help to bring it closer? I have tried to indicate some steps that might point in the right direction: a rediscovery of our biblical heritage, an openness to other cultures and religions, and an awareness of the ties to our natural environment. The Hebrew and Christian Scriptures see the child as "leading" adults, and many other faith traditions honor a divine presence in the child. This divinity, however, appears in humble human form: it begins with dirty diapers; it brings us down to earth. Children can revive our relationship to body, nature, and place and remind us of our rather humble place in the intricate weave of the cosmos. As Brian Swimme said, "We will discover our larger role only by reinventing the human as a dimension of the emergent universe."[3]

Unfortunately, the world around us teaches us the opposite: we seem to be lords of the universe. We are the adults in charge who teach less grown-up people in faraway places the values of freedom, wealth, power, and security. We absorb the gospel of individualism and independence, of market laws and preemptive wars. The worldwide expenditure for military matters increased from $870 billion in 2001 to $900 billion in 2002 and continues to increase rapidly.[4] At the same time the feeling of security has diminished, and the most basic social services, including those for children, have been drastically reduced in the United States as in many other countries. So in thinking about the suffering of child workers and child soldiers, we have to ask ourselves what we are teaching our children about work and war, how our lifestyle might be related to conditions in distant countries, and why "war holds a deep attraction for large numbers of people in most cultures around the world."[5] Also, our understandable fear of terror—and of running out of natural resources—is not a valid excuse for building bigger bunker-busting bombs and futuristic missile defense shields, and in so doing neglecting millions of children at home and abroad.

The Children's Defense Fund's most recent report gives a devastating overview of our shortcomings while challenging us with realistic proposals for change. It does point out where progress has been made in the care for children, but the statistics are still staggering. Twelve million children in the United States (one in six) live in poverty; 7.5 million of them are white, 3.6 million black, and 3.7 million brown. Among industrialized countries the United States ranks first in military technology and military exports and eighteenth in the percent of children in poverty. U.S. children under fifteen years of age are nine times more likely to die in a firearm accident than children in twenty-five other industrialized countries combined. Over 2.5 million households with children live in substandard housing. As of 2002, there were thirteen million children in this country who live in households suffering from hunger or "food insecurity without hunger."[6]

We cannot distance ourselves from this reality, because we are part of it. Only in relationship with those who are suffering are we really alive, are we truly "coworkers with God." Even in our secular daily affairs we are inexorably connected. When in August of 2003 the huge, cascading power failure occurred in the northeast of the United States, it taught us "an often ignored aspect of our globalized world: vulnerability due to interconnectivity."[7] The same pertains to our spiritual lives. "Everything exists, lives and moves in others, in one another, with one another, for one another, in the cosmic interrelations of the divine Spirit."[8] When churches welcome children, they are learning to be attentive also to each other as adults. As Bradley Wigger says,

> Attention is the key to care and attachment; being there, holding, seeing, tending, listening. We are made to attend to one another, to attach, to care.[9]

The terrorist attacks of September 11, 2001, have made it especially urgent to think about the global situation of children. More than a third of the world's people, or 35 percent, are children, meaning 2.1 billion are minors. Every year 120 million are born. A quarter of them live in bitter poverty. Every third child is not registered at birth and therefore does not have an official citizenship. Thirty-two of every one hundred children suffer malnutrition in their first five years of life, eighteen do not have access to safe water, and twenty-seven are not immunized against any disease. Of one hundred children worldwide, eighteen never go to school, and eleven of them are girls.[10] War's impact on girls is particularly damaging to future generations. AIDS is increasingly affecting adolescent girls, and an estimated two million girls are at risk of female genital mutilation.[11]

When we compare these estimates with the luxuries that most Western children enjoy, like tennis, horseback riding, dancing lessons, or shopping for clothes, videos, laptops, and handys, in addition to good education and health care, it becomes understandable that the poor will rise up and call for justice, sometimes with the voice of a strident fundamentalism. Benjamin Barber has stated that if our only choice is between "the mullahs and the mall, between the hegemony of religious absolutism and the hegemony of market determinism, neither liberty nor the human spirit is likely to flourish." He also thinks "the only war worth winning is the struggle for democracy."[12] This very democracy, however, is in danger of being eroded by measures taken against the threat of terrorism, and the increasing emphasis on military power and expenditure is making the reduction of poverty and ecological damage extremely difficult.[13] The future of the planet will be determined by the way children are taken care of and not by the most sophisticated weapons.

The global situation of children is especially critical because in almost all of the poor developing countries half of the population is below fourteen years of age. While in the European nations, except for Ireland and Luxembourg, the population is rapidly aging, demographic research indicates that in countries like Syria, Iraq, Jordan, and the Palestinian areas the population will show a massive increase during the next decades. These young populations will either be productive or destructive.[14] In some countries, a religious totalitarianism takes hold of them, unless other nations learn to be inspiring models of integrating foreign policy and social concern. Where masses of children do not have a future, no amount of military power will solve their problems. "A little child shall lead them," was the vision of the Hebrew prophet. However, we are called by grace to participate in the realization of Isaiah's "peaceable kingdom." If we don't become like little children, letting children "lead" us, then big, hopeless, landless, hungry, and desperate children will rebel against us instead of bringing reconciliation and peace.

It does not even take a Christian or other religious argument to prove that countries or persons are responsible for each other. Judith Butler, for example, argues from a philosophical point of view that we have a responsibility toward all because we are all vulnerable. There is no ethical norm that requires this, but acting responsibly without a norm is the ethically radical thing to do. Ethics is nonviolence without any reciprocation.[15] All the more, Christians and other people of faith will have reason to consider anew the importance of children in their midst and in the world at large.

Learning from children to become like children will mean becoming more curious, frank, hopeful, trusting, and eager to relate and communicate, and being full of vitality and imagination. What we teach children already lies hidden in them—as in us—by grace and just has to be awakened. There is a legend in the Talmud that says that an angel takes every newly conceived child out of the mother's womb at night, showing it first the Garden of Eden with its righteous people and then all the places the child will see in its real life. Every evening the angel returns the child to its mother's womb. At the time of birth, the angel just gives the child a little slap on the back of its head to let it forget what it saw. However, once in a while the growing child will have spells of memory, recognizing thoughts and places, because the angelic slap was gentle.

This legend, according to a German theologian, might lead to the pedagogic idea that all learning is remembering. We do not have to fill the child's brain with facts, figures, and rules. Parents and teachers only revive, concretize, actualize, and increase what the child has been given and what the angel with kind intentions made it forget. The birth process is thus being continued throughout a lifetime.[16]

> As long as we live, we are being born. As long as we are adults, we may be children. We are dead if we are no longer children.[17]

Our lives as well as those of the children of this world can be changed if we understand this continuing birth process, this "theology of becoming." Jesus is said to have started his preaching with the assertion: the time is fulfilled, the reign of God is near: so go and change! (Mark 1:15).

Can the children be our saviors because they show us daily how to be born, how to grow and change, and so to be agents of God's reign? The reign of God is not transcendent or utopic, but is as concrete and vital as the life of a child. "The reign of God is life, life in its fullness and the fulfillment of life."[18] There is no list of requirements for entering, no categorical imperative to get us going. The apostle Paul had the wisdom of a child when he insisted that good works will not bring us close to God. We live by grace like a baby that lives only by the love and care of some adult. Only a child can lead us toward true life.

> Like a vulnerable child, "God comes to us from the future and has only one godlike gift: the lure. We are lured toward truth, beauty and goodness . . . the lure is pulling at our hearts like some lucid joy inside every actual occasion, and all we have to do is . . . say yes."[19]

There is no time to lose. As Gabriela Mistral said, "The name of the child is *today*."

# NOTES

## INTRODUCTION

1. UNICEF Key Figures 2005, UNICEF office, Köln, Germany. Regarding September 11, 2001, see the excellent work by Jon L. Berquist, ed., *Strike Terror No More: Theology, Ethics, and the New War* (St. Louis, Mo.: Chalice Press, 2002).

2. See, e.g., the Introduction to Patricia Eichenbaum Karetzky, *The Life of the Buddha: Ancient Scriptural and Pictorial Traditions* (Lanham, Md.: University Press of America, 1992), and Huston Smith, *The World's Religions: Our Great Wisdom Traditions* (New York: Harper Collins, 1991), 82ff.

3. See Paul Martin-Dubost, *Ganeśa: The Enchanter of the Three Worlds* (Mumbai: Project for Indian Cultural Studies, 1997), 42, 94.

4. See *Heraclitus, Fragments: A Text and Translation with a Commentary* by T. M. Robinson (Toronto: University of Toronto Press, 1987), 37, 116, 119ff.; Eduard Norden, *Die Geburt des Kindes: Geschichte einer religiösen Idee* (Leipzig: Teubner, 1924); and William Berg, *Early Virgil* (University of London: Athlone Press, 1974).

5. *The State of America's Children 2004* (Washington, D.C.: The Children's Defense Fund, 2004), 2.

6. *The Christian Century* (June 28, 2003), 38.

7. ABC News, January 2, 2000.

8. UNICEF Key Figures, 2005.

9. Ibid.; terre des hommes, *Kinderarbeit: Kein Kinderspiel* (Osnabrück, 2001), 2; and *Frankfurter Rundschau* (May 31, 1998), 6.

10. *The Christian Century* (April 19–26, 2000), 449.

11. *Generalanzeiger*, Bonn, July 14, 2004, quoting UNICEF, UNAIDS, and USAID.

12. Information from Alliance of AIDS Services-Carolina, Raleigh, N.C., December 2003.

13. World Food Organization and UNICEF, quoted in *The Christian Century* (October 25, 2000), 1092.

14. See Pauline Hunt and Ronald Frankenberg, "It's a Small World: Disneyland, the Family and the Multiple Re-presentations of American Childhood," in *Constructing and Reconstructing Childhood: Contemporary Issues in the Sociological Study of Childhood*, ed. Allison James and Alan Prout (London: Falmer Press, 1997).

15. Diana Gittens, *The Child in Question* (New York: St. Martin's Press, 1998), 4.

16. Ed Cairns, *Children and Political Violence* (Cambridge, Mass.: Blackwell Publications, 1996), 9. Cairns too uses the limit of eighteen years to define children.

17. Philippe Ariès, *Centuries of Childhood: A Social History of Family Life* (New York: Knopf, 1962).

18. Lloyd de Mause, ed., *The History of Childhood* (New York: Psychohistory Press, 1974). See also Nicholas Orme, *Medieval Children* (New Haven, Conn.:Yale University Press, 2002), for a picture of medieval childhood that is very different from Ariés's, and Willem Koops and Michael Zuckerman, eds., *Beyond the Century of the Child: Cultural History and Developmental Psychology* (Philadelphia: University of Pennsylvania Press, 2003). For other critics of Ariès, see Gittens, *The Child in Question*, 13, 26ff.

19. De Mause, *History of Childhood*, 5.

20. Rex Stainton Rogers and Wendy Stainton Rogers, *Stories of Childhood: Shifting Agendas of Child Concern* (Toronto: University of Toronto Press, 1992), 66; and see Nancy Scheper-Hughes, *Death Without Weeping: The Violence of Everyday Life in Brazil* (Berkeley: University of California Press, 1992).

21. Claudia Castañeda, *Figurations: Child, Bodies, Worlds* (Durham, N.C.: Duke University Press, 2002), 5.

22. Ibid., 27–29.

23. Ibid., 5.

24. Gittens, *The Child in Question,* 6.

25. Ibid., 43.

26. Ibid., 17.

27. Allison James, Chris Jenks, and Alan Prout, eds., *Theorizing Childhood* (New York: Teacher's College, Columbia University, 1998), 28.

28. Ibid., 24.

**CHAPTER 1**

1. Rainer Lachmann, s.v. "Kind," *Theologische Realencyclopädie,* vol. 18 (Berlin/New York: 1989), 168. Translation is mine.

2. Rita Nakashima Brock, "And a Little Child Will Lead Us: Christology and Child Abuse," in *Christianity, Patriarchy and Abuse: A Feminist Critique,* ed. Joanne Carlson Brown and Carol R. Bohn (New York: Pilgrim Press, 1989), 42.

3. Dawn DeVries, "Toward a Theology of Childhood," *Interpretation* 55, 2 (April 2001), 162.

4. For example, the *New International Dictionary of the Christian Church,* ed. J. D. Douglas (Grand Rapids, Mich.: Zondervan, 1974), has no entry for "child" or "children," just for "Children's Crusade" (!), even though it does have an entry for "Women in the Church, Place of."

5. Marcia J. Bunge, Introduction, *The Child in Christian Thought,* ed. Marcia J. Bunge (Grand Rapids, Mich.: Eerdmans, 2001), 3f. See also Catherine Maresca, "Children and Theology," *Sewanee Theological Review* 48, 1 (Christmas 2004), 11–15, about Schubert Ogden's focus on theology as a scientific task, whereas in James Cone's work it is growing out of the Christian community.

6. Bonnie Miller-McLemore, "'Let the Children Come' Revisited: Contemporary Feminist Theologians on Children," in *The Child in Christian Thought,* ed. Marcia J. Bunge (Grand Rapids, Mich.: Eerdmans, 2001), 465, 447, 452.

7. See, e.g., Nakashima Brock, "And a Little Child Will Lead Us" (see note 2).

8. Ulrich Luz, *Das Evangelium nach Matthäus,* EKK I, 3 (Zürich/Neukirchen-Vluyn: Neukirchener Verlag, 1997), 115. See also Kurt Sier, "Die Dialektik des 'Noch-Nicht'—Zur Representation des Kindes in der griechischen Literatur und Philosophie," in *Schau auf die Kleinen . . . : Das Kind in Religion, Kirche und Gesellschaft,* ed. Rüdiger Lux (Leipzig: Evangelische Verlagsanstalt, 2002), 54–81, where Hans Herter's emphasis on the uniqueness of Jesus' attitude toward children is relativized.

9. See Milan Machoveč, *A Marxist Looks at Jesus* (Philadelphia: Fortress Press, 1976), 99–100. I have asked Professor Machoveč where one could find a quote on Jesus' attitude toward children in Marx's works. He answered

that his reference was not to one of Marx's books, but that the sentence he had in mind is "absolutely proven to be accurate" because it is quoted by all the biographers who still knew Marx personally and also by one of his daughters: "One has to forgive Christianity a lot, because it taught the love for children." (Personal letter from Machoveč, of July 11, 2001.)

10. Judith Gundry-Volf, "Mark 9:33–37: Discipleship of Equals at the Cradle and the Cross," *Interpretation* 53, 1 (Jan. 1999), 61.

11. See UNICEF, *The State of the World's Children 2002: Leadership* (New York: UNICEF, 2002), 52: "Between 60 million and 100 million women are 'missing' from the world's population—victims of gender-based infanticide, feticide, malnutrition, and neglect." See also UNICEF, *The State of the World's Children 2004*, dedicated to "Girls, Education, and Development" (New York: UNICEF, 2003).

12. Robert Coles, *The Political Life of Children* (Boston: Houghton Mifflin, 1986).

13. Gerhard Krause, *Kinder im Evangelium* (Stuttgart: Ehrenfried Klotz Verlag, 1973); Hans-Ruedi Weber, *Jesus and the Children: Biblical Resources for Study and Preaching* (Geneva: World Council of Churches, 1979). The Spanish translation of this book has been widely used in Latin America.

14. Diana Wood, ed., *The Church and Childhood*, in *Studies in Church History*, vol. 31 (Oxford: Blackwell, 1994).

15. *Concilium* 32, 2 (1996).

16. Judith Gundry-Volf, "'To Such as These Belongs the Reign of God': Jesus and Children," *Theology Today* 56, 4 (Jan. 2000), 469–80; "Discipleship of Equals at the Cradle and the Cross," *Interpretation* 53, 1 (Jan. 1999): 57–61.

17. Bonnie Miller-McLemore, "'Let the Children Come' Revisited: Contemporary Feminist Theologians on Children," in Bunge, ed., *The Child in Christian Thought*, 472. In addition, see her *Also a Mother: Work and Family as Theological Dilemma* (Nashville: Abingdon Press, 1994), and her more recent volume, *Let the Children Come: Reimagining Childhood from a Christian Perspective* (San Francisco: Jossey-Bass, 2003).

18. Pamela D. Couture, *Seeing Children, Seeing God: A Practical Theology of Children and Poverty* (Nashville: Abingdon Press, 2000).

19. Peter Müller, *In der Mitte der Gemeinde: Kinder im Neuen Testament* (Neukirchen-Vluyn: Neukirchener Verlag, 1992).

20. Martin Ebner et al., eds., *Gottes Kinder: Jahrbuch für biblische Theologie* 17 (Neukirchen-Vluyn: Neukirchener Verlag, 2002).

21. Rüdiger Lux, ed., *Schau auf die Kleinen . . . Das Kind in Religion, Kirche und Gesellschaft* (Leipzig: Evangelische Verlagsanstalt, 2002). A more recent German publication and a goldmine of historical information is Marc Kleijwegt's article "Kind" in the *Reallexicon für Antike und Christentum* (2004).

22. David H. Jensen, *Graced Vulnerability: A Theology of Childhood* (Cleveland: Pilgrim Press, 2005). The book appeared after I had finished my own manuscript.

23. Jacquelyn Grant, "A Theologial Framework," in Charles R. Foster and Grant S. Shockley, eds., *Working with Black Youth: Opportunities for Christian Ministry* (Nashville: Abingdon Press, 1989), 55–76.

24. Joan Martin, "Public Education and the Battle over the Nature of Social Responsibility to the Nation's Children and Schools," *Journal of the American Academy of Religion*, 70, 4 (December 2002); and Evelyn L. Parker, *Trouble Don't Last Always: Emancipatory Hope among African American Adolescents* (Cleveland: Pilgrim Press, 2003). See also Parker's essay, "Hungry for Honor: Children in Violent Youth Gangs," *Interpretation* 55, 2 (April 2001): 148–60.

25. *The Journal of the Interdenominational Center*, vol. 30, 1 and 2 (Fall 2002/Spring 2003).

26. Danna Nolan Fewell, *The Children of Israel: Reading the Bible for the Sake of Our Children* (Nashville: Abingdon Press, 2003).

27. E-mail message from Agencia Latinoamericana y Caribeña de Comunicación, Lima, Peru, September 26, 2003.

28. E-mail from Agencia Latinoamericana y Caribeña de Comunicación, February 1 and 2, 2004.

29. For more information about the project, contact Dr. Reidar Aasgaard, e-mail: reidar.aasgaard@teologi.uio.no.

30. See Jonathan Fineberg, with Helmut Friedel and Josef Helfenstein, eds., *Mit dem Auge des Kindes: Kinderzeichnung und moderne Kunst* (München, Bern: Verlag Gerhard Hatje, 1995). See also *Kindheit und Moderne von Klee bis Boltanski*, ed. Städtische Galerie Bietigheim-Bissingen, 2001).

31. The exhibit was also shown in Aschaffenburg. The catalog, *"Kinder des zwanzigsten Jahrhunderts: Malerei, Skulptur, Photographie,"* ed. Christa Murken et al. (2000), is available from the Mittelrhein Museum Koblenz.

32. Elise Boulding, *Children's Rights and the Wheel of Life* (New Brunswick, N.J.: Transaction Books, 1979), 85.

33. Personal communication, April 5, 2000. Bartlett confirmed the statement in March of 2003.

34. Bartlett mentioned Barbara Woodhouse, Martha Minow, James Dwyer, and Mary Ann Mason. The recent interdisciplinary volume *Rethinking Childhood*, ed. Peter B. Pufall and Richard P. Unsworth (New Brunswick, N.J.: Rutgers University Press, 2004), contains the excellent article by Barbara Bennett Woodhouse, " Re-Visioning Rights for Children."

35. See Nina Bernstein, "Children Alone and Scared, Fighting Deportation," *New York Times*, March 28, 2003.

36. See notes 17 and 18 of my introduction.

37. Barbara Tuchman, *A Distant Mirror: The Calamitous 14th Century* (New York: Alfred Knopf, 1978).

38. Paula S. Fass and Mary Ann Mason, eds., *Childhood in America* (New York: New York University Press, 2000). See also Mary Ann Mason, *From Fathers' Property to Children's Rights: The History of Child Custody in the U.S.* (New York: Columbia University Press, 1994).

39. Gareth B. Matthews, *The Philosophy of Childhood* (Cambridge, Mass.: Harvard University Press, 1994), and his earlier works, *Philosophy and the Young Child* (1980) and *Dialogues with Children* (1984).

40. See chapter 6, notes 40 and 41 on this and other titles on the topic.

41. Anita Hamilton, "All the Right Questions: Discussion Groups Based on the Teachings of Socrates Are Reviving the Art of Conversation," *Time* (April 5, 2004), 65f.

42. Eileen W. Lindner, "Children as Theologians," in Peter B. Pufall and Richard P. Unsworth, eds., *Rethinking Childhood* (New Brunswick, N.J.: Rutgers University Press, 2004).

43. Robin Maas, "Christ as the Logos of Childhood: Reflections on the Meaning and Mission of the Child," *Theology Today* 56, 4 (January 2000): 458.

44. Bonnie Miller-McLemore makes the point that the subject matter of children "requires a radical rethinking of the theological encyclopedia. . . . To think about children theologically requires movement across the conventionally separated disciplines." Bonnie Miller-McLemore, *Let the Children Come: Reimagining Childhood from a Christian Perspective* (San Francisco: Jossey-Bass, 2003), xxix.

45. Dietrich Bonhoeffer, *Act and Being* (New York: Harper & Brothers, 1961), 182.

46. Jürgen Moltmann, "Child and Childhood as Metaphors of Hope," *Theology Today* (January 2000): 603.

47. Elisabeth Moltmann-Wendel, "Natalität und die Liebe zur Welt. Hannah Arendt's Beitrag zu einer immanenten Transzendenz," *Evangelische Theologie* 58 (1998): 283–95.

48. Elisabeth Moltmann-Wendel, *Wer die Erde nicht berührt, kann den Himmel nicht erreichen . . . Autobiographie* (Zürich: Benziger Verlag, 1997), 253.

49. Grace M. Jantzen, *Becoming Divine: Towards a Feminist Theology of Religion* (Bloomington: Indiana University Press, 1999), 150.

50. Karin Ulrich-Eschemann, *Vom Geborenwerden des Menschen: Theologische und philosophische Erkundungen* (Münster: LIT-Verlag, 2000), 33. Translation is mine. The reference is to Arendt's "Freiheit und Politik" in her *Zwischen Vergangenheit und Zukunft* (München, 1994), 206.

51. Maas, "Christ as the Logos of Childhood," 458.
52. Quoted from Johann Christoph Arnold, *Endangered: Your Child in a Hostile World* (Farmington, Pa.: Plough Publishing, 2000), 132.
53. Hermann L. Strack und Paul Billerbeck, *Das Evangelium des Matthäus erläutert aus Talmud und Midrasch* (München: C.H. Beck, 1926, 1956), 781.
54. Janusz Korczak, *Leben für andere: Gedanken und Meditationen von Janusz Korczak,* ed. Friedhelm Beiner and Erich Dauzenroth (Gütersloh: Kiefel, 1997), 5. Translation is mine. About Korczak's life and work, see also Aleksander Lewin, *So war es wirklich: Die letzten Lebensjahre und das Vermächtnis Janusz Korczaks* (Gütersloh: Gütersloher Verlagshaus, 1998).
55. See Korczak as quoted by Arnold, *Endangered,* 56.
56. Thich Nhat Hanh, *Going Home: Jesus and Buddha as Brothers* (New York: Penguin Putnam, 1999), 66f.
57. Czeslaw Z. Prokopczyk, ed., *Bruno Schulz: New Documents and Interpretations* (New York: Peter Lang, 1999), 101. For Schulz, creative ideas, the courage for invention, are rooted in our childhood dreams and memories. We have to tap into these reserves, this "frozen capital" (ibid., 124). See also Jerzy Ficowski, ed., *Letters and Drawings of Bruno Schulz* (New York: Harper & Row, 1988).

**CHAPTER 2**

1. UNICEF Key Figures 2005. See also http://www.unicef.org/media /media_9475.html.
2. Sharon Ringe called my attention to the fact that these texts have to be seen against the background of Israel's exile when the study of the Torah, now practiced also by childless women and eunuchs, became the defining characteristic of Judaism.
3. Erhard Gerstenberger and Wolfgang Schrage, *Frau und Mann* (Stuttgart: Kohlhammer, 1980), 24.
4. Carol Meyers, "The Family in Early Israel," in *Families in Ancient Israel,* ed. Leo G. Perdue, Joseph Blenkinsopp, John J. Collins, and Carol Meyers (Louisville, Ky.: Westminster John Knox Press, 1998), 27.
5. Ibid., 31. About punishment of children in Israel, see James L. Crenshaw, *Education in Ancient Israel: Across the Deadening Silence* (New York: Doubleday, 1998), 149, 165–167, 203, 208.
6. Hans-Ruedi Weber, *Jesus and the Children: Biblical Resources for Study and Preaching* (Geneva: World Council of Churches, 1979), 6. See also Judith M. Gundry-Volf, "Discipleship of Equals at the Cradle and the Cross," *Interpretation* 53, 1 (Jan. 1999), 58. While the abandoning of children was mostly a primitive way of population control—with girls as the

more numerous victims because they did not guarantee the financial stability of the family that the male breadwinner represented—cultic motives may also have played a part, as Albrecht Oepke suggests in Gerhard Kittel, *Theologisches Wörterbuch zum Neuen Testament* (Grand Rapids: Eerdmans, 1964–76), vol. 5, 639.

About the legal and practical details concerning the abandoning of newborn children in antiquity, see Marc Kleijwegt, s.v. "Kind," in *Reallexikon für Antike und Christentum*, ed. Georg Schöllgen et al. (Stuttgart: Anton Hiersmann, 2004), 866–947, specifically 924–31.

7. Hans Wildberger, *Jesaja Kapitel 1–12*, Biblischer Kommentar. Altes Testament (Neukirchen-Vluyn: Neukirchener Verlag, 1972), 377, assumes that the texts in Isaiah 9 and 11 definitely relate to the birth of a royal child, an event that has already occurred and that will guarantee the continuation of YHWH's covenant and the Davidian line. *The Interpreter's Bible*, vol. 5 (New York/Nashville: Abingdon, 1956), 247, asserts that the texts are related to the royal accession ceremony described in 2 Kings 11:12–19 and that they may have been composed by Isaiah for the anointing of Hezekiah.

8. Jon D. Levenson, *The Death and Resurrection of the Beloved Son: The Transformation of Child Sacrifice in Judaism and Christianity* (New Haven, Conn.: Yale University Press, 1993), 205.

9. Wildberger, *Jesaja*, 383–88.

10. Actually Hicks (1780–1849) painted this scene in at least twenty-five versions, often with Penn and the Indians in the background. He was a self-taught painter of houses and coaches and a Quaker preacher in various states of the country. The painting I have in mind is dated around 1840–45. See the picture in my chapter 3.

For the interpretation of Isaiah 9 and 11 see *The Interpreter's Bible*, vol. 5 (see note 7); and Sharon Ringe and Carol Newsom, *Women's Bible Commentary*, expanded edition (Louisville, Ky.: Westminster John Knox Press, 1998), 169–77.

11. T. M. Robinson, *Heraclitus: Fragments: A Text and Translation with a Commentary* (Toronto: University of Toronto Press, 1987), 37, 166, 119f. About Virgil, see Eduard Norden, *Die Geburt des Kindes : Geschichte einer religiösen Idee* (Leipzig: Teubner, 1924), and William Berg, *Early Virgil* (University of London: Athlone Press, 1974).

12. Lam. Rabba, 1,33, at 1,6; quoted from Charlotte Klein, *Theologie und Anti-Judaismus: Eine Studie zur deutschen theologischen Literatur der Gegenwart* (München: Kaiser, 1975), 17. Translation is mine.

13. *The Book of Jubilee* 23, 28. I have translated the sentence from the German edition in P. Riessler, *Altjüdisches Schrifttum ausserhalb der Bibel* (Augsburg, 1928), 601.

14. See, e.g., Carol Delaney, *Abraham on Trial: The Social Legacy of Biblical Myth* (Princeton, N.J.: Princeton University Press, 1998).

15. The vessel is located in the Museum für Völkerkunde, Preussischer Kulturbesitz, Berlin, and is probably from about 700 B.C.E. See the illustration in my chapter 3. The Andean people practiced human sacrifices only at special occasions, like the ascent or death of a ruler, the beginning of war, or the threat of an epidemic. At one occasion more than two hundred children between four and twelve years were buried alive, two by two, boys and girls. They were sacrificed to Sun, Moon, Thunder, or Earth. See María Rostworowski, *La mujer en la época prehispánica* (Lima: Instituto de Estudios Peruanos, 1988), 10.

16. Levenson, *Death and Resurrection*, 189–99.

17. Ibid., 173f.

18. In ancient Rome some state officials had their sons executed because they had committed a crime against the state, and the loyalty to the *res publica* was considered above the loyalty to a child. See Kleijwegt, "Kind," 891.

19. See Milton Schwantes, "Do Not Extend Your Hand against the Child": Observations on Genesis 21 and 22," in *Subversive Scriptures: Revolutionary Readings of the Christian Bible in Latin America*, ed. Leif E. Vaage (Valley Forge, Pa.: Trinity Press International, 1997), 101–23.

20. Phyllis Trible, review of Carol Delaney, "Abraham on Trial: The Social Legacy of Biblical Myth," *Journal of the American Academy of Religion* 69, 4 (Dec. 2001), 926.

21. Associated Press article in the *Herald-Sun*, Durham, N.C., April 4, 2004, A7.

22. Frank Crüsemann, "Gott als Anwalt der Kinder!? Zur Frage von Kinderrechten in der Bibel," in *Gottes Kinder*, Jahrbuch für biblische Theologie, ed. Martin Ebner et al. (Neukirchen-Vluyn: Neukirchener Verlag, 2002), 190. Anthropologically it is interesting that other religious traditions also imagine a duality in God. The indigenous Tarahumaras of northwestern Mexico see themselves as physically descended from the "Corn Mother" as well as symbolically and morally from "the one who is the father." This dual descent influences their attitudes toward violence and nonviolence. There is a constant tension between the need for violent sacrifices that give strength to the divine father and the insight that violence should be avoided because it might destroy the very life of the tribe as it is represented by "Corn Mother." See Evelyne Puchegger-Ebner, "Uniendo Fronteras: Violence and Non-Violence as Strategies for Demarcating and Crossing Boundaries," *European Review of Native American Studies* 16:2 (2002), 29–38.

23. Danna Nolan Fewell, *The Children of Israel: Reading the Bible for the Sake of Our Children* (Nashville: Abingdon, 2003), 110–13, has made the good point that hard-to-understand biblical stories can be helpful "interruptions" in our life and in the life of children. I will come back to her argument in chapter 6.

Today the story of Abraham and Isaac can trigger fruitful discussions between Jews, Christians, and Muslims, all of whom interpret it differently. See Bruce Feiler, *Abraham: A Journey to the Heart of Three Faiths* (New York: HarperCollins, 2002), and the article, "The Legacy of Abraham," *Time*, Sept. 30, 2002. I will refer to Feiler's book in chapter 3.

24. The connection between Isaac and the Suffering Servant of Isaiah 40–55 is discussed in Levenson, *Death and Resurrection*, 200ff.

25. Sharon Ringe, *Wisdom's Friends: Community and Christology in the Fourth Gospel* (Louisville, Ky.: Westminster John Knox Press, 1999), 36. About the imaging of Wisdom as daughter, see Athalia Brenner, "Some Observations on the Figurations of Woman in Wisdom Literature," in Athalia Brenner, ed., *A Feminist Companion to Wisdom Literature* (Sheffield: Sheffield Academic Press, 1995), 55.

26. See Carol R. Fontaine on the personification of Wisdom in "Proverbs," in *Harper's Bible Commentary*, ed. J. L. Mays (San Francisco: Harper & Row, 1988), 508: "Maat is both playful child and master plan for creation."

27. *The New Interpreter's Bible*, vol. 5 (Nashville: Abingdon, 1999), 94.

28. Otto Plöger, *Sprüche Salomos (Proverbia)* (Neukirchen-Vluyn: Neukirchener Verlag, 1984), 95f. As Sharon Ringe states, the redaction of this text is post-exilic, probably from the late sixth or early fifth century, when the crisis of exile was still a fresh memory, the focus on the Torah not yet as sharp as later, and the social context providing a dramatic increase in the authority of women. (Ringe, *Wisdom's Friends*, 33–34.)

29. Ringe, ibid., 46. See *Philo*, "On Flight and Finding," vol. V, trans. F. H. Colson and G. H. Whitaker (London; Cambridge, Mass.: William Heinemann/Harvard University Press, 1958), 69. Cf. also in the same edition, Supplement I, "Questions and Answers," trans. Ralph Marcus, 381.

30. Wolfgang Schrage, *Unterwegs zur Einheit und Einzigkeit Gottes: Zum "Monotheismus" des Paulus und seiner alttestamentlich-frühjüdischen Tradition* (Neukirchen-Vluyn: Neukirchener Verlag, 2002), 109.

31. Elizabeth A. Johnson, *She Who Is: The Mystery of God in Feminist Discourse* (New York: Crossroad, 1992), 95.

32. See Schrage, *Unterwegs zur Einheit*, 109, referring to Ethiopian Henoch 42.2 in its German translation (*Jüdische Schriften aus hellenistisch-römischer Zeit*, vol. V, 6 [Gütersloh: Gütersloher Verlagshaus, 1984], 584).

33. At the same time Wisdom has immediate political ramifications, as Claudia Camp points out in "Woman Wisdom as Root Metaphor: A Theological Consideration," in *The Listening Heart: Essays in Wisdom and the Psalms Presented to Roland E. Murphy*, ed. K. G. Hoglund et al. (JSOT Sup, 58; Sheffield: JSOT Press, 1987), 66–70.

34. 11Q5, Col. XVIII (Psalm 154), 3–5 in *The Dead Sea Scrolls Translated: The Qumran Texts in English*, ed. Florentino García Martínez (Leiden: E. J. Brill, 1994), 304.

35. Carol Meyers points to the lack of knowledge about everyday family life because the biblical authors were elite males, mostly from urban areas. *The Family in Ancient Israel*, 4.

36. On children in Roman society, see T. E. J. Wiedemann, *Adults and Children in the Roman Empire* (New Haven: Yale University Press, 1989), and Kleijwegt, "Kind," 866–91.

37. Andries van Aarde, *Fatherless in Galilee: Jesus as Child of God* (Harrisburg, Pa.: Trinity Press International, 2001), 129, 154.

38. See Exod. 22:22; Ps. 82:3; Isa. 1:17; Hos. 14:3.

39. See Frank Crüsemann, "Die Macht der kleinen Kinder: Ein Versuch, Psalm 8, 2b.3 zu verstehen," in *Was ist der Mensch? Festschrift für Hans-Walter Wolff*, ed. Frank Crüsemann (München: Kaiser, 1992), 54f.

40. Van Aarde, *Fatherless in Galilee*, 106, 98.

41. See John P. Meier, *A Marginal Jew: Rethinking the Historical Jesus*, vol. I (New York: Doubleday, 1991), 222.

42. Van Aarde, *Fatherless in Galilee*, 73f.

43. This is of course not just a modern idea. The apocryphal Gospel of Philip sees the "virgin birth" not as something that happened once to Jesus. "Philip suggests instead that Jesus' resurrection, like his virgin birth, is not only something that occurred in the past but is a paradigm of what happens to each person who undergoes spiritual transformation." Elaine Pagels, *Beyond Belief: The Secret Gospel of Thomas* (New York: Random House, 2003), 132.

44. Jane Schaberg, *The Illegitimacy of Jesus: A Feminist Theological Interpretation of the Infancy Narratives* (San Francisco: Harper & Row, 1987), 45f., 50, 67.

45. Schaberg, *The Illegitimacy of Jesus*, 57.

46. Meier, *A Marginal Jew*, 230, 246.

47. Ibid., 213, 217, 220–30, 331.

48. Virgilio Elizondo, *The Future Is Mestizo: Life Where Cultures Meet*, rev. ed. (Boulder: University Press of Colorado, 2000), 77, 79.

49. Kleijwegt, "Kind," 905. Translation is mine.

50. The gnostically influenced Gospel of Thomas (saying 22) does contain some cryptic allusion to infants as lacking sexual differentiation and

therefore representing some divine innocence or union of opposites. See the text in Pagels, *Beyond Belief,* 231. I find it surprising that Pagels—given the subtitle of her book—does not discuss the view of childhood in the *Gospel of Thomas.*

51. Cranach's painting (dated 1538) is found in the Kunsthalle Hamburg. (See the illustration in my chapter 3.) Since the pronoun "them" in the phrase, "the disciples rebuked them," is masculine in the Greek text, it is likely that the children were not just brought by mothers. See William Lane, *The Gospel According to Mark* (Grand Rapids, Mich.: Eerdmans, 1974), 358f. The baptism of infants cannot be definitely ascertained before the third century. See Kleijwegt, "Kind," 930.

52. Weber, *Jesus and the Children,* 16.

53. Luz, *Das Evangelium nach Matthäus,* 114–17; Gundry-Volf, "To Such as These Belongs the Reign," 471; Joseph A. Fitzmyer, S.J., *The Gospel According to Luke (X–XXIV)* (Garden City, N.Y.: Doubleday, 1985), 1193. See also Ingetraut Ludolphy, "Zur Geschichte der Auslegung des Evangelium infantium," in Gerhard Krause, ed., *Die Kinder im Evangelium* (Stuttgart: Ehrenfried Klotz Verlag, 1973), 32: "Neither in the early church nor in the Middle Ages can documents be found that relate the text of Mark 10:13ff. to the baptism of children." Translation is mine.

54. Weber, *Jesus and the Children,* 15.

55. Ibid., 46.

56. Elisabeth Moltmann-Wendel, "Natalität und die Liebe zur Welt: Hannah Arendts Beitrag zu einer immanenten Transzendenz," *Evangelische Theologie* 58 (1998): 283–95.

57. See Kleijwegt, "Kind," 866.

58. See Albrecht Oepke in Gerhard Kittel, *Theologisches Wörterbuch zum Neuen Testament,* vol. 5, 637; and Walter Zimmerli in the same volume, 655ff.

59. Judith Gundry-Volf, "Mark 9:33–37: Discipleship of Equals at the Cradle and the Cross," *Interpretation* 53, 1 (Jan. 1999): 59–60.

60. Sharon Ringe, private communication of April 15, 2003.

61. Quoted from Johnson, *She Who Is,* 99.

62. Quoted from Thomas Wiedemann, *Adults and Children in the Roman Empire* (New Haven, Ct.: Yale University Press, 1989), 104, referring to Augustine's Letters 69, 1; 93, 50.

63. Mary Grey, "Beyond the Dark Night—A *Kenotic* Church Moves On . . . ?" in Johannes Brosseder, ed., *Verborgener Gott—Verborgene Kirche: Die kenotische Theologie und ihre ekklesiologischen Implikationen* (Stuttgart: Kohlhammer, 2001), 54. Emphasis is Grey's.

64. Annie Dillard, *Holy the Firm* (New York: Harper & Row, 1977), 47.

65. Gershom Sholem, *Major Trends in Jewish Mysticism* (New York: Schocken Books, 1946), 260–65, 271, 273, 297, 411ff. The idea of *Tzimtzum* was developed by Isaac Luria (1534–1572).

66. Grey, "Beyond the Dark Night," 62. On page 55 Grey mentions Philip Newell's phrase that "justice is the heartbeat of God."

67. Abraham Joshua Heschel, in a speech to the White House Council on Aging, January 9, 1961, Washington, D.C.

68. See my reference to Danna Nolan Fewell in note 23.

69. See Kleijwegt, "Kind," 871f.

70. Wolfgang Schrage, *The Ethics of the New Testament* (Philadelphia: Fortress Press, 1988, 1990), 253.

71. I have quoted these texts from Elaine Pagels, *Beyond Belief*, 231, 227.

72. Mark 5:22–24, 35–43; Luke 7:11–17; Mark 7:24–30; John 4:46–54.

## CHAPTER 3

1. Confucius, *The Analects*, IX, 23, trans. David Hinton (Washington, D.C.: Counterpoint, 1998), 96.

2. Ulrich Luz, *Das Evangelium nach Matthäus* (Neukirchen/Vluyn: Benziger/Neukirchener Verlag, 1997), 115.

3. Milan Machoveč, *A Marxist Looks at Jesus* (Philadelphia: Fortress Press, 1976), 99–100. See note 9 of my chapter 1 concerning the authenticity of Karl Marx's statement.

4. I agree in this regard with the arguments of David H. Jensen, *In the Company of Others: A Dialogical Christology* (Cleveland: Pilgrim Press), 2001.

5. See *The Book of Discipline of the Methodist Church* (Nashville: United Methodist Publishing House, 1988), 82–86.

6. *Religious Studies News*, American Academy of Religion, Fall 2000, 6.

7. See Joseph Epes Brown, *The Spiritual Legacy of the American Indian* (New York: Crossroad, 1987), x.

8. Willard G. Oxtoby, ed., *World Religions: Eastern Traditions* (Toronto, New York, Oxford: Oxford University Press, 1996), 16ff.

9. Richard A. Horsley, "Religion and Other Products of Empire," *Journal of the American Academy of Religion* 71, 1 (March 2003): 13–44.

10. Rosemary Radford Ruether, introduction to Daniel C. Maguire and Larry L. Rasmussen, *Ethics for a Small Planet: New Horizons on Population, Consumption, and Ecology* (Albany: State University of New York Press, 1998), xii. Jeannine Hill Fletcher has made the good point that every "religion" comprises a great variety of ideas and practices, and every member of a certain religion actually has a hybrid identity because we belong to

different ethnic or economic groups and different cultures and genders while confessing the same "religion." Since feminism has long insisted on this hybridity, it can make a special contribution to a solidarity with members of other "religions" who are just as much characterized by a web of identity and are not just "Jews," Hindus," or "Confucians." Jeannine Hill Fletcher, "Shifting Identity: The Contribution of Feminist Thought to Theologies of Religious Pluralism," *Journal of Feminist Studies in Religion* 19, 2 (Fall 2003): 5–24.

11. Vasudha Narayanan, "Embodied Cosmologies: Sights of Piety, Sites of Power," *Journal of the American Academy of Religion*, 71, 3 (September 2003), 495.

12. I will repeat here some points from the introduction and chapters 1 and 2 in order to tie the biblical considerations to the pictures under discussion.

13. See illustration 1. Emil Nolde, *Jesus and the Children*, 1910, Museum of Modern Art, New York.

14. Gerhard Krause, ed., *Die Kinder im Evangelium* (Stuttgart: Ehrenfried Klotz, 1973), 24, suggests that Mark's statement that Jesus was "indignant" may have been left out by Matthew and Luke because it appeared to be too harsh.

15. Weber, *Jesus and the Children*, 46.

16. See illustration 2. Lukas Cranach the Elder, *Christ Blessing the Children*, 1538, Kunsthalle Hamburg.

17. On Heraclitus and Virgil, see note 4 of the introduction.

18. See Associated Press articles in *The Herald-Sun*, Durham, N.C., Jan. 8 and 16, 2000, and Feb. 19, 2000. The interview was reported by the German *Spiegel*, May 7, 2001, 192.

19. See illustration 3. About Hicks and this picture, see note 10 of chapter 2. Besides being a painter, Hicks was a Quaker minister much in demand for his sermons.

20. See illustration 4 and see Thomas F. Mathews, *The Clash of the Gods: A Reinterpretation of Early Christian Art* (Princeton, N.J.: Princeton University Press, rev. ed., 1993), 29, 124ff.

21. See illustration 5, taken from Hans Wolfgang Schumann, *Buddhistische Bilderwelt: Ein ikonographisches Handbuch des Mahāyāna-und Tantrayāna-Buddhismus* (Köln: Eugen Diederichs Verlag, 1986), 51.

22. Patricia Eichenbaum Karetzky, *The Life of the Buddha: Ancient Scriptural and Pictorial Traditions* (Lanham, Md.: University Press of America, 1992), introduction (no page number); Roy C. Amore in Oxtoby, ed., *World Religions: Eastern Traditions*, 221–23; and Huston Smith, *The World's Religions: Our Great Wisdom Traditions* (New York: HarperCollins, 1991), 82f.

23. See Zacharias P. Thundy, *Buddha and Christ: Nativity Stories and Indian Traditions* (Leiden: E.J. Brill, 1993), esp. 106–24, 151–54.

24. The Puranas are compilations of the ancient Brahmanic cosmogonies, describing also the lineage of the gods, the great sages, and the royal dynasties. Parts of the Sanskrit scriptures were recorded before the Christian era, but some Puranas—in vernacular languages—originated as late as the eighteenth century.

25. Paul Martin-Dubost, *Gaṇeśa: The Enchanter of the Three Worlds* (Mumbai: Project for Indian Cultural Studies, 1997), 42.

26. Ibid., 44.

27. The picture can be found in Martin-Dubost, *Gaṇeśa,* 40.

28. Ibid., 232.

29. For example, in the pictures of Chagall's Exodus cycle, Moses is shown repeatedly with an angel who has an animal head while holding the Torah, indicating the unity of nature, humans, and divine law. Chagall's twelve windows of the Hadassa hospital in Jerusalem are teeming with animals and plants: dancing pigeons, flying fishes, a grim lion, a patient donkey, merging with Torah, menorah, and iron serpent as well as trees, flowers, and stars, all representing the twelve Hebrew tribes.

30. See illustration 7. The Pharaoh Akhenaten and his wife Nefertiti with three of their daughters, 1350–1334 B.C.E. Ägyptisches Museum Berlin.

31. See the catalogue of the Egyptian Museum in Cairo, picture #168 in the German edition. I thank Ute Honecker for this reference.

32. John Stratton Hawley, *Krishna the Butter Thief* (Princeton, N.J.: Princeton University Press, 1983). My illustration 8 shows a calendar picture from the front page of Hawley's book. Krishna steals "butter," because India's traditional butter is white, semiliquid, churned from curd rather than cream, and is sweeter than our butter (5).

33. Ibid. 298f., 48f., 119, 132f.

34. Ibid., 17.

35. Jürgen Moltmann, *God in Creation: An Ecological Doctrine of Creation* (London: SCM Press, 1985), 110.

36. Huston Smith, *The World's Religions: Our Great Wisdom Traditions* (New York: Harper Collins, 1991), 71.

37. See Ana Castillo, Introduction to *Goddess of the Americas: Writings on the Virgin of Guadalupe,* ed. Ana Castillo (New York: Riverhead Books, 1996), xix.

38. Paula Richman, *Extraordinary Child: Poems from a South Indian Devotional Genre* (Honolulu: University of Hawaii Press, 1997), 21. I follow Richman for my whole discussion of the *pillaittamil.*

39. Ibid., 162.

40. Ibid., 164–67.

41. Margaret Trawick, *Notes on Love in a Tamil Family* (Berkeley: University of California Press, 1990), 215.

42. See Sudhir Kakar, *The Inner World: A Psychoanalytic Study of Childhood and Society in India* (Delhi: Oxford University Press, 1978), 20.

43. Thich Nhat Hanh, *Going Home: Jesus and Buddha as Brothers* (New York: Penguin Putnam, 1999), 108.

44. Ibid., 92.

45. See H. Saddhatissa, *The Life of the Buddha* (New York: Harper & Row, 1976), 23, 34, 53. Also, we should remember that even Jesus is supposed to have said, "Whoever comes to me and does not hate father and mother, wife and children . . . yes, and even life itself, cannot be my disciple" (Luke 14:26), although in Matt. 19:29 and Mark 10:29–30 this word has a different emphasis: whoever gives up all this will receive it back "a hundredfold." Children ought to be honored and loved, but not idolized or put in the place of God. A too strong tie to a child can be a temptation to forget about truth and integrity. This idea can also be found among Tamil Indians who believe that, if a mother gazed too lovingly at her child, it could bring harm. (See Trawick, *Notes on Love*, 93f.).

46. Gustav Mensching, ed., *Leben und Legende der Religionsstifter* (Darmstadt: Holle Verlag, no date), 237–39.

47. See illustration 9, the *arhat Hvāsáng*. Woodcut from Schumann, *Buddhistische Bilderwelt*, 232. Another image of Hvāsháng is a Tibetan portable icon from the seventeenth century, depicted in *Worlds of Transformation: Tibetan Art of Wisdom and Compassion*, ed. Marilyn M. Rhie and Robert A. F. Thurman (New York: Tibet House, 1999), 168.

48. Willard G. Oxtoby, ed., *World Religions: Western Traditions* (Toronto, etc.: Oxford University Press, 1996), 370.

49. Koran, Sura 19:35; 19:91–94; 21:26; 10:69. I have used the translation by N. J. Dawood, *The Koran* (London: Penguin Books, 1956).

50. Sura 3:40–44; 10:109–15; 19:30–34.

51. Mensching, *Leben und Legende der Religionsstifter*, 144–46.

52. Sura 6:137, 140, 151; 16:57–62; 17:34; 81:8.

53. Sura 3:193; 4:124; 33:35. Concerning the education of girls, a text from the Hadith, the later tradition (ninth century), says that the person who brings up two or three daughters or sisters, who educates them, is good to them, and provides them with a spouse, will enter paradise. (From the Hadith collections of Abu Dawud and Tirmidhi, quoted in the appendix of the German Koran translation by Adel Theodor Khoury (Gütersloh: Gütersloher Verlagshaus, 1987), 532.

54. Sura 24:32–33.

55. Sura 4:11–12, 176.

56. Sura 4:10, 127.

57. For stories about the prophet's tender love of children, see, e.g., William E. Phipps, *Muhammad and Jesus: A Comparison of the Prophets and Their Teaching* (New York: Continuum, 1996), 120.

58. Oxtoby, *World Religions*, 385.

59. Bruce Feiler, *Abraham: A Journey to the Heart of Three Faiths* (New York: HarperCollins, 2004, 2002), 84.

60. Ibid., 35.

61. Ibid., 108.

62. Mensching, *Leben und Legende der Religionsstifter*, 278.

63. See Mark Csikszentmihalyi, "Confucius," in *The Rivers of Paradise: Moses, Buddha, Confucius, Jesus, and Muhammad as Religious Founders*, ed. Noel Freedman and Michael McClymond (Grand Rapids, Mich.: Eerdmans, 2001), 304f. "Heaven" is something like destiny in Confucius, "the inevitable evolution of things according to the principle inherent in them," according to David Hinton, ed., *Confucius, The Analects*, xxix.

64. Csikszentmihalyi, 255. *The Analects* were written down by Confucius' successors of the first and second generation "Confucius." A helpful article on the Western failure to understand the legacy of Confucianism today is Mary I. Bockover, "The Internet in China: A Confucian Critique," *Religion East and West: Journal of the Institute of World Religions* 2 (June 2002): 91–100.

65. Kirill O. Thompson, review of *Confucius and the Analects: New Essays*, ed. Bryan W. Van Norden. *Journal of the American Academy of Religion*, 72, 1 (March 2004): 285.

66. Kurtis Hagen, "Xunzi and the Nature of Confucian Ritual," *Journal of the American Academy of Religion* 71, 2 (June 2003): 377, quoting Roger T. Ames and Henry Rosemont, Jr., *The Analects of Confucius: A Philosophical Translation* (New York: Ballentine Books, 1998), 51.

67. Csikszentmihalyi, "Confucius," 254. See illustration 10. This picture of 1826 is from Gu Yuan, *Shengji tu*. Beijing: Xianzhuang.

68. *Tao te Ching: The Definitive Edition*, Translation and commentary by Jonathan Star (New York: Jeremy P. Tarcher/Putnam, 2001), 1. My quotations are from this edition. A more easily read, free translation is Ursula K. Le Guin, *Lao Tzu Tao te Ching: A Book about the Way and the Power of the Way*. A new English version by Ursula K. Le Guin with the collaboration of J. P. Seaton (Boston and London: Shambhala, 1997).

69. Star, *Tao te Ching*, 2.

70. John C. Raines, Introduction to *What Men Owe to Women: Men's Voices from World Religions*, ed. John C. Raines and Daniel C. Maguire (Albany, N.Y.: State University of New York Press, 2001), 1.

71. The UNICEF office in Köln, Germany, confirmed in June 2005 that the number they are working with is still thirty thousand. Several years ago it was thirty-four thousand.

72. Philip Ariès, *Centuries of Childhood: A Social History of Family Life* (New York: Knopf, 1962). Neil Postman, *The Disappearance of Childhood* (New York: Vintage Books, 1994).

73. Feiler, *Abraham*, 49, quoting an Irish Catholic priest.

74. See illustration 11. About child sacrifice among the Aztecs, see David Carrasco, *City of Sacrifice: The Aztec Empire and the Role of Violence in Civilization* (Boston: Beacon Press, 1999), 196.

75. Feiler, *Abraham*, 99. Feiler explained that in medieval Judaism some rabbis taught that Abraham actually killed Isaac and that he was then resurrected. Ibid.

76. Some religious groups are waking up to their responsibility. The Global Religious Network for Children, founded by the Arigatou Foundation in Japan, held its second international meeting in Geneva in May of 2004. About three hundred members of various religions signed a "Letter to the Children of Iraq and Their Parents," expressing their pain in view of the suffering of the Iraqi children and the conviction that the God proclaimed by the invaders of Iraq is not the God of truth, mercy, and justice. They also expressed the hope that suffering and desperation would not lead to more violence. E-mail message from Agencia de Noticias Prensa Ecumenica, May 24, 2004.

77. See illustration 12, Joseph Beuys, *Family*, 1961. Schloss Moyland, Kleve, Germany.

78. See illustration 13, Walter Williams (1920– ), *Roots*, undated. University Galleries of Fisk University.

79. See illustration 14.

## CHAPTER 4

1. I presented a shorter form of this chapter at the International Conference of Independent Scholars in Vancouver, B.C., on October 5, 2002. It was then directed to scholars of various disciplines and countries, Christians, Jews, and atheists, but in its present form it is meant mainly for scholars of religion in the United States.

2. UNICEF, Key Figures of February 2005.

3. For the statistics, see UNICEF, Key Figures of February 2005, and *Sojourners* (May/June 2002), 22, 24. For discussions of globalization, see Thomas Friedman, *The Lexus and the Olive Tree* (Farrar, Straus & Giroux, 1999) and John Gray, *False Dawn: The Delusions of Globalization* (New York:

New Press, 1998). See also the criticism of the World Bank in Ken Ringle's essay, "Bank Shot," *Washington Post*, March 20, 2002, reviewing the book by William Easterly, *The Elusive Quest for Growth*, and commenting on the World Bank's own analysis of its assistance efforts titled *Assessing Aid*.

4. Pierre Bourdieu, "For a Scholarship with Commitment," *Profession 2000* (New York: PMLA, 2000), 41.

5. Claudia Castañeda, *Figurations: Child, Bodies, Worlds* (Durham, N.C.: Duke University Press, 2002), 5.

6. See the excellent argument by Ariel Dorfman, who knows about torture from his homeland Chile, in his article, "Are there times when we have to accept torture?" The *New York Times*, May 8, 2004, reprinted from the Guardian Weekly. The office of the U.S. Attorney General as early as 2002 prepared a memo for the White House that practically allowed torture if the president would authorize it (*New York Times*, June 15, 2004). In Germany, some legal scholars have used convoluted language in interpreting the German constitution in such a way that torture can be used in some cases (*Frankfurter Rundschau*, May 28, 2004).

7. *Amnesty Now*, Spring 2001. See also the Amnesty International report of summer 2003 in *Amnesty Now*, "Tortured Logic: Thumbscrewing International Law," 20–25, 28, and the annual report of 2004 that strongly condemns torture.

8. *New York Times*, August 26, 2004.

9. The problems connected with having the United States ratify the Convention on the Rights of the Child are discussed in Cynthia Price Cohen, "Children's Rights: An American Perspective," in Bob Franklin, ed., *The Handbook of Children's Rights: Comparative Policy and Practice* (London and New York: Routledge, 1995), 163–71. See especially page 169: "Many unresolved children's rights issues could be more effectively settled through USA ratification of the Convention on the Rights of the Child." Some conservative Roman Catholics have seriously criticized UNICEF's way to fight for the rights of women and children. See www.OneWorld.net for the story by Barabara Crossette, "Rightist Catholic Group Launches Attack on UNICEF," Sept. 5, 2003.

10. *New York Times*, June 9, 2000. The U.S. Senate ratified the ILO Convention #182 on November 5, 1999. See "Protocols to the Convention on the Rights of the Child, July 25, 2000, Treaty Document 106-37 (Washington: U.S. Government Printing Office, 2000), 10. By July 2003, 130 countries had ratified the treaty (terre des hommes, *Kinderarbeit: Kein Kinderspiel* [Children's Work: No Child's Play] (Osnabrück, August 2003), 4.

11. Statistics are from a publication of the German organization terre des hommes, *Kinderarbeit: Was Verbraucher und Unternehmer tun können*

[Childworkers: What Consumers and Employers Can Do] (Osnabrück, 2001), 2–3.

12. ZEITzeichen, January 2004, 47, and terre des hommes, Kinderarbeit: Kein Kinderspiel (Osnabrück, 2003), 7.

13. terre des hommes, Kinderarbeit: Kein Kinderspiel (2001 edition), 1–3. The Christian Century reported on prostitution and slave labor of children in vol. 19, 26 (April 2000), 449. See also the Frankfurter Rundschau of July 15, 2000, about European trading of women and children.

14. Rita Nakashima Brock and Susan Thistlethwaite, Casting Stones: Prostitution and Liberation in Asia and the United States (Minneapolis: Fortress Press, 1996), 26, 38–43, 60–63, 138, 191. A University of Pennsylvania study of 2001 estimates that 40 percent of the young girls who engaged in prostitution in the United States were sexually abused at home, as were 30 percent of the boys. (Knight Ridder report, Herald-Sun, Durham, N.C., September 11, 2001, A6).

15. terre des hommes, Kinderarbeit: Was Verbraucher und Unternehmer tun können, 2–3.

16. Latinamerica Press, July 17, 2000, quoting estimates by the Royal Canadian Mounted Police.

17. Most of my examples are from Christliche Initiative Romero, "Arbeitende Kinder achten statt Kinderarbeit ächten" [Honoring Working Children instead of Outlawing Children's Work] (Münster, 1999), 12–18. More stories of working children are found in terre des hommes, Kinderarbeit: Kein Kinderspiel (edition of 2003).

18. Amnesty Now, Fall 2004.

19. Latinamerica Press, Nov. 19, 2001, 6, and terre des hommes, "Kinderarbeit: Kein Kinderspiel," (edition of 2001), 9.

20. Latinamerica Press, October 22, 2003, 8f.

21. Latinamerica Press, June 28, 1999, 7.

22. Ibid., 5.

23. Ibid., and terre des hommes, Kinderarbeit: Kein Kinderspiel (2003 edition), 6.

24. Latinamerica Press, June 28, 1999, 5.

25. See Bruce Robbins, "The Sweatshop Sublime," quoting from Gayatri Chacravorty Spivak's A Critique of Postcolonial Reason: Western human rights discourse "flattens out the complexity and difference of Third World society to suit a First World standard of ethical rationality." PMLA 117, 1 (Jan. 2002), 95. See also Judith Ennew, "Outside Childhood: Street Children's Rights," in Bob Franklin, ed., Handbook of Children's Rights: Comparative Policy and Practice (London and New York: Routledge, 1995), 201–26.

26. terre des hommes, *"Kinderarbeit: Was Verbraucher und Unternehmer tun können,"* 10f.

27. See Christliche Initiative Romero, *"Arbeitende Kinder achten,"* 8–10.

28. Ibid., 22f.

29. *Freitag* (Berlin), April 30, 2004, 5, reporting on an international symposion on child labor in Berlin, where forty scholars from twenty countries in Africa, North and South America, Asia, and Europe gathered.

30. terre des hommes, *"Kinderarbeit: Kein Kinderspiel,"* 23f., and personal communication from Alejandro Cussianovich, November 2003.

31. Christliche Initiative Romero, "Arbeitende Kinder achten," 26f., and terre des hommes, *Kinderarbeit: Kein Kinderspiel* (2003 edition), 5, where eleven demands formulated at the meeting in Kundapur, India, are quoted. Increasing international interest is indicated by the fact that in May 2004, two thousand nongovernmental organizations from 140 countries met at the World Congress against Child Labor in Florence, Italy. (noticias@ecupres.com.ar, May 11, 2004). For Islamic rules concerning child labor, see Regina Wentzel Wolfe, "For the Good of the Children," in *Ethics and World Religions: Cross-Cultural Case Studies,* ed. Regina Wentzel Wolfe and Christine E. Gudorf (Maryknoll, N.Y.: Orbis Books, 1999), 310–18.

32. Jo Boyden, "Childhood and the Policy Makers: A Comparative Perspective on the Globalization of Childhood," in *Constructing and Reconstructing Childhood: Contemporary Issues in the Sociological Study of Childhood,* ed. Allison James and Alan Prout (London: Falmer Press, 1990), 208.

33. See Margot Roosevelt Huatusco, "The Coffee Clash," *Time,* March 8, 2004, quoting the marketing director of Dunkin' Donuts: "We expect to serve 30 million Fair Trade Lattes and cappuccinos this year."

34. "Fair Trade Gains Ground," *Latinamerica Press,* October 8, 2003, 6.

35. *Latinamerica Press,* Feb. 22, 1999, 5.

36. *Durham Herald Sun* (Associated Press), April 29, 2004.

37. terre des hommes, *Albtraum ohne Ende: Kinder zwischen den Fronten [Nightmare Without End: Children between the Fronts]* (Osnabrück, November 2002), 2.

38. UNICEF Key Figures of 2005, and the global overview of child soldiers by the Coalition to Ban the Use of Child Soldiers, to be found on the website of terre des hommes, www.kindersoldaten.de.

39. For the role of religious and ideological indoctrination of children, see Ilene Cohn and Guy S. Goodwin-Gill, *Child Soldiers: The Role of Children in Armed Conflict* (Oxford and New York: Oxford University Press, 1994), 37f.

40. UNICEF, "Kinder im Krieg und auf der Flucht," Deutsches Komitee für UNICEF, 2002, 5. About the experiences of girl soldiers, see Susan McKay and Dyan Mazurana, *Where Are the Girls? Girls in Fighting Forces in Northern Uganda, Sierra Leone, and Mozambique: Their Lives During and After War* (Montreal: International Centre for Human Rights and Democratic Development, 2004).

41. See www.kindersoldaten.de.

42. Ilene Cohn and Guy S. Goodwin-Gill state that child soldiers often have experienced or witnessed "extremes of physical violence, including summary executions, death squad killings, disappearances, torture, arbitrary arrest or detention, sexual abuse, bombings, forced displacement, destruction of home or property, and massacres." *Child Soldiers*, 32. See also terre des hommes, *Albtraum ohne Ende* (2002), 2–3, 23f.

43. *Generalanzeiger*, Bonn, May 23, 2003, 4.

44. terre des hommes, *Albtraum ohne Ende* (2002), 2.

45. President Clinton signed the first special Protocol on Children in Armed Conflict and the second Protocol on the Sale of Children, Child Prostitution, and Child Pornography on July 5, 2000. This action does not imply that the United States is thereby bound by the Convention on the Rights of the Child, but it is a separate international agreement. The first Protocol stipulates not only that young people under eighteen cannot be forcibly drafted , but also that even voluntary soldiers (who in the United States are allowed to be drafted from seventeen years on with consent of a parent or guardian) will not "directly" participate in armed conflict when they are under eighteen. It also establishes rules for reintegrating former child soldiers into civilian society. See "Protocols to the Convention on the Rights of the Child," July 25, 2000, Treaty Document 106-37 (Washington: U.S. Government Printing Office, 2000), VII–VIII.

Extensive excerpts from the text of both protocols can be found in *The State of the World's Children 2002: Leadership* (New York: UNICEF, 2002), 62–65.

46. See http://www.unicef.org/crc/crc.htm for a list of countries that have not signed the optional protocol concerning "no draft under 18" and a list of those that have signed, but not ratified it. The website continually updates these lists.

47. A fourteen-year-old girl from a rebel movement in Sierra Leone recounted: I have seen how people had their hands cut off, how a ten-year-old girl was raped and then died, and how many people were burned alive. I have often cried quietly inside, because I did not dare to weep aloud. See www.kindersoldaten.de.

48. Dietmar Ostermann, "Mit dem Joystick die Freiheit verteidigen," *Frankfurter Rundschau*, May 27, 2002, 1. The CBS News of March 30, 2004, called "America's Army" a "sanitized view of violence" and a top sales item.

49. Krystian Woznicki, "Hollywood Wants You: From Ecological Activist to Actor—Soldiers as Protagonists of Globalization," *Frankfurter Rundschau*, July 3, 2002.

50. Ironically, British youngsters cannot legally drink or vote before age eighteen, but they can die in combat. See www.kindersoldaten.de.

51. Ibid. Canada accepts volunteers for its army at sixteen years of age, but forbids their participation in armed conflict. Germany affirmed in June of 2003 the same rule for seventeen-year-olds (*Frankfurter Rundschau*, June 26, 2003). In terms of "volunteer" soldiers we have to realize, especially in relation to the Third World, that children's volunteerism is often not really the wish of the child, but the force of circumstances like poverty or societal pressure.

52. See Arlie Hochschild, "Arrested Development," *New York Times*, June 29, 2005.

53. Gerhard Spörl, "Die Achse des Guten," *Der Spiegel*, 29/2002, 152–55.

54. German television featured a detailed program on early military training in Russia on July 31, 2003, and a German radio program (WDR Köln) reported on June 18, 2000, about the Soldier Mothers of Petersburg.

55. *Time*, March 4, 2002, 50. An excellent article by Scott Button on the problem of recruiting soldiers in schools can be found on the website of the Bruderhof Communities, http://www.bruderhof.com/articles/teenvoices/.

56. See Ed Cairns, *Children and Political Violence* (Cambridge, Mass.: Blackwell Publishers, 1996), 135.

57. Peter Lock, "Vom Wandel bewaffneter Konflikte—Kinder und Gewehre," in *Ich will endlich Frieden: Kinder im Krieg*, ed. Hans-Martin Grosse-Oetringhaus (Münster: Westfälisches Dampfboot, 1998), 29–31. See also UNICEF, "Stoppt Kleinwaffen!" Eine Aktion von UNICEF, Deutsches Komitee für UNICEF, 2001.

58. terre des hommes, *Albtraum ohne Ende: Kinder und Krieg* (Osnabrück, 1997), 6. See also the previously quoted update of this brochure of November 2002, 1f.

59. *Die Zeit*, June 5, 2003, 28. French President Jacques Chirac endorsed the plan.

60. *Kölner Stadtanzeiger*, July 15, 2003. A new UN treaty concerning the marking and tracing of small weapons was drafted in July of 2005 and criticized by human rights groups as very weak. *Frankfurter Rundschau*, July 15, 2005.

61. UNICEF Information of 2001. Every fifth victim of landmines worldwide is a child (UNICEF Key Figures 2005). See also terre des

hommes, *Albtraum ohne Ende* (2002), 9–11, about the political discussions concerning landmines.

62. See www.landmines.org for "Adopting a Minefield."

63. Rex Stainton Rogers and Wendy Stainton Rogers, *Stories of Childhood: Shifting Agendas of Child Concern* (Toronto: University of Toronto Press, 1992), 197.

64. *Amnesty Now* (Fall 2002), 4–7. A German journal reports that the McDonald company, while advertising Ronald McDonald houses and other charitable deeds, has actually been buying plastic little figures made by children under fourteen years in China for their popular "Happy Meals." Human rights organizations in Hong Kong have discovered that the rural Chinese children working for the "City Toys" company producing these figures are being ruthlessly exploited. When the Mattel company was criticized for having their Barbie dolls dressed by child laborers in Indonesia, they started overseeing production more carefully. *Der Gesundheitsberater* 3/2002, 12–13.

65. terre des hommes, *Die Zeitung*, March 2003, 7.

66. terre des hommes, *Albtraum ohne Ende*, 1997 edition, 32.

67. *Kölner Stadtanzeiger*, July 15, 2003, 2.

68. *Frankfurter Rundschau*, July 2, 2003, 7.

69. terre des hommes, *Die Zeitung*, November 2003, 3, and the special project study of terre des hommes, *Ehemalige Kindersoldaten als Flüchtlinge in Deutschland*, by Michaela Ludwig (Osnabrück, October 2003), where interviews with former child soldiers, of whom an estimated three hundred to five hundred live in Germany, are describing their legal and psychological difficulties.

70. *Frankfurter Rundschau*, May 15, 2004, 7.

71. Amnesty International estimated that by early fall of 2004 and since the beginning of the present *intifada* 450 Palestinian children and one hundred Israeli children have died. *Amnesty Now*, Fall 2004, 19.

72. "Die Seele der Welt: Auch die Psychotherapie stellt sich den Herausforderungen der Globalisierung," *Frankfurter Rundschau*, July 24, 2002.

73. *Duke Dialogue* (Duke University), August 9, 2002, 9.

74. Children's Defense Fund, *The State of America's Children* (Boston: Beacon, 2001), x. The figure of 35 percent is from UNICEF Key Figures of 2005: 617 million of these children are under five years old. Ibid.

**CHAPTER 5**

1. UN Population Fund Report, chap. 1, quoted by Werner Sollors, "Cooperation between English and Foreign Languages in the Area of Multilingual Literature," PMLA 117, 5 (Oct. 2002), 1287.

2. *Time*, December 15, 2003, 51–53.

3. Ivone Gebara, *Longing for Running Water: Ecofeminism and Liberation* (Minneapolis: Augsburg/Fortress, 1999), 197.

4. Tobias Hecht, "Children and Contemporary Latin America," in *Minor Omissions: Children in Latin American History and Society,* ed. Tobias Hecht (Madison: University of Wisconsin Press, 2002), 242.

5. Samuel Blixen, "'War' Waged on Latin American Street Kids," *Latinamerica Press,* November 7, 1991, 3.

In early February, 2004, a conference took place in Tegucigalpa, Honduras, bringing together Christian young people from Guatemala, Nicaragua, El Salvador, and Honduras, discussing the causes of juvenile delinquency, listening to testimonies from street children, denouncing government laws and police practices that violate children's rights, and pleading for education, prevention and rehabilitation programs instead of careless incarceration. *Agencia Latinoamericana y Caribeña de Comunicación,* February 1, 2004.

6. UNICEF, German report on the Children's World Summit 2002.

7. UNICEF, Key Figures 2005.

8. *Latinamerica Press,* May 1, 2000.

9. Hal Crowther, "Friends of the Earth," *The Independent Weekly,* Durham, N.C., March 28–April 3, 2001, 11.

10. Associated Press report, *Durham Herald-Sun,* Nov. 4, 2002, 7B.

11. David Alexander, "Feeding the Hungry and Protecting the Environment," in Carol J. Dempsey and Russell A. Butkus, eds., *All Creation Is Groaning: An Interdisciplinary Vision for Life in a Sacred Universe* (Collegeville, Minn.: Liturgical Press, 1999), 80 (quoting Alan B. Durning).

12. See Rüdiger Siebert, *Indonesien—Inselreich in Turbulenzen* (Bad Honnef: Horlemann-Verlag, 1998).

13. Pablo Richard, "Teología de la solidaridad en el contexto actual de economía neoliberal de libre mercado," in *El huracán de la globalización,* ed. Franz J. Hinkelammert (San José, Costa Rica: DEI, 1999), 224.

14. About the apostle Paul and the neoliberal market, see Elsa Tamez, "Libertad neoliberal y libertad paulina," in *El huracán de la globalización,* ed. Franz J. Hinkelammert (San José, Costa Rica: DEI, 1999), 209–21.

15. An excellent overview of these issues is Dempsey and Butkus, eds., *All Creation Is Groaning* (see note 11).

16. Ibid., viii, Walter Brueggemann in his foreword summarizing the core argument of the book.

17. Robert Dreyfuss, "Apocalypse Still," *Mother Jones* (Jan.–Feb. 2000), 40–51, 90.

18. Associated Press report in *Durham-Herald Sun,* Jan. 24, 2003, A6.

19. See Susan Steingraber, *Having Faith: An Ecologist's Journey into Motherhood* (Cambridge, Mass.: Perseus Publishing, 2003).

20. *New York Times*, December 3, 2003. See also Paul Krugman, "The Mercury Scandal," *New York Times*, April 6, 2004, and "Mercury Wars," *The New York Times*, April 15, 2004. The website http://cleanairnow.org gave an overview of the mercury issue on March 18, 2004.

21. Richard Rothstein, "Students in a Fog," *New York Times*, April 25, 2003. See also Margot Roosevelt, "The tragedy of Tar Creek," about toxic waste dumps, *Time*, April 26, 200, 42–47.

22. "The Plague of Lead Poisoning," *New York Times*, September 13, 2003.

23. Margaret Lamberts Bendroth, *Growing Up Protestant: Parents, Children, and Mainline Churches* (New Brunswick, N.J.: Rutgers University Press, 2002), 43.

24. *Frankfurter Rundschau*, May 10, 2001, 2. The Nuclear Policy Research Institute (Washington, D.C.), in a message of October 15/16, 2004, pointed out that nuclear power plants continuously emit radiation, and that children and fetuses are ten to twenty times more susceptible to the carcinogenic effects of radiation than adults.

25. See Robin Kirk, *More Terrible Than Death: Massacres, Drugs, and America's War in Colombia* (New York: Public Affairs, 2003), 265–66.

26. Ibid.

27. Kirk stated her view during a public reading from her book in Chapel Hill, N.C., in January 2003.

28. terre des hommes, *Die Zeitung* (April 2002), 5.

29. *Durham Herald-Sun*, November 25, 2000.

30. John Cort, quoting from Eileen Egan, *Peace Be with You* (Maryknoll, N.Y.: Orbis Books, 2000), in *Religious Socialism*, Autumn 2000, 12.

31. Dempsey and Butkus, eds., *All Creation Is Groaning*, 80–81, quoting Anita Gordon and David Suzuki, *It's a Matter of Survival* (Cambridge, Mass.: Harvard University Press, 1990), 92–93. These issues were widely discussed in the seventies, for example, in the book by Frances Moore Lappé, *Diet for a Small Planet* (New York: Ballantine Books, 1971). The worldwide meat production has increased between 1950 and 2002 from 44 million tons to 242 million tons. (Information from State Garden Exhibit, Leverkusen, Germany, July 2005.)

32. *Utne Reader* (Nov.–Dec. 2002), 29.

33. Ibid. The article points to www.fairtrade.org/html/english or www.globalexchange.org. See also the e-mail addresses: info@divine chocolate.com and Marilyn@ShamanChocolates.com. The firm Newman's Own Organics certifies that their chocolate is produced without forced labor.

34. Children's Defense Fund, *The State of America's Children* (Boston: Beacon, 2001), 2.

35. Ibid., 1.

36. Barbara Kingsolver, "Either life is precious or it's not," *The Plough Reader* (Fall 1999), 28. The article appears in a slightly different form in Kingsolver's *Small Wonder: Essays* (New York: HarperCollins, 2002), 180–83.

37. *Time*, April 7, 2003, 40.

38. *Time*, February 17, 2003, 44.

39. I have quoted the first text from The Koran, translated with notes by N. J. Dawood (London: Penguin Classics, 1956–1999), and the second from "An Islamic Perspective on the Environment," in Dempsey and Butkus, eds., *All Creation Is Groaning*, 46, which has the more beautiful translation.

40. Ibid., 56.

41. Kwok Pui-lan, "Ecology and the Recycling of Christianity," in *Ecotheology: Voices from South and North*, ed. David G. Hallman (Maryknoll, N.Y.: Orbis Books, 1994), 110. See also Anna L. Peterson, *Being Human: Ethics, Environment, and Our Place in the World* (Berkeley: University of California Press, 2001), chapters 4–7, on Asian, Native American, feminist, and ecological approaches to the relationship of human beings to nature.

42. William Blake, "Auguries of Innocence," in *English Romantic Writers*, ed. David Perkins (New York: Harcourt, Brace & World, 1967), 113.

43. See Ellen Dissanayake, "Aesthetic Incunabula," *Philosophy and Literature* 25, 2 (Oct. 2001), 335–44, and Martin Spiewak, "Die Botschaft der Babyrassel," *Die Zeit*, July 8, 2004.

44. Margot Kässmann, "Covenant, Praise, and Justice in Creation: Five Bible Studies," in *Ecotheology: Voices from the South and North*, ed. David G. Hallman (Maryknoll, N.Y.: Orbis Books, 1994), 36.

45. Elise Boulding, *Cultures of Peace: The Hidden Side of History* (Syracuse, N.Y.: Syracuse University Press, 2000), 223.

46. Ibid. Sally McFague speaks of an "extinction of experience," a lack of close encounters with the earth, in many children and adults. *Super, Natural Christians: How We Should Love Nature* (Minneapolis: Fortress Press, 1997), 118.

47. Roger Ebert, "Forget myth and metaphysics: 'Matrix Revolutions' is a great action film," *Durham Herald Sun* (United Press Syndicate), November 7, 2003, 15.

48. See Markus Günther, "Ihr seid Sklaven der Matrix," *General-Anzeiger*, Bonn, May 21, 2003, 3; and Katja Nicodemus, "Nichts als digitale Dönekes," *Die Zeit*, May 22, 2003, 34.

49. *Time*, Dec. 20, 1999, 40f.

50. "'The Matrix': Global Opening," *New York Times*, November 7, 2003.

51. Justine Cassell and Henry Jenkins, eds., *From Barbie to Mortal Kombat: Gender and Computer Games* (Cambridge, Mass.: MIT Press, 1998).

52. Cornelia Brunner, Dorothy Bennett, and Margaret Honey, "Girl Games and Technological Desire," in Cassell and Jenkins, eds., *From Barbie to Mortal Kombat*, 81f. Henry Jenkins, in his own article in this volume, "'Complete Freedom of Movement': Video Games as Gendered Play Spaces," puts it succinctly: "We need to design digital play spaces that allow girls to do more than stitch doll clothes, [love] mother nature, or heal their friends' hurts, and boys to do more than battle barbarian hordes." Ibid., 290.

53. James T. Hamilton, *Channeling Violence: The Economic Market for Violent Television Programming* (Princeton, N.J.: Princeton University Press, 1998), xvii, 26–27. See also Noreen Herzfeld, "Video Shootout," *The Christian Century*, May 4, 2004, 23: "When the average American child spends nine hours a week playing [these video games], we need to ask what sort of worldview the games are furthering." Herzfeld admits that not all video games are violent, but all promote viewing oneself as managing alone. Even those requiring a group to solve a quest are not in any real sense collaborative.

54. I am referring here to some comments Hamilton made at a conference in Chapel Hill, N.C., in April 2004.

55. Kingsolver, "The One-Eyed Monster, and Why I Don't Let Him In." *Small Wonder* (see note 36), 131–43.

56. Carol J. Adams, *Neither Man nor Beast: Feminism and the Defense of Animals* (New York: Continuum, 1994), 161.

57. Temple Grandin stated this in an interview on National Public Radio, January 30, 2003. See also her book *Thinking in Pictures and Other Reports from My Life with Autism* (New York: Random House, 1995), 194–206.

58. Deane Curtin, "Toward an Ecological Ethic of Care," in *Beyond Animal Rights: A Feminist Caring Ethic for the Treatment of Animals*, ed. Josephine Donovan and Carol J. Adams (New York: Continuum, 1996), 72.

59. Carol J. Adams, *The Pornography of Meat* (New York: Continuum, 2003).

60. Ibid., 113, 98.

61. Ibid., 20, 122. Barbara Kingsolver has described this problem and the way she dealt with it in her essay, "Lily's Chickens," *Small Wonder*, 109–30.

62. Clara Sue Kidwell, Homer Noley, and George E. "Tink" Tinker, eds., *A Native American Theology* (Maryknoll, N.Y.: Orbis Books, 2001), 41.

63. Ibid., 44.

64. See "Indigenous Survival Threatened" (by oil drilling, free trade, and fumigation among Amazonian natives), *Latinamerica Press*, March 24, 2004, 11.

65. Ibid., 42.

66. Ibid., 50f. Sally McFague similarly suggests that we should love nature like we want to love God and neighbor: as subjects, not as objects for our use. *Super, Natural Christians*, 1.

67. *Frankfurter Rundschau*, May 7, 2003, WB3. About the cruelty of animal experiments, see Tom Regan, "The Myth of 'Humane' Treatment," *The Independent Weekly* (Durham, N.C.), February 4–10, 2004, 19.

68. Riane Eisler, *Tomorrow's Children: A Blueprint for Partnership Education in the 21st Century* (Boulder: Westview Press, 2000), 404.

69. Associated Press report, *Durham Herald-Sun*, April 3, 2003.

70. Associated Press report, *News & Observer*, Raleigh, N.C., March 20, 2003.

71. William Styron, *The Confessions of Nat Turner*, quoted from Frederick Herzog, "Who Speaks for the Animals?" in *Theology from the Belly of the Whale: A Frederick Herzog Reader*, ed. Jörg Rieger (Harrisburg, Pa.: Trinity Press International, 1999), 259.

72. See, e.g., Silko's novel *Ceremony* (New York: New American Library, 1978).

73. Quoted from Luis N. Rivera, *A Violent Evangelism: The Political and Religious Conquest of the Americas* (Louisville, Ky.: Westminster John Knox Press, 1992), 222.

74. See Kidwell, Noley, Tinker, eds., *A Native American Theology*, 55–61.

75. Ibid., 75.

76. Sarah L. Holloway and Gill Valentine, eds., *Children's Geographies: Playing, Living, Learning* (London and New York: Routledge, 2000), 12.

77. Nancy Scheper-Hughes and Daniel Hoffman, "Brazilian Apartheid: Street Kids and the Struggle for Urban Space," in *Small Wars: The Cultural Politics of Childhood*, ed. Nancy Scheper-Hughes and Carolyn Sargent (Berkeley: University of California Press, 1998), 353.

78. Henry Jenkins makes the good point that we sometimes blame video games for problems they do not cause. Rather, there are material conditions and economic policies that create a lack of play spaces. "Video games . . . offer children some way to respond to domestic confinement." "'Complete Freedom of Movement': Gendered Play Spaces," in Cassell and Jenkins, eds., *From Barbie to Mortal Kombat*, 266.

79. See Anna L. Peterson and Kay Almere Read, "Victims, Heroes, Enemies: Children in Central American Wars," in *Minor Omissions:*

*Children in Latin American History and Society,* ed. Tobias Hecht (Madison: University of Wisconsin Press, 2002), 218. See also Key Figures of UNICEF for 2005.

80. Peterson and Read, "Victims, Heroes, Enemies," 219.

81. Ibid., 229, quoting Florentino Moreno Martín, "Infancia y guerra en Centroamérica (San José, Costa Rica: FLACSO, 1991).

82. The U.S. policy on land mines was improved in 2004, but still steers clear of banning all land mines. See the editorial "A Bad Shift in Land Mines," *New York Times,* March 1, 2004.

83. Arnd Festerling, "Kampf gegen Kinder," *Frankfurter Rundschau,* June 11, 2003), 2.

84. Ibid.

85. See a report on the Congo situation in *Generalanzeiger* (Bonn), June 13, 2003, 4, and a report on child workers and child soldiers in Liberia, the Congo, and the Sudan in *Die Zeit,* August 28, 2003.

86. The meteorologist Edward Lorenz first drew attention to this "butterfly effect." "Does the flap of a butterfly wing in Tokyo, Lorenz queried, affect a tornado in Texas (or a thunderstorm in New York)? Though unfortunate for the future of accurate weather prediction, his answer was 'yes.'" Margaret J. Wheatley, *Leadership and the New Science: Learning about Organization from an Orderly Universe* (San Francisco: Berrett-Koehler Publishers, 1992, 1994), 126. See also Paul Davies, *The Cosmic Blueprint: New Discoveries in Nature's Creative Ability to Order the Universe* (New York: Simon & Schuster, 1988), 52.

87. Wheatley, *Leadership and the New Science,* 8.

88. Ibid., 9f.

89. Ibid., 75.

90. Paul Davies, *The Mind of God: The Scientific Basis for a Rational World* (New York: Simon & Schuster, 1992), 30.

91. William Wordsworth, "The Prelude: or, Growth of a Poet's Mind," Book Fifth, in *English Romantic Writers,* ed. David Perkins (New York: Harcourt, Brace & World, 1967), 236.

92. See Ron O'Grady, *The Hidden Shame of the Church: Sexual Abuse of Children and the Church* (Geneva: World Council of Churches Publications, 2001).

93. Tony Brun, "Social Ecology: A Timely Paradigm for Reflection and Praxis for Life in Latin America," in *Ecotheology: Voices from South and North,* ed. David G. Hallman (Maryknoll, N.Y.: Orbis Books, 1994), 80.

94. Associated Press report, *Herald-Sun,* Durham, N.C., April 12, 1999, 4A.

95. Reported in *Latinamerica Press*, April 3, 2000, 7.

96. *terre des hommes*, Jahresbericht 2002, 7, 16. See also an article on Cambodian girls traded and abused in Thailand in *Generalanzeiger* (Bonn), June 26–27, 2004, and the UNICEF Key Figures of 2004 and 2005, stating that worldwide every year about 1.2 million children are being sold, and in Asia alone about one million are sexually exploited, most of them girls.

97. See "JonBenét, Inc.: Books, Movies, TV, Careers," *Brill's Content*, February 2000, 97–107. "In the year of JonBenét's death, 804 children ages 12 and under were murdered in the United States, according to the FBI's 1996 Uniform Crime Report. Her killing should never have been more than a Denver-area story" (ibid., 97). Meanwhile the number of people getting famous and rich from dealing with the case has continuously increased, as a Google search of JonBenét's name shows.

98. UNICEF, *The State of the World's Children 2003* (New York: UNICEF, 2003), 78.

99. UNICEF Key Figures 2005.

100. *Latinamerica Press*, quoting UNICEF, December 3, 2003, 2.

101. Sheryl Gay Stolberg, "War, Murder and Suicide: A Year's Toll Is 1.6 Million," *New York Times* (October 3, 2002), A12.

102. Arthur Waskow, "Judaism, Violence, and Nonviolence," *Fellowship*, 69, 5–6 (May–June 2003), 12f. Emphasis is mine.

103. Murray Polner and Naomi Goodman, eds., *The Challenge of Shalom: The Jewish Tradition of Peace and Justice* (Philadelphia: New Society Publishers, 1994). For environmental concerns, see especially pages 127–38.

104. See Frederick Herzog, *European Pietism Reviewed* (San Jose, Calif.: Pickwick Publications, 2003), 105–8, about Oetinger's theology.

105. Ivone Gebara, *Longing for Running Water: Ecofeminism and Liberation* (Minneapolis: Fortress Press, 1999), 206–10.

106. *Thomas Merton, Essential Writings*, selected and introduced by Christine M. Bochen (Maryknoll, N.Y.: Orbis Books, 2000), 142.

107. Ibid., 134.

108. See note 57 of chapter 1 about Bruno Schulz's term "maturing into childhood."

## CHAPTER 6

1. Dorothee Soelle, "Aus der Schule plaudern," *Spiel doch von Brot und Rosen: Gedichte* (Berlin: Fietkau Verlag, 1983), 121. Translation is mine.

2. Judith M. Gundry-Volf emphasizes that the Greek word for "welcoming" (*dechomai*) is used especially for hospitality to guests and implies service, not just affection. "The Least and the Greatest: Children in the

New Testament," in *The Child in Christian Thought*, ed. Marcia J. Bunge (Grand Rapids, Mich.: Eerdmans, 2001), 43.

3. Christine D. Pohl, *Making Room: Recovering Hospitality as a Christian Tradition* (Grand Rapids, Mich.: Eerdmans, 1999), 3.

4. Ibid., 69.

5. See Frederick Herzog, "New Birth of Conscience," in *Theology and Corporate Conscience: Essays in Honor of Frederick Herzog*, ed. M. Douglas Meeks, Jürgen Moltmann, and Frederick Trost (Minneapolis: Kirk House Publishers, 1999), 410.

6. See Marcia J. Bunge's comment on Schleiermacher in her introduction to *The Child in Christian Thought*, ed. Marcia J. Bunge (Grand Rapids, Mich.: Eerdmans, 2001), 22.

7. Hubertus Lutterbach emphasizes that Philippe Ariès was one of the few scholars who appreciated the role of the church in the history of education, whereas others have simply pointed to the Enlightenment as the strongest proponent of schooling. "'Was ihr einem dieser Kleinen getan habt, das habt ihr mir getan,'" in *Gottes Kinder*, ed. Martin Ebner et al. (Neukirchen-Vluyn: Neukirchener Verlag, 2002), 201.

8. Margaret Lamberts Bendroth, *Growing Up Protestant: Parents, Children, and Mainline Churches* (New Brunswick, N.J.: Rutgers University Press, 2002), 28f.

9. Ibid., 34.

10. Ibid., 70.

11. Quoted from ibid., 108.

12. See Bonnie J. Miller-McLemore's comments on "othermothering" in black communities and congregations in her *Let the Children Come: Reimagining Childhood from a Christian Perspective* (San Francisco: Jossey Bass, 2003), 165, 200.

13. Bendroth, *Growing Up Protestant*, 88.

14. Miller-McLemore, *Let the Children Come*, 164.

15. Bendroth, *Growing Up Protestant*, 158.

16. See Herbert Anderson et al., eds., *Mutuality Matters: Family, Faith, and Just Love* (Lanham, Md.: Rowman & Littlefield, 2003).

17. Bendroth, *Growing Up Protestant*, 28.

18. Rita Nakashima Brock quotes Alice Miller in this regard, who suggested that virtually all child rearing in our culture is control-oriented. The parents shape the child into a being who reflects the parents' needs and wishes. Rita Nakashima Brock, "And a Little Child Will Lead Us: Christology and Child Abuse," in *Christianity, Patriarchy, and Abuse: A Feminist Critique*, ed. Joanne Carlson Brown and Carol R. Bohn (New York: Pilgrim Press, 1989), 46.

19. Ralph Koerrenz, "'Vom Kinde aus'—Nachdenken über einen Anspruch," in *Gottes Kinder*, ed. Martin Ebner et al. (Neukirchen-Vluyn: Neukirchener Verlag, 2002), 379f.

20. Ibid., 381f. Bonnie Miller-McLemore uses the term "transitional hierarchy," "a temporary inequity between persons—whether of power, authority, expertise, responsibility, or maturity—that is moving toward but has not yet arrived at genuine mutuality." *Let the Children Come*, 130.

21. Koerrenz, "'Vom Kinde aus,'" 386. Translation is mine.

22. See Brita L. Gill-Austern's comments on "Feminist Pedagogues as Midwives" in her essay, "Pedagogy Under the Influence of Feminism and Womanism," *Feminist and Womanist Pastoral Theology*, ed. Bonnie J. Miller-McLemore and Brita L. Gill Austern (Nashville: Abingdon Press, 1999), 152f.

23. Sofia Cavalletti, "Die Katechese des guten Hirten," in *Gottes Kinder*, ed. Martin Ebner et al. (Neukirchen-Vluyn: Neukirchener Verlag, 2002), 292f.

24. Ibid., 297.

25. Cf. Miller-McLemore stating that some people consider learning from children to be as difficult as learning a kind of religious practice, like meditation or Zen. *Let the Children Come*, 39.

26. Dorothee Soelle, *The Silent Cry: Mysticism and Resistance* (Minneapolis: Fortress Press, 2001), 11.

27. See my chapter 2, note 65.

28. Quoted from Dawn DeVries, "'Be Converted and Become as Little Children': Friedrich Schleiermacher on the Religious Significance of Childhood," in *The Child in Christian Thought*, ed. Marcia J. Bunge (Grand Rapids: Eerdmans, 2001), 329.

29. Elisabeth Moltmann-Wendel used this anonymous German saying as title of her autobiography, *Wer die Erde nicht berührt, kann den Himmel nicht erreichen . . . Autobiographie* (Zürich: Benziger Verlag, 1997).

30. See Carl J. Friedrich, ed., *The Philosophy of Hegel* (New York: Random House, 1953/1954), 404–07, about "Master and Servant."

31. Evelyn L. Parker, *Trouble Don't Last Always: Emancipatory Hope among African American Adolescents* (Cleveland: Pilgrim Press, 2003), 24.

32. Elizabeth J. Walker, "Pastoral Counseling with African-American Male Youth Offenders," and Bridgette Hector, "Womanist Model: Crossing Class Barriers: Middle-Class Black Women Relating with Inner-City Black Female Youth," *The Journal of the Interdenominational Theological Center*, 30, 1 and 2 (Fall 2002/Spring 2003), 109–27 and 129–45.

33. Jonathan Kozol, *Ordinary Resurrections: Children in the Years of Hope* (New York: Crown Publishers, 2000), 42.

34. Ibid., 132.

35. Ibid., 244f.

36. Cavalletti, "Die Katechese des guten Hirten," 300.

37. Brett P. Webb-Mitchell, *Christly Gestures: Learning to Be Members of the Body of Christ* (Grand Rapids, Mich.: Eerdmans, 2003).

38. Quoted from ibid., 120.

39. Ibid., 220.

40. About children as philosophers, see the works by Gareth B. Matthews, e.g., *The Philosophy of Childhood* (Cambridge, Mass.: Harvard University Press, 1994); also Hans Ludwig Freese, *Kinder sind Philosophen* (Weinheim and Berlin: Quadriga, 1989, 1992), and E. Marteens and H. Schreier, *Philosophieren mit Schulkindern* (Heinsberg: Agentur Dieck, 1994).

41. Helmut Hanisch, "Kinder als Philosophen und Theologen," in "Schau auf die Kleinen . . . ," ed. Rüdiger Lux (Leipzig: Evangelische Verlagsanstalt, 2002), 157f. Gareth Matthews had used the same example by Christa Wolf in *The Philosophy of Childhood*, 37. See Christa Wolf, *Störfall: Nachrichten eines Tages* (Frankfurt: Luchterhand, 1987, 1989), 105f.

42. Hanish, "Kinder als Philosophen," 160f.

43. Parker, *Trouble Don't Last Always*, 75–77, refers to Danna Nolan Fewell's *The Children of Israel* concerning the relevance of these and other Bible stories for young people today.

44. See Antonio Damasio, *Looking for Spinoza: Joy, Sorrow, and the Feeling Brain* (New York: Harcourt, 2003), and the article about him, "I Feel, Therefore I Am," *New York Times*, April 19, 2003, 1.

45. See Sarah Boxer, "McLuhan's Messages, Echoing in Iraq Coverage," *New York Times,* April 3, 2003, 1; and Marshall McLuhan and Quentin Fiore, *The Medium Is the Massage* (New York: Random House, 1967), 8–10.

46. Jeanette Rodríguez, "Latina Activists: Toward an Inclusive Spirituality of Being in the World," in *A Reader in Latina Feminist Theology: Religion and Justice*, ed. María Pilar Aquino et al. (Austin: University of Texas Press, 2002), 127. In the same volume Carmen Marie Nanco reminds us that the Hispanic population in the United States "is characterized demographically by its youthfulness." "Justice Crosses the Border: The Preferential Option for the Poor in the United States," 195. Appealing in teaching to all human senses is especially important for ethnic children because many of them have not as yet experienced the full impact of abstract technological thought.

47. Edward Farley, "Being Human and the Arts: A Sacramental Reflection," *ARTS: The Arts in Religious and Theological Studies*, 15, 1, 2003, 5.

48. Ibid., 8.

49. Ibid., 9.

50. Bärbel Wartenberg-Potter, ed., *Was tust du, fragt der Engel: Mystik im Alltag* (Freiburg: Herder, 2004), 177.

51. Vincent Van Gogh, *Letters to Emile Bernard* (New York: Museum of Modern Art, 1938), 44f.

52. Rosemarie Garland-Thomson delivered a splendid slide presentation at the American Academy of Religion conference in Atlanta on November 24, 2003, about advertisements that hide or glorify physical handicaps in order to entice the viewer to give money to a charity or to buy extravagant items of clothing or convenience for disabled people. Disability is shown only in being overcome or cheerfully displayed.

53. John M. Buchanan, "Stopwatch," *The Christian Century*, Sept. 20, 2003), 3.

54. Quoted in ibid. from Abraham Joshua Heschel, *I Asked for Wonder.*

55. Rita Nakashima Brock, "And a Little Child Will Lead Us" (see note 18), 59.

56. For the latter see Donna E. Schaper, *Raising Interfaith Children: Spiritual Orphans or Spiritual Heirs?* (New York: Crossroad, 1999).

57. Marsha Snulligan Haney, "The Urban Child, Congregational Ministry and the Challenge of Religious Diversity," *The Journal of the Interdenominational Theological Center*, 30, 1 and 2 (Fall 2002/Spring 2003), 21.

58. Yann Martel, *Life of Pi* (Orlando, etc.: Harcourt Inc., 2003). Martel describes a teenager in India who wants to worship the Christian, the Muslim, and the Hindu way, something his parents do not approve of or understand.

59. ABC News Report of April 11, 2004.

60. Jörg Rieger has described this "outreach" and "inreach" in "Theology and Mission in a Postcolonial World," *Mission Studies: Journal of the International Association for Mission Studies* 21, 2 (2004): 201–27. See also Frederick Herzog, "Full Communion Training," in *Theology from the Belly of the Whale: A Frederick Herzog Reader*, ed. Jörg Rieger (Harrisburg, Pa.: Trinity Press International, 1999), 286.

61. Martin Luther King Jr., quoted from *Episcopal Life*, April 2003.

62. Ralph Waldo Emerson, "Merlin II," from *Early Poems of Ralph Waldo Emerson* with Introduction by Nathaniel Haskel Dole (New York, Boston: Thomas Y. Crowell, 1899); http://www.emersoncentral.com/poems/merlin_ii.htm.

63. Rabbi Steven S. Schwarzschild, "Shalom," in *The Challenge of Shalom: The Jewish Tradition of Peace and Justice*, ed. Murray Polner and Naomi Goodman (Philadelphia: New Society Publishers, 1994), 17.

64. Ibid., 18. The translation is Schwarzschild's.

65. I owe this comparison to a sermon by Teresa Berger in the spring of 2003.

66. Schwarzschild, "Shalom," 21.

67. For example, the German organization "Komitee für Grundrechte und Demokratie" (Aquino Strasse 7–11, 50670 Köln, Germany) every year brings together young people from war zones like Albania and Serbia, Israel and Palestine. Private sponsors help to give these teenagers the opportunity to spend a vacation away from their home countries with their peers from "enemy" territory. There are organizations in Jerusalem that still manage encounters between Israeli and Palestinian youth under most difficult circumstances.

68. Ardys Dunn, "Development of Environmental Responsibility in Children," in *All Creation Is Groaning: An Interdisciplinary Vision for Life in a Sacred Universe*, ed. Carol J. Dempsey and Russell Butkus (Collegeville, Minn.: Liturgical Press, 1999), 193–211.

69. Ibid., 199.

70. Ibid., 200.

71. William Raspberry, "Connected children are healthier," *Herald-Sun*, Durham, N.C., Sept. 22, 2003. The Commission on Children at Risk is a creature of the YMCA of the U.S.A., Dartmouth Medical School, and the Institute for American Values. Ibid.

72. Charlene Spretnak, *The Resurgence of the Real: Body, Nature, and Place in a Hypermodern World* (New York: Routledge, 1999), 51.

73. See, for example, Elisabeth Moltmann-Wendel, *Macht der Mütterlichkeit: Die Geschichte der Henriette Schrader-Breymann* (Berlin: Wichern Verlag, 2003).

74. See, e.g., Fritjof Capra, *The Web of Life: A New Scientific Understanding of Living Systems* (New York: Anchor Books/Doubleday, 1996).

75. Larry Rasmussen, "Theology of Life and Ecumenical Ethics," in *Ecotheology: Voices from South and North*, ed. David G. Hallman (Maryknoll, N.Y.: Orbis Books, 1994, 1995), 115; referring to Michael Lerner, "Jewish Liberation Theology," in Michael Zweig, ed., *Religion and Economic Justice* (Philadelphia: Temple University Press, 1991), 31.

76. Ralph Waldo Emerson, "Nature," in *Eight American Writers: An Anthology of American Literature* (New York: W.W. Norton, 1963), 219.

77. Pauline Hunt and Ronald Frankenberg, "It's a Small World: Disneyland, the Family and the Multiple Re-presentations of American Childhood," in *Constructing and Reconstructing Childhood: Contemporary Issues in the Sociological Study of Childhood*, ed. Allison James and Alan Prout (London: Palmer Press, 1990), 116.

78. Ibid.

## CHAPTER 7

1. David Batstone in *Sojourners*, March 24, 2004.

2. A government-appointed Truth and Reconciliation Commission issued a report on August 28, 2003, stating that 69,000 people died between 1980 and 2000, more than half of them through the violence of Shining Path, the Maoist rebels, and Tupac Amaru, the Cuban-style rebels, but the rest through three different governments who gave too much power to the armed forces and failed to stem abuses by the military. Three of every four people that died were Quechua-speaking Indians. *New York Times*, August 29, 2003.

3. UNICEF, *The State of the World's Children 2004* (New York: UNICEF, 2003), 104, 108.

4. Ibid., 106. The percentage of the Peruvian population living on less than $1.00 a day is given as 15 percent for 1990–1999, "at 1985 international prices, adjusted for purchasing power parity." The higher figure for 2002 came from the Agencia Latinoamericana y Caribeña de Comunicación.

5. "Invasión" is a common practice among the poor or homeless population of Peru, referring to the taking over of land or of a single piece of real estate that is unused, for which the owner cannot prove a clear title, or which is owned by the government or a city without being occupied.

6. UNICEF, *The State of the World's Children 2003* (New York: UNICEF, 2002), 98.

7. Esther Hammer of Rochester, N.Y., developed the program in English and Spanish and donated the materials.

8. *Latinamerica Press*, July 30, 2003, 10.

9. Ivone Gebara, *Out of the Depths: Women's Experience of Evil and Salvation* (Minneapolis: Augsburg/Fortress, 2002), 56f.

10. Wolfgang Wiedlich, "Wieder führt Eva's Spur nach Afrika," *Generalanzeiger* (Bonn), July 12/13, 2003. The variability of the chimpanzee genes are, however, four times as high as those of the six billion of humans, so that two people living in Lima and New York are more closely related than two chimpanzees living a few yards from each other. Ibid.

11. Larry Rasmussen, "Theology of Life and Ecumenical Ethics," in *Ecotheology: Voices from South and North*, ed. David. G. Hallman (Geneva: WCC Publications, and Maryknoll, N.Y.: Orbis Books, 1994), 119.

12. See Rosa del Carmen Bruno-Jofré, *Methodist Education in Peru: Social Gospel, Politics, and American Ideological and Economic Penetration, 1888–1930* (Waterloo, Ont.: Canadian Corporation for Studies in Religion, 1988).

13. *Generalanzeiger* (Bonn), July 10, 2003, 18.

14. Scott McPherson, "War on Drugs Aids Terrorists," *Durham Herald-Sun*, from Knight Ridder/Tribune, Feb. 21, 2003, A13. In 2004 the United Nation's chief of antidrug efforts announced a drastic decline in the coca

production in Colombia's heartland, due to increased spraying, and also a reduction of cocaine consumption in the United States, but he admitted that coca fields have sprung up in other regions and along the borders of Colombia. Other observers have discerned an increase in coca cultivation in Peru and Bolivia.

15. Gayatri Chakravorty Spivak, *A Critique of Postcolonial Reason: Toward a History of the Vanishing Present* (Cambridge, Mass.: Harvard University Press, 1999), 382f.

16. See Yersu Kim, "World Change and the Cultural Synthesis of the West," in *Justice and Democracy: Cross-Cultural Perspectives*, ed. Ron Bontekoe and Marietta Stepaniants (Honolulu: University of Hawaii Press, 1997), 431–33.

17. Fred Dallmayr, "Justice and Global Democracy," in *Justice and Democracy* (see note 16), 443.

## CHAPTER 8

1. Elise Boulding, *Cultures of Peace: The Hidden Side of History* (Syracuse, N.Y.: Syracuse University Press, 2000), 139.

2. Christoph Kähler, "'Wenn ihr nicht werdet wie die Kinder . . .': Kindsein als Metapher im Neuen Testament," in *Schau auf die Kleinen . . . : Das Kind in Religion, Kirche, und Gesellschaft*, ed. Rüdiger Lux (Leipzig: Evangelische Verlagsanstalt, 2002), 104. Translation is mine.

3. Anne Primavesi makes the same point in *Sacred Gaia: Holistic Theology and Earth System Science* (London and New York: Routledge, 2000), 54f.

4. Riane Eisler, *Tomorrow's Children: A Blueprint for Partnership Education in the 21st Century* (Boulder: Westview Press, 2000), ix, 21, 37, 69.

5. Boulding, *Cultures of Peace*, 139.

6. See Priscilla Ferguson Clement, review of Joseph E. Illick, *American Childhoods* (Philadelphia: University of Pennsylvania Press, 2002), published online by H-Childhood, January 2003. See also David Halberstam, *The Children* (New York: Random House, 1998), about the young people who provided national leadership to the civil rights movement.

7. A German news report emphasized this point in describing the uprising at the anniversary celebrations on August 1, 2004.

8. *Sojourners*, July–August 2003, 10.

9. See Ulrich Janssen and Ulla Steuernagel, *Kinder-Uni: Forscher erklären die Rätsel der Welt* (München: DVA, 2004).

10. Elizabeth Rusch, *Generation Fix: Young Ideas for a Better World* (Hillsboro, Ore.: Beyond Words Publishing, 2002).

11. Children from poor families are often at a disadvantage because they cannot afford computers, cell phones, DVD players, etc. In recent years social workers and nonprofit groups at home and abroad have increasingly given cameras to underprivileged children and asked them to be photographers of their surroundings, giving them the possibility to be agents in their communities and families instead of being photographed as victims of poverty and neglect. See *Duke Magazine*, Duke University, September/October 2003, 40–45.

12. Barbara Feinberg in *New York Times*, July 18, 2004.

13. Ilias Yocaris, "Harry Potter, Market Wiz," *New York Times*, July 18, 2004.

14. This point is made in Anna L. Peterson and Kay Almere Read, "Victims, Heroes, Enemies: Children in Central American Wars," in Tobias Hecht, ed., *Minor Omissions: Children in Latin American History and Society* (Madison: University of Wisconsin Press, 2002), 226–28.

15. See my comments on Ivone Gebara's thoughts on the subject in chapter 7, and see Delores S. Williams, "A Womanist Perspective on Sin," in Emily M. Townes, ed., *A Troubling in My Soul: Womanist Perspectives on Evil and Suffering* (Maryknoll, N.Y.: Orbis Books, 1993), 130–49.

16. See Peterson and Read, "Victims, Heroes, Enemies," 222–25.

17. On March 1, 2005, the U.S Supreme Court decided to outlaw the death penalty for juvenile offenders, finally joining the opinion of most countries, many U.S. states, and countless organizations that have fought for this goal for many years.

18. Agencia Latinoamericana y Caribeña de Comunicación, August 19, 2004.

19. Kofi A. Annan, Foreword to *The State of the World's Children 2003* (New York: UNICEF), 2002.

20. Alex Stock has given an excellent interpretation of this story, using its representations in art history, in "Junglehrer und Musterknabe—Zur Bildgeschichte des zwölfjährigen Jesus," in *Schau auf die Kleinen . . . Das Kind in Religion, Kirche und Gesellschaft*, ed. Rüdiger Lux (Leipzig: Evangelische Verlagsanstalt, 2002), 118–40.

21. Catherine Keller, *Face of the Deep: A Theology of Becoming* (London/New York: Routledge, 2003), 233.

22. The figure is from Kofi Annan, *We the Children: Meeting the Promises of the World Summit for Children* (New York: UNICEF, 2001), 8.

23. Justine Cassell, "'We Have These Rules Inside': The Effects of Exercising Voice in a Children's Online Forum," in *Rethinking Childhood*, ed. Peter B. Pufall and Richard P. Unsworth (New Brunswick, N.J.: Rutgers University Press, 2004).

24. Martin Buber, quoted in Dorothee Sölle, *Against the Wind: Memoir of a Radical Christian* (Minneapolis: Fortress Press, 1995), 27.

25. Quoted in Ellen Stubbe, "Im Netz der Schänder: Der Skandal der Kinderpornographie in Deutschland," *Evangelische Kommentare*, Nov. 1998, 641.

26. William Dietrich, "Work Is Just a Word for Life," *Durham Herald Sun* (Knight Ridder), August 8, 2004, F2.

27. M. Douglas Meeks has presented a convincing theology of work in his *God the Economist: The Doctrine of God and Political Economy* (Minneapolis: Augsburg/Fortress, 1989), 127–55, and Armand Larive has continued and elaborated the topic in his *After Sunday: A Theology of Work* (New York: Continuum, 2004).

28. Jack Zimmerman in Jacqueline McCandless, *Children with Starving Brains: A Medical Treatment Guide for Autism Spectrum Disorder*, 2nd ed. (Thousand Oaks, Calif.: Bramble Books, 2003), 223–26.

29. Ibid.

30. See William E. Connolly, *Why I Am Not a Secularist* (Minneapolis: University of Minnesota Press, 1999), 47–71, "Suffering, Justice, and the Politics of Becoming." Connolly finds examples of the politics of becoming in "antislavery movements, feminism, gay/lesbian rights movements, the introduction of secularism, the effort to put 'Judeo' in front of the 'Christian tradition,' the right to die, and so on." Ibid., 59.

31. Giles Deleuze and Felix Guattari, *A Thousand Plateaus: Capitalism and Schizophrenia* (Minneapolis: University of Minnesota Press, 1998), 211, quoted from Keller, *Face of the Deep*, 216.

32. The story and the whole debate can be found in *Frankfurter Rundschau*, June 13, 2003, June 23, 2003, and June 30, 2003. In 2005 Eva Kor has still given talks in German high schools about her experiences. See *Frankfurter Rundschau*, June 21, 2005. See a similar story of difficult forgiving and a theological interpretation of it in L. Gregory Jones, *Embodying Forgiveness: A Theological Analysis* (Grand Rapids, Mich.: Eerdmans, 1995), 283–90. See also Marc Lacey, "Atrocity Victims in Uganda Choose to Forgive," *New York Times*, April 18, 2005.

33. See the title of John P. Meier's book, *A Marginal Jew: Rethinking the Historical Jesus* (New York: Doubleday, 1991).

## CONCLUSION

1. Marian Wright Edelman, *Hold My Hand: Prayers for Building a Movement to Leave No Child Behind*. Children's Defense Fund, *The State of America's Children 2004* (Washington, D.C., 2004), x.

2. Karl Rahner, "Ideas for a Theology of Childhood," in his *Theological Investigations*, vol. 8 (New York: Seabury Press, 1977), 35f., 37.

3. Quoted in Riane Eisler, *Tomorrow's Children*, 60, from Brian Swimme's *The Universe Is a Green Dragon*.

The emphasis on ecology in theological reflections on childhood is of course another parallel to the history of feminist and womanist research. We only have to think of Rosemary Radford Ruether's *Gaia and God: An Ecofeminist Theology of Earth Healing* (New York: HarperCollins, 1992) and of Delores Williams' comment, "Womanist theology can claim a definite parallel between the defilement of Black women's bodies and the defilement of the health of earth's body (the land, air, and water) by the people who own the means of production." "A Womanist Perspective of Sin," in *A Troubling in my Soul: Womanist Perspectives on Evil and Suffering*, ed. Emily Townes (Maryknoll, N.Y: Orbis Books, 1993), 145.

4. Yearbook 2003 of the Bonn International Center for Conversion, reviewed in *Generalanzeiger* (Bonn), May 14, 2003. The *New York Times* of July 25, 2004, reported on "indefensible defense budgeting."

5. See Lawrence LeShan, "Why we love war and what we can do to prevent it," *Utne Reader*, Jan.–Feb. 2003, 53–58.

6. Children's Defense Fund, *The State of America's Children 2004*, xxii, xxv, 20, 28.

7. Albert-László Barabási, "We're All on the Grid Together," *New York Times*, August 16, 2003.

8. Jürgen Moltmann, *God in Creation: An Ecological Doctrine of Creation* (London: SCM Press, 1985), 11.

9. J. Bradley Wigger, *The Power of God at Home: Nurturing Our Children in Love and Grace* (San Francisco: Jossey-Bass, 2003), 160.

10. United Nations statistics as reported in *Honnefer Volkszeitung* (Bad Honnef), May 3, 2002.

11. Kofi Annan, *We the Children: Meeting the Promises of the World Summit for Children* (New York: UNICEF, 2001), 83, 10, 78.

12. Benjamin R. Barber, "Jihad Vs. McWorld: On Terrorism and the New Democratic Realism," *The Nation*, Jan. 21, 2002, 17.

13. This is the conclusion drawn by Internationales Konversionszentrum Bonn (BICC). See "Milliarden leben in permanenter Unsicherheit," *Frankfurter Rundschau*, May 14, 2003, 7.

14. Richard Meng, "Sprengkraft oder kreatives Potential," *Frankfurter Rundschau*, July 16, 2003.

15. Judith Butler, *Kritik der ethischen Gewalt*, reviewed in *ZEITLiteratur*, June 2003.

16. Teresa Berger has emphasized the thought that God's interaction with a child starts in the mother's womb, not just at birth, in her *Sei geseg-*

*net, meine Schwester: Frauen feiern Liturgie* (Würzburg: Echter, 1999), 183–94.

17. Wolfgang Teichert, "Solange wir leben, werden wir geboren," *Publik-Forum Extra: Kindsein-Erwachsenwerden* (Oberursel: Verlagsgesellschaft Publik-Forum, 1992), 34.

18. Jon Sobrino, quoted from Jürgen Moltmann, "Political Theology and Theology of Liberation," in Jörg Rieger, ed., *Liberating the Future: God, Mammon, and Theology* (Minneapolis: Fortress Press, 1998), 79.

19. Haven Kimmel, *The Solace of Leaving Early* (New York: Random House, 2002), 34.

# Selected Bibliography

✦

Adams, Carol J. *Neither Man Nor Beast: Feminism and the Defense of Animals.* New York: Continuum, 1994.

———. *The Pornography of Meat.* New York: Continuum, 2003.

Adams, Carol J., and Marie M. Fortune, eds. *Violence Against Women and Children: A Christian Theological Sourcebook.* New York: Continuum, 1995.

Alexander, David. "Feeding the Hungry and Protecting the Environment." In *All Creation Is Groaning.* Ed. Carol J. Dempsey and Russell A. Butkus. Collegeville, Minn.: Liturgical Press, 1999.

Annan, Kofi A. *We, the Children. Meeting the Promises of the World Summit for Children.* New York: UNICEF, 2001.

Arditti, Rita. *Searching for Life: The Grandmothers of the Plaza de Mayo and the Disappeared Children of Argentina.* Berkeley: University of California Press, 1999.

Ariès, Philippe. *Centuries of Childhood: A Social History of Family Life.* New York: Knopf, 1962.

Arnold, Johann Christoph. *Endangered: Your Child in a Hostile World.* Farmington, Pa.: Plough Publishing, 2000.

Baldermann, Ingo. *Wer hört mein Weinen? Kinder entdecken sich selbst in den Psalmen.* Neukirchen-Vluyn: Neukirchener Verlag, 1986.

von Balthasar, Hans-Urs. "Jesus as Child and His Praise of the Child." *Communio* 22 (1995): 625–34.

Barber, Benjamin R. *Jihad vs. McWorld: How Globalism and Tribalism Are Reshaping the World.* New York: Ballentine Books, 1996.

Bendroth, Margaret Lamberts. *Growing Up Protestant: Parents, Children, and Mainline Churches.* New Brunswick, N.J.: Rutgers University Press, 2002.

Berg, William. *Early Virgil.* University of London: Athlone Press, 1974.

Berquist, Jon L. *Strike Terror No More: Theology, Ethics, and the New War.* St. Louis, Mo.: Chalice Press, 2002.

Berry, Thomas. *The Great Work: Our Way into the Future.* New York: Bell Tower, 1999.

Bérubé, Michael. *Life As We Know It: A Father, a Family, and an Exceptional Child.* New York: Vintage Books, 1996.

Black, Vicky K. "And a Little Child Shall Teach Them: Lessons in Diakonia." *The Anglican Theological Review* 86, 1 (Winter 2004): 95–101.

Bockover, Mary I. "The Internet in China: A Confucian Critique." *Religion East and West: Journal of the Institute of World Religions* 2 (June 2002): 91–100.

Bonhoeffer, Dietrich. *Act and Being.* New York: Harper & Brothers, 1961.

Bonteko, Ron, and Marietta Stepaniants, eds. *Justice and Democracy: Cross-Cultural Perspectives.* Honolulu: University of Hawai'i Press, 1997.

Boulding, Elise. *Cultures of Peace: The Hidden Side of History.* Syracuse, N.Y.: Syracuse University Press, 2000.

————. *Children's Rights and the Wheel of Life.* New Brunswick, N.J.: Transaction Books, 1979.

Bourdieu, Pierre. "For a Scholarship of Commitment." *Profession 2000* (New York: PMLA) (2000): 40–45.

Boyden, Jo. "Childhood and Policy Makers: A Comparative Perspective on the Globalization of Childhood." In *Constructing and Reconstructing Childhood.* Ed. Allison James and Alan Prout. London: Falmer Press, 1990.

Brenner, Athalia, ed. *A Feminist Companion to Wisdom Literature.* Sheffield, U.K.: Sheffield Academic Press, 1995.

Brock, Rita Nakashima. "And a Little Child Will Lead Us: Christology and Child Abuse." In *Christianity, Patriarchy, and Abuse.* Ed. Joanne Carlson Brown and Carole R. Bohn. New York: Pilgrim Press, 1989.

Brock, Rita Nakashima, and Susan Brooks Thistlethwaite. *Casting Stones: Prostitution and Liberation in Asia and the United States.* Minneapolis: Augsburg/Fortress, 1996.

Brown, Joanne Carlson, and Carole R. Bohn, eds. *Christianity, Patriarchy, and Abuse: A Feminist Critique.* New York: Pilgrim Press, 1989.

Brown, Joanne Carlson, and Rebecca Parker. "For God So Loved the World?" In *Violence Against Women and Children.* Ed. Carol J. Adams and Marie M. Fortune. New York: Continuum, 1995.

Brown, Joseph Epes. *The Spiritual Legacy of the American Indian.* New York: Crossroad, 1987.

Browning, Don S., et al. *From Culture Wars to Common Ground: Religion and the American Family.* Louisville, Ky.: Westminster John Knox Press, 1997.

Brun, Toni. "Social Ecology: A Timely Paradigm for Reflection and Praxis for Life in Latin America." In *Ecotheology.* Ed. David G. Hallman. Maryknoll, N.Y.: Orbis Books, 1994.

Bruno-Jofré, Rosa del Carmen. *Methodist Education in Peru: Social Gospel, Politics, and American Ideological and Economic Penetration, 1888–1930.* Waterloo, Ont.: Canadian Corporation for Studies in Religion, 1988.

Bunge, Marcia J., ed. *The Child in Christian Thought.* Grand Rapids, Mich.: Eerdmans, 2001.

Cairns, Ed. *Children and Political Violence.* Cambridge, Mass.: Blackwell Publications, 1996.

Caldwell, Elizabeth F. *Leaving Home with Faith: Nurturing the Spiritual Life of Our Youth.* Cleveland: Pilgrim Press, 2002.

Cameron, Sara. *Constructores de paz: Relatos verídicos de los fundadores del movimiento de los niños y niñas por la paz.* Bogotá: Editorial Norma and UNICEF, 2001.

Camp, Claudia. "Woman Wisdom as Root Metaphor: A Theological Consideration." In *The Listening Heart: Essays in Wisdom and the Psalms Presented to Roland E. Murphy.* Ed. K. J. Hoglund et al. JSOT Sup., 58. Sheffield, U.K.: JSOT Press, 1987.

Carrasco, David. *City of Sacrifice: The Aztec Empire and the Role of Violence in Civilization.* Boston: Beacon Press, 1999.

Cassell, Justine, and Henry Jenkins, eds. *From Barbie to Mortal Kombat: Gender and Computer Games.* Cambridge, Mass.: MIT Press, 1998.

Castañeda, Claudia. *Figurations: Child, Bodies, Worlds.* Durham, N.C.: Duke University Press, 2002.

Castillo, Ana, ed. *Goddess of the Americas: La Diosa de las Americas. Writings on the Virgin of Guadalupe.* New York: Riverhead Books, 1996.

Cavaletti, Sofia. "Die Katechese des guten Hirten. Ein Abenteuer." In *Gottes Kinder*. Ed. Martin Ebner et al. Jahrbuch für biblische Theologie 17. Neukirchen-Vluyn: Neukirchener Verlag, 2002.

Children's Defense Fund. *The State of America's Children*. Yearbook. Washington, D.C.: Children's Defense Fund, 2000.

————. *The State of America's Children*. Boston: Beacon, 2001.

————. *The State of America's Children*. Washington, D.C.: Children's Defense Fund, 2004.

Cohn, Ilene, and Guy S. Goodwin-Gill. *Child Soldiers: The Role of Children in Armed Conflict*. Oxford/New York: Oxford University Press, 1994.

Coles, Robert. *The Political Life of Children*. Boston: Houghton Mifflin, 1986.

————. *The Spiritual Life of Children*. Boston: Houghton Mifflin, 1990.

Confucius. The Analects. Trans. David Hinton. Washington, D.C.: Counterpoint, 1998.

Couture, Pamela. *Seeing Children, Seeing God: A Practical Theology of Children and Poverty*. Nashville: Abingdon, 2000.

Crenshaw, James L. *Education in Ancient Israel: Across the Deadening Silence*. New York: Doubleday, 1998.

Crüsemann, Frank. "Gott als Anwalt der Kinder!? Zur Frage von Kinderrechten in der Bibel." In *Gottes Kinder*. Ed. Martin Ebner et al. Jahrbuch für biblische Theologie 17. Neukirchen-Vluyn: Neukirchener Verlag, 2002.

————. "Die Macht der kleinen Kinder: Ein Versuch, Psalm 8, 2b.3 zu verstehen." In *Was ist der Mensch? Festschrift für Hans-Walter Wolf*. Ed. Frank Crüsemann. München: Kaiser, 1992.

Csikszentmihalyi, Mark. "Confucius." In *The Rivers of Paradise: Moses, Buddha, Confucius, Jesus, and Muhammad as Religious Founders*. Ed. Noel Freedman and Michael McClymond. Grand Rapids, Mich.: Eerdmans, 2001.

Davies, Paul. *The Cosmic Blueprint: New Discoveries in Nature's Creative Ability to Order the Universe*. New York: Simon and Schuster, 1988.

————. *The Mind of God: The Scientific Basis for a Rational World*. New York: Simon and Schuster, 1992.

Delaney, Carol. *Abraham on Trial: The Social Legacy of Biblical Myth*. Princeton, N.J.: Princeton University Press, 1998.

Dempsey, Carol J., and Russell A. Butkus, eds. *All Creation Is Groaning: An Interdisciplinary Vision for Life in a Sacred Universe*. Collegeville, Minn.: Liturgical Press, 1999.

DeVries, Dawn. "'Be Converted and Become as Little Children': Friedrich Schleiermacher on the Religious Significance of Childhood." In *The

*Child in Christian Thought.* Ed. Marcia J. Bunge. Grand Rapids, Mich.: Eeerdmans, 2001.

————. "Toward a Theology of Childhood." *Interpretation* 55, 2 (April 2001): 161–73.

Dillard, Annie. *Holy the Firm.* New York: Harper & Row, 1977.

Donovan, Josephine, and Carol J. Adams, eds. *Beyond Animal Rights: A Feminist Caring Ethic for the Treatment of Animals.* New York: Continuum, 1996.

Dorfman, Ariel. "Are There Times When We Have to Accept Torture?" *New York Times,* May 8, 2004.

Dunn, Ardys. "Development of Environmental Responsibility in Children." In *All Creation Is Groaning.* Ed. Carol J. Dempsey and Russell Butkus. Collegeville, Minn.: Liturgical Press, 1999.

Ebner, Martin, et al., eds. *Gottes Kinder.* Jahrbuch für biblische Theologie 17. Neukirchen-Vluyn: Neukirchener Verlag, 2002.

Eisler, Riane. *Tomorrow's Children: A Blueprint for Partnership Education in the 21st Century.* Boulder: Westview Press, 2000.

Farley, Edward. "Being Human and the Arts; A Sacramental Reflection." *A.R.T.S. The Arts in Religious and Theological Studies* 15, 1 (2003): 4–9.

Fass, Paula S., and Mary Ann Mason, eds. *Childhood in America.* New York: New York University Press, 2000.

Feiler, Bruce. *Abraham: A Journey to the Heart of Three Faiths.* New York: HarperCollins, 2002.

Fernea, Elizabeth, ed. *Children in the Muslim Middle East.* Austin: University of Texas Press, 1995.

Fewell, Danna Nolan. *The Children of Israel: Reading the Bible for the Sake of Our Children.* Nashville: Abingdon, 2003.

Fineberg, Jonathan, et al., eds. *Mit dem Auge des Kindes: Kinderzeichnung und moderne Kunst.* München, Bern: Verlag Gerhard Hatje, 1995.

Fitzmyer, Joseph A., S.J. *The Gospel According to Luke (X–XXIV).* Garden City, N.Y: Doubleday, 1985.

Fletcher, Jeannine Hill. "Shifting Identities: The Contribution of Feminist Thought to Theologies of Religious Pluralism." *Journal of Feminist Studies in Religion* 19, 2 (Fall 2003): 5–24.

Fontaine, Carol R. "The Personification of Wisdom in 'Proverbs.'" In *Harper's Bible Commentary.* Ed. J. L. Mays. San Francisco: Harper & Row, 1988.

Franklin, Bob, ed. *Handbook of Children's Rights: Comparative Policy and Practice.* London and New York: Routledge, 1995.

Freedman, David Noel, and Michael J. McClymond, eds. *The Rivers of Paradise: Moses, Buddha, Confucius, Jesus, and Muhammad as Religious Founders.* Grand Rapids, Mich.: Eerdmans, 2001.

Friedman, Thomas. *The Lexus and the Olive Tree: Understanding Globalization.* New York: Farrar, Straus & Giroux, 1999.

Friedrich, Carl J., ed. *The Philosophy of Hegel.* New York: Random House, 1953/1954.

Gebara, Ivone. *Longing for Running Water: Ecofeminism and Liberation.* Minneapolis: Fortress Press, 1999.

————. *Out of the Depths: Women's Experience of Evil and Salvation.* Minneapolis: Augsburg/Fortress, 2002.

Gerstenberger, Erhard, and Wolfgang Schrage. *Frau und Mann.* Stuttgart: Kohlhammer, 1980.

Gittens, Diana. *The Child in Question.* Basingstoke: Macmillan Press; New York: St. Martin's Press, 1998.

Grandin, Temple. *Thinking in Pictures and Other Reports from My Life with Autism.* New York: Random House, 1995.

Grant, Jacqueline. "A Theological Framework." In *Working with Black Youth: Opportunities for Christian Ministry.* Ed. Charles R. Foster and Grant S. Shockley. Nashville: Abingdon, 1989.

Gray, John. *False Dawn: The Delusions of Globalization.* New York: New Press, 1998.

————. "Beyond the Dark Night—A Kenotic Church Moves On . . . ?" In *Verborgener Gott—Verborgene Kirche: Die kenotische Theologie und ihre ekklesiologischen Implikationen.* Ed. Johannes Brosseder. Stuttgart: Kohlhammer, 2001.

Grey, Mary C. *Sacred Longings: The Ecological Spirit and Global Culture.* Minneapolis: Fortress Press, 2004.

Grosse-Oetringhaus, Hans-Martin, ed. *Ich will endlich Frieden: Kinder im Krieg.* Ein terre des hommes Buch. Münster: Verlag Westfälisches Dampfboot, 1998.

de Gruchy, John W. "Holy Beauty: A Reformed Perspective on Aesthetics within a World of Ugly Injustice." In *Reformed Theology for the Third Christian Millennium.* Louisville, Ky.: Westminster John Knox Press, 2003.

Gundry-Volf, Judith M. "Discipleship of Equals at the Cradle and the Cross." *Interpretation* 53, 1 (Jan. 1999): 57–61.

————. "The Least and the Greatest: Children in the New Testament." In *The Child in Christian Thought.* Ed. Marcia J. Bunge. Grand Rapids, Mich.: Eerdmans, 2001.

————. "To Such as These Belongs the Reign of God: Jesus and Children." *Theology Today* 56, 4 (Jan. 2000): 469–80.

Gutiérrez, Gustavo. *The God of Life.* Maryknoll, N.Y.: Orbis Books, 1991.

Hagen, Kurtis. "Xunzi and the Nature of Confucian Ritual." *Journal of the American Academy of Religion* 71, 2 (June 2003): 371–403.

Hallman, David G., ed. *Ecotheology: Voices from South and North.* 2nd ed. Maryknoll, N.Y.: Orbis Books, 1994.

Hamilton, James T. *Channeling Violence: The Economic Market for Violent Television Programming.* Princeton: Princeton University Press, 1998.

Haney, Marsha Snulligan. "The Urban Child, Congregational Ministry and the Challenge of Religious Diversity." *The Journal of the Interdenominational Theological Center 30*, 1 & 2 (Fall 2002/ Spring 2003): 9–35.

Hanh, Thich Nhat. *Going Home: Jesus and Buddha as Brothers.* New York: Penguin Putnam, 1999.

Hanisch, Helmut. "Kinder als Philosophen und Theologen." In *Schau auf die Kleinen.* . . . Ed. Rüdiger Lux. Leipzig: Evangelische Verlagsanstalt, 2002.

Hawley, John Stratton. *Krishna, the Butter Thief.* Princeton, N.J.: Princeton University Press, 1983.

Hecht, Tobias. *Minor Omissions: Childhoods in Latin America.* Madison: University of Wisconsin Press, 2002.

Hector, Bridgette. "Womanist Model: Crossing Class Barriers: Middle-Class Black Women Relating with Inner-City Black Female Youth." *The Journal of the Interdenominational Theological Center 30*, 1 & 2 (Fall 2002/ Spring 2003): 129–45.

Heraclitus. *Heraclitus, Fragments. A Text and Translation with a Commentary* by T. M. Robinson. Toronto: University of Toronto Press, 1987.

Herzog, Frederick. "New Birth of Conscience." In *Theology and Corporate Conscience: Essays in Honor of Frederick Herzog.* Ed. M. Douglas Meeks, Jürgen Moltmann, and Frederick Trost. Minneapolis: Kirk House Publishers, 1999.

———. "New Birth of Conscience." In *Theology from the Belly of the Whale: A Frederick Herzog Reader.* Ed. Jörg Rieger. Harrisburg, Pa.: Trinity Press International, 1999.

Hinkelammert, Franz J. *El huaracán de la globalización.* San José, Costa Rica: DEI, 1999.

Hinton, David, ed. *Confucius. The Analects.* Washington, D.C.: Counterpoint, 1998.

Holloway, Sarah L., and Gill Valentine, eds. *Children's Geographies: Playing, Living, Learning.* London and New York: Routledge, 2000.

Horsley, Richard A. "Religion and Other Products of Empire." *Journal of the American Academy of Religion* 71, 1 (March 2003): 13–44.

Hunt, Pauline, and Ronald Frankenberg, "It's a Small World: Disneyland, the Family and Multiple Re-presentations of American Childhood." In

*Constructing and Reconstructing Childhood.* Ed. Allison James and Alan Prout. London: Falmer Press, 1997.

Huizinga, Johan. *Homo Ludens: A Study of the Play-Element in Culture.* London: Routledge & Kegan Paul, 1949.

Inness, Sherrie A., ed. *Running for Their Lives: Girls, Cultural Identity, and Stories of Survival.* Lanham, Md.: Rowman & Littlefield, 2000.

James, Allison, and Alan Prout, eds. *Constructing and Reconstructing Childhood: Contemporary Issues in the Sociological Study of Childhood.* London: Falmer Press, 1990.

James, Allison, Chris Jenks, and Alan Prout, eds. *Theorizing Childhood.* New York: Teacher's College, Columbia University, 1998.

Jantzen, Grace. *Becoming Divine: Toward a Feminist Philosophy of Religion.* Bloomington: Indiana University Press, 1999.

Jenkins, Henry. *The Children's Culture Reader.* New York: New York University Press, 1998.

Jensen, David H. *Graced Vulnerability: A Theology of Childhood.* Cleveland: Pilgrim Press, 2005.

————. *In the Company of Others: A Dialogical Christology.* Cleveland: Pilgrim Press, 2001.

Johnson, Elizabeth A. *She Who Is: The Mystery of God in Feminist Discourse.* New York: Crossroad, 1992.

Jones, L. Gregory. *Embodying Forgiveness: A Theological Analysis.* Grand Rapids, Mich.: Eerdmans, 1995.

Jung, C. G., and C. Kerényi. *Essays on a Science of Mythology: The Myths of the Divine Child and the Divine Maiden.* Rev. ed. New York: Harper, 1963.

Kähler, Christoph. "'Wenn ihr nicht werdet wie die Kinder . . .'—Kindsein als Metapher im Neuen Testament." In *Schau auf die Kleinen . . . .* Ed. Rüdiger Lux. Leipzig: Evangelische Verlagsanstalt, 2002.

Kakar, Sudhir. *The Inner World: A Psychoanalytic Study of Childhood and Society in India.* Delhi: Oxford University Press, 1978.

Karetzky, Patricia Eichenbaum. *Early Buddhist Narrative Art: Illustrations of the Life of the Buddha from Central Asia to China, Korea and Japan.* Lanham, Md.: University Press of America, 1992.

————. *The Life of the Buddha: Ancient Scriptural and Pictorial Traditions.* Lanham, Md.: University Press of America, 1992.

Kässmann, Margot. *Overcoming Violence: The Challenge to the Churches in All Places.* Geneva: World Council of Churches, 1998.

Keitetsi, China. *Sie nahmen mir die Mutter und gaben mir ein Gewehr.* Berlin: Ullstein, 2002.

Keller, Catherine. *Face of the Deep: A Theology of Becoming.* London and New York: Routledge, 2003.

Kidwell, Clara Sue, Homer Noley, and George E. "Tink" Tinker, eds., *A Native American Theology.* Maryknoll, N.Y.: Orbis Books, 2001.

Kingsolver, Barbara. *Small Wonder: Essays.* New York: HarperCollins, 2002.

Kirk, Robin. *More Terrible than Death: Massacres, Drugs, and America's War in Colombia.* New York: Public Affairs, 2003.

Kleijwegt, Marc. s.v. "Kind." In *Reallexikon für Antike und Christentum.* Ed. Georg Schöllgen et al. Stuttgart: Anton Hiersmann, 2004, 866–947.

Klein, Charlotte. *Theologie und Anti-Judaismus: Eine Studie zur deutschen theologischen Literatur der Gegenwart.* München: Kaiser, 1975.

Koerrenz, Ralf. "'Vom Kinde aus'—Nachdenken über einen Anspruch." In *Gottes Kinder.* Ed. Martin Ebner et al. Jahrbuch für biblische Theologie 17. Neukirchen-Vluyn: Neukirchener Verlag, 2002.

Koops, Willem, and Michael Zuckerman, eds. *Beyond the Century of the Child: Cultural History and Developmental Psychology.* Philadelphia: University of Pennsylvania Press, 2003.

*Koran, The.* Translated with notes by N. J. Dawood. London: Penguin Books, 1999.

Korczak, Janusz. *Leben für andere. Gedanken und Meditationen von Janusz Korczak.* Ed. Friedhelm Beiner and Erich Dauzenroth. Gütersloh: Kiefel, 1997.

Kozol, Jonathan. *Ordinary Resurrections: Children in the Years of Hope.* New York: Crown Publishers, 2000.

Krause, Gerhard, ed. *Die Kinder im Evangelium.* Stuttgart: Ehrenfried Klotz, 1973.

Lachmann, Rainer. s.v. "Kind." *Theologische Realenzyklopädie.* Vol. 18. Ed. Gerhard Müller et al. Berlin/New York: Walter de Gruyter, 1989.

Lao Tzu. *Tao Te Ching.* The Definitive Edition. Translated and Commentary by Jonathan Star. New York: Penguin Putnam, 2001.

Larive, Armand. *After Sunday: A Theology of Work.* New York: Continuum, 2004.

Le Guin, Ursula. *Lao Tzu: Tao te Ching.* Boston: Shambhala Publications, 1997.

Levenson, Jon. *The Death and Resurrection of the Beloved Son: The Transformation of Child Sacrifice in Judaism and Christianity.* New Haven, Ct.: Yale University Press, 1993.

Lindner, Eileen W. "Children as Theologians," in *Rethinking Childhood.* Ed. Peter B. Pufall and Richard P. Unsworth. Brunswick, N.J.: Rutgers University Press, 2004.

Ludolphy, Ingetraut. "Zur Geschichte der Auslegung des Evangelium infantium." In *Die Kinder im Evangelium.* Ed. Gerhard Krause. Stuttgart: Ehrenfried Klotz, 1973.

Ludwig, Michaela. *Ehemalige Kindersoldaten als Flüchtlinge in Deutschland.* Osnabrück: terre des hommes, 2003.

Lux, Rüdiger, ed. *Schau auf die Kleinen . . . Das Kind in Religion, Kirche und Gesellschaft.* Leipzig: Evangelische Verlagsanstalt, 2002.

Luz, Ulrich. *Das Evangelium nach Matthäus.* Zürich/Neukirchen-Vluyn: Neukirchener Verlag, 1997.

Maas, Robin. "Christ as the Logos of Childhood: Reflections on the Meaning and Mission of the Child." *Theology Today* 56, 4 (Jan. 2000): 456–68.

Machoveč, Milan. *A Marxist Looks at Jesus.* Philadelphia: Fortress Press, 1976.

Maguire, Daniel C., and Larry L. Rasmussen. *Ethics for a Small Planet: New Horizons on Population, Consumption, and Ecology.* Albany: State University of New York Press, 1998.

Martin, Joan. "Public Education and the Battle over the Nature of Social Responsibility to the Nation's Children and Schools." *Journal of the American Academy of Religion* 70, 4 (Dec. 2002): 833–41.

Martin-Dubost, Paul. *Ganésa: The Enchanter of the Three Worlds.* Mumbai: Project for Indian Cultural Studies, 1997.

Mathews, Thomas F. *The Clash of Gods: A Reinterpretation of Early Christian Art.* Rev. ed. Princeton, N.J.: Princeton University Press, 1993.

Matthews, Gareth B. *The Philosophy of Childhood.* Cambridge, Mass.: Harvard University Press, 1994.

de Mause, Lloyd., ed. *The History of Childhood.* New York: Psychohistory Press, 1974.

Mazurana, Dyan. "Where Are the Girls?" *The Women's Review of Books,* 21, 12 (Sept. 2004): 21f.

McFague, Sallie. *Super, Natural Christians: How We Should Love Nature.* Minneapolis: Fortress Press, 1997.

McKay, Susan, and Dyan Mazurana. *Where Are the Girls? Girls in Fighting Forces in Northern Uganda, Sierra Leone, and Mozambique: Their Lives During and After War.* Montreal: International Center for Human Rights and Democratic Development, 2004.

McKenna, Megan. *Not Counting Women and Children: Neglected Stories from the Bible.* Maryknoll, N.Y.: Orbis Books, 1994.

McLuhan, Marshall, and Quentin Fiore. *The Medium is the Massage.* New York: Random House, 1967.

Meeks, M. Douglas. *God the Economist: The Doctrine of God and Political Economy.* Minneapolis: Augsburg Fortress, 1989.

Meier, John P. *A Marginal Jew: Rethinking the Historical Jesus.* Vol. 1. New York: Doubleday, 1991.

Mensching, Gustav. *Leben und Legende der Religionsstifter.* Darmstadt: Holle Verlag, n.d.

Meyers, Carol L. "The Family in Early Israel." In *Families in Ancient Israel.* Ed. Leo G. Perdue et al. Louisville, Ky.: Westminster John Knox Press, 1998.

Miller-McLemore, Bonnie J. *Also a Mother: Work and Family as Theological Dilemma.* Nashville: Abingdon, 1994.

————. *Let the Children Come: Reimagining Childhood from a Christian Perspective.* San Francisco: Jossey-Bass, 2003.

————. "'Let the Children Come' Revisited: Contemporary Feminist Theologians on Children." In *The Child in Christian Thought.* Ed. Marcia J. Bunge. Grand Rapids, Mich.: Eerdmans, 2001.

Miller-McLemore, Bonnie J., and Brita L. Gill-Austern, eds. *Feminist and Womanist Pastoral Theology.* Nashville: Abingdon, 1999.

Mintz, Steven. *Huck's Raft: A History of American Childhood.* Cambridge, Mass.: Belknap, 2004).

Moltmann, Jürgen. "Child and Childhood as Metaphors of Hope." *Theology Today* (Jan. 2000): 592–603.

————. *Science and Wisdom.* Minneapolis: Fortress Press, 2003.

————. *God in Creation: An Ecological Doctrine of Creation.* London: SCM Press, 1985.

Moltmann-Wendel, Elisabeth. *Macht der Mütterlichkeit: Die Geschichte der Henriette Schrader-Breymann.* Berlin: Wichern Verlag, 2003.

————. "Natalität und die Liebe zur Welt. Hannah Arendt's Beitrag zu einer immanenten Transzendenz." *Evangelische Theologie* 58 (1998): 283–95.

————. *Wer die Erde nicht berührt, kann den Himmel nicht erreichen . . . Autobiographie.* Zürich: Benziger Verlag, 1997.

Müller, Peter. *In der Mitte der Gemeinde: Kinder im Neuen Testament.* Neukirchen-Vluyn: Neukirchener Verlag, 1992.

Norden, Eduard. *Die Geburt des Kindes.* Leipzig: B.G. Teubner, 1924.

O'Grady, Ron. *The Hidden Shame of the Church: Sexual Abuse of Children and the Church.* Geneva: World Council of Churches Publications, 2001.

Orme, Nicholas. *Medieval Children.* New Haven, Conn.: Yale University Press, 2002.

Osmer, Richard R., and Friedrich Schweitzer, *Religious Education Between Modernization and Globalization: New Perspectives on the United States and Germany.* Grand Rapids, Mich.: Eerdmans, 2003.

Oxtoby, Willard G., ed. *World Religions: Eastern Traditions.* Toronto and New York: Oxford University Press, 1996.

————. *World Religions: Western Traditions*. Toronto: Oxford University Press, 1996.

Pagels, Elaine. *Beyond Belief: The Secret Gospel of Thomas*. New York: Random House, 2003.

Parker, Evelyn L. "Hungry for Honor: Children in Violent Youth Gangs." *Interpretation* 55, 2 (April 2001): 148–60.

————. *Trouble Don't Last Always: Emancipatory Hope among African American Adolescents*. Cleveland: Pilgrim Press, 2003.

Perdue, Leo G., et al., eds. *Families in Ancient Israel*. Louisville, Ky.: Westminster John Knox Press, 1998.

Peterson, Anna L. *Being Human: Ethics, Environment, and Our Place in the World*. Berkeley: University of California Press, 2001.

Peterson, Anna L., and Kay Almere Read. "Victims, Heroes, Enemies: Children in Central American Wars." In *Minor Omissions: Children in Latin American History and Society*. Ed. Tobias Hecht. Madison: University of Wisconsin Press, 2002.

Phipps, William E. *Muhammad and Jesus: A Comparison of the Prophets and Their Teachings*. New York: Continuum, 1996.

Plöger, Otto. *Sprüche Salomos (Proverbia)*. Neukirchen-Vluyn: Neukirchener Verlag, 1984.

Pohl, Christine. *Making Room: Recovering Hospitality as a Christian Tradition*. Grand Rapids, Mich.: Eerdmans, 1999.

Polner, Murray, and Naomi Goodman, eds. *The Challenge of Shalom: The Jewish Tradition of Peace and Justice*. Philadelphia: New Society Publishers, 1994.

Postman, Neil. *The Disappearance of Childhood*. New York: Vintage Books, 1994.

Prigogine, Ilya. *Order Out of Chaos: Man's New Dialogue with Nature*. New York: Bantam Books, 1984.

Primavesi, Anne. *Sacred Gaia*. London: Routledge, 2000.

Pufall, Peter B., and Richard P. Unsworth, eds. *Rethinking Childhood*. Brunswick, N.J.: Rutgers University Press, 2004.

Pui-lan, Kwok. "Ecology and the Recycling of Christianity." In *Ecotheology*. Ed. David G. Hallman. Maryknoll, N.Y.: Orbis Books, 1994.

Rahner, Karl. "Ideas for a Theology of Childhood." In his *Theological Investigations*. Vol. 8. New York: Seabury Press, 1977.

Raines, John C., and Daniel C. Maguire, eds. *What Men Owe to Women: Men's Voices from World Religions*. Albany, N.Y.: State University of New York Press, 2001.

Rassmussen, Larry. "Theology of Life and Ecumenical Ethics." In *Ecotheology*. Ed. David. G. Hallman. Maryknoll, N.Y.: Orbis Books, 1994.

Raymond, Alan, and Susan Raymond. *Children in War.* New York: TV Books, L.L.C., 2000.

Ress, Mary Judith. *Without a Vision the People Will Perish: Reflections on Latin-American Ecofeminist Theology.* Santiago, Chile: Sociedad Conspirando, 2003.

Rhie, Marilyn M., and Robert A. F. Thurman, eds. *Worlds of Transformation: Tibetan Art of Wisdom and Compassion.* New York: Tibet House, 1999.

Richard, Pablo. "Teología de la solidaridad en el contexto actual de economía de libre mercado." In *El huaracán de la globalización.* Ed. Franz J. Hinkelammert. San José, Costa Rica: DEI, 1999.

Richman, Paula. *Extraordinary Child: Poems from a South Indian Devotional Genre.* Honolulu: University of Hawaii Press, 1997.

Rieger, Jörg, ed. *Theology from the Belly of the Whale: A Frederick Herzog Reader.* Harrisburg, Pa.: Trinity Press International, 1999.

Ringe, Sharon H. *Wisdom's Friends: Community and Christology in the Fourth Gospel.* Louisville, Ky.: Westminster John Knox Press, 1999.

Ringe, Sharon H., and Carol Newsom, eds. *Women's Bible Commentary.* Louisville, Ky.: Westminster John Knox Press, 1998.

Rivera, Luis N. *A Violent Evangelism: The Political and Religious Conquest of the Americas.* Louisville, Ky.: Westminster John Knox Press, 1992.

Robbins, Bruce. "The Sweatshop Sublime." PMLA 117, 1 (Jan. 2002): 84–97.

Rostworowski, María. *La mujer en la época prehispánica.* Lima: Instituto de Estudios Peruanos, 1988.

Ruether, Rosemary Radford. *Christianity and the Making of the Modern Family.* Boston: Beacon, 2000.

Rusch, Elizabeth. *Generation Fix: Young Ideas for a Better World.* Hillsboro, Ore.: Beyond Words Publishing, 2002.

Saddhatissa, H. *The Life of the Buddha.* New York: Harper & Row, 1976.

Schaberg, Jane. *The Illegitimacy of Jesus: A Feminist Theological Interpretation of the Infancy Narratives.* San Francisco: Harper & Row, 1987.

Schaper, Donna. *Raising Interfaith Children: Spiritual Orphans or Spiritual Heirs?* New York: Crossroad, 1999.

Scheper-Hughes, Nancy. *Death Without Weeping: The Violence of Everyday Life in Brazil.* Berkeley: University of California Press, 1992.

――――. "Maternal Thinking and the Politics of War." In *The Women and War Reader.* Ed. Lois Ann Lorentzen and Jennifer Turpin. New York: New York University Press, 1998.

Scheper-Hughes, Nancy, and Carolyn Sargent, eds. *Small Wars: The Cultural Politics of Childhood.* Berkeley: University of California Press, 1998.

Schrage, Wolfgang. *The Ethics of the New Testament.* Philadelphia: Fortress Press, 1988, 1990.

————. *Unterwegs zur Einheit und Einzigkeit Gottes: Zum "Monotheismus" des Paulus und seiner alttestamentlich-frühjüdischen Tradition.* Neukirchen-Vluyn: Neukirchener Verlag, 2002.

Schulz, Bruno. *Bruno Schulz: New Documents and Interpretations.* Ed. Czeslaw Z. Prokopczyk. New York: Peter Lang, 1999.

Schumann, Wolfgang. *Buddhistische Bilderwelt: Ein ikonographisches Handbuch des Mahāyāna- und Tantrayāna-Buddhismus.* Köln: Eugen Diederichs, 1986.

Schwantes, Milton. "'Do Not Extend Your Hand against the Child': Observations on Genesis 21 and 22." In *Subversive Scriptures: Revolutionary Readings of the Christian Bible in Latin America.* Ed. Leif E. Vaage. Valley Forge, Pa.: Trinity Press International, 1997.

Schweitzer, Friedrich, and Richard Robert Osmer. *Religious Education Between Modernization and Globalization.* Grand Rapids, Mich.: Eerdmans, 2003.

Sholem, Gershom. *Major Trends in Jewish Mysticism.* New York: Schocken Books, 1946.

Sier, Kurt. "Die Dialektik des 'Noch-Nicht'—Zur Representation des Kindes in der griechischen Literatur und Philosophie." In *Schau auf die Kleinen. . . .* Ed. Rüdiger Lux. Leipzig: Evangelische Verlagsanstalt, 2002.

Smith, Huston. *The World's Religions: Our Great Wisdom Traditions.* New York: HarperCollins, 1991.

Soelle, Dorothee. *The Silent Cry: Mysticism and Resistance.* Minneapolis: Fortress Press, 2001.

Spivak, Gayatri Chakravorty. *A Critique of Postcolonial Reason: Toward a History of the Vanishing Present.* Cambridge, Mass.: Harvard University Press, 1999.

Spretnak, Charlene. *The Resurgence of the Real: Body, Nature, and Place in a Hypermodern World.* New York: Routledge, 1999.

Stainton Rogers, Rex, and Wendy Stainton Rogers. *Stories of Childhood: Shifting Agendas of Child Concern.* Toronto, Buffalo, N.Y.: University of Toronto, 1992.

Steingraber, Susan. *Having Faith: An Ecologist's Journey into Motherhood.* Cambridge, Mass.: Perseus Publishing, 2003.

Stock, Alex. "Junglehrer und Musterknabe—Zur Bildgeschichte des zwölfjährigen Jesus." In *Schau auf die Kleinen . . . .* Ed. Rüdiger Lux. Leipzig: Evangelische Verlagsanstalt, 2002.

Tamez, Elsa. "Libertad neoliberal y libertad paulina." In *El huaracán de la globalización.* Ed. Franz J. Hinkelammert. San José, Costa Rica: DEI, 1999.

Tanner, Kathryn. "Incarnation, Cross, and Sacrifice: A Feminist-Inspired Reappraisal." *The Anglican Theological Review* 86, 1 (Winter 2004): 35–56.

terre des hommes. *Albtraum ohne Ende: Kinder zwischen den Fronten.* Osnabrück: terre des hommes, 1997, 2002.

———. *Kinderarbeit: Kein Kinderspiel.* Osnabrück: terre des hommes, 2001.

———. *Kinderarbeit: Was Verbraucher und Unternehmer tun können.* Osnabrück: terre des hommes, 2001.

Thundy, Zacharias P. *Buddha and Christ: Nativity Stories and Indian Traditions.* Leiden: E.J. Brill, 1993.

Townes, Emily M. *A Troubling in My Soul: Womanist Perspectives on Evil and Suffering.* Maryknoll, N.Y.: Orbis Books, 1993.

Trawick, Margaret. *Notes on Love in a Tamil Family.* Berkeley: University of California Press, 1990.

Tuchman, Barbara W. *A Distant Mirror: The Calamitous 14th Century.* New York: Knopf, 1978.

Ulrich-Eschemann, Karin. *Vom Geborenwerden des Menschen: Theologische und Philosophische Erkundungen.* Münster: LIT-Verlag, 2000.

UNICEF. *The State of the World's Children 2003.* New York: UNICEF, 2002.

———. *The State of the World's Children 2004: Girls, Education and Development.* New York: UNICEF, 2003.

United Nations. *World Youth Report 2003.* New York: United Nations Publications, 2004.

Van Aarde, Andries G. *Fatherless in Galilee: Jesus as Child of God.* Harrisburg, Pa.: Trinity Press International, 2001.

Van Norden, Bryan W., ed. *Confucius and the Analects: New Essays.* Oxford, New York: Oxford University Press, 2002.

Walker, Elizabeth J. "Pastoral Counseling with African-American Male Youth Offenders." *The Journal of the Interdenominational Theological Center* 30, 1 & 2 (Fall 2002/Spring 2–3): 109–27.

Waskow, Arthur. "Judaism, Violence, and Nonviolence." *Fellowship* 69, 5–6 (May–June 2003): 12–19.

Webb-Mitchell, Brett P. *Christly Gestures: Learning to be Members of the Body of Christ.* Grand Rapids, Mich.: Eerdmans, 2003.

Weber, Hans-Ruedi. *Jesus and the Children: Biblical Resources for Study and Preaching.* Geneva: World Council of Churches, 1979.

Wheatley, Margaret. *Leadership and the New Science: Learning About Organization from an Orderly Universe.* San Francisco: Berrett-Koehler Publishers, 1994.

Wiedemann, T. E. J. *Adults and Children in the Roman Empire.* New Haven, Conn.: Yale University Press, 1989.

Wigger, J. Bradley. *The Power of God at Home: Nurturing Our Children in Love and Grace.* San Francisco: Jossey-Bass, 2003.

Wildberger, Hans. *Jesaja Kapitel 1–12.* Biblischer Kommentar, Altes Testament. Neukirchen-Vluyn: Neukirchener Verlag, 1972.

Wolfe, Regina Wentzel. "For the Good of the Children." In *Ethics and World Religions.* Ed. Regina Wentzel Wolfe and Christine E. Gudorf.

———, and Christine E. Gudorf, eds. *Ethics and World Religions: Cross-Cultural Case Studies.* Maryknoll, N.Y.: Orbis Books, 1999.

Wood, Diana. *The Church and Childhood.* Vol. 31 of *Studies in Church History.* Oxford: Blackwell, 1994.

Woodhouse, Barbara Bennett. "Re-Visioning Rights for Children," in *Rethinking Childhood.* Ed. Peter B. Pufall and Richard P. Unsworth. Brunswick, N.J.: Rutgers University Press, 2004.

# I N D E X

➳ ✷ ⬱